To: Daddy
From Nida + Harold
Christmas 1987

TALMADGE

TALMADGE

A Political Legacy,
A Politician's Life

A MEMOIR

Herman E. Talmadge

with Mark Royden Winchell

Peachtree Publishers, Ltd.

Published by
PEACHTREE PUBLISHERS, LTD.
494 Armour Circle, N.E.
Atlanta, GA 30324

Manufactured in the United States of America

10 9 8 7 6 5 4 3 2

Library of Congress Catalog Card Number 87-80973

ISBN 0-934601-23-2

To my father and mother:

Eugene Talmadge
"The bravest man I ever knew."
and
Mattie (Miss Mitt) Thurmond Talmadge
"The most remarkable woman I ever knew."

Acknowledgments

I wish to acknowledge several persons who rendered valuable assistance in the preparation of this book.

Professors Mel Steely and Don Wagner of the oral history project of West Georgia College helped to jog my memory by conducting a series of taped interviews, which they then made available for my use.

My former aide and longtime friend Jimmy Bentley also provided me with valuable taped interviews.

In addition to being a skilled secretary, Mrs. Jane Harris read and commented on early drafts of this book. Mrs. Betsy Dendy of Clemson University did a superb job of compiling an index on very short notice. Other forms of technical assistance were rendered by Kim Hunter, Pearl Parker, Charles Toney, Sharon Sifford, and Bernard K. Duffy, all of Clemson University.

Special thanks to the *Atlanta Journal and Constitution*, particularly to reference manager Diane Hunter and photographer Bud Skinner, for use of photographs from their files; and to Sheryl Vogt of the University of Georgia Libraries for use of photographs from the Herman Talmadge files.

I am also grateful to Professor Bill Koon of Clemson University for bringing this project to the attention of my collaborator and to Chuck Perry of Peachtree Publishers for getting the book off the ground and seeing it through every step of the way.

My collaborator Mark Winchell did a remarkable job of overcoming his Yankee background to understand the life and times of a Southern politician. He and I are both eternally grateful to our wives—Lynda Cowart Talmadge and Donna Haisty Winchell—for reading and responding to every draft of this book and for sustaining us personally every day of our lives.

Herman E. Talmadge

Part One

The
Georgia
Years

Prologue

Going Home

I AWOKE ON THE MORNING of November 5, 1980, to a newspaper headline proclaiming, "Talmadge Walks Away With Fifth Term." By noon I knew it wasn't so. I had served twenty-four years in the United States Senate (in addition to another decade or so in state politics), but by the time the last returns were in the majority of voters in Georgia had decided they no longer required my services.

It was the first election I had ever lost and I didn't like the feeling. But as I have done often in my lifetime, I took some comfort from history: Winston Churchill, the most remarkable man of this century, held the British people together during the darkest days of World War II and defied the forces of Naziism with little more than stirring rhetoric and fiery determination. So what did the electorate do as soon as victory was within sight? They replaced Churchill with a political lightweight by the name of Clement Atlee. If a man as great as Sir Winston could take defeat, then so could Herman Talmadge.

Several days later I began the disquieting task of moving out of my senate office. I suppose it would make for a more dramatic story if I could say I stood at my office window and looked out over the Capitol Mall at the Lincoln and Jefferson Memorials, pondering the theories and realities of our democratic system

3

of government. But the truth is that my office was at ground level, and I kept the curtains drawn all the time. Had I bothered to look out the window, all I would have seen was dirt and the back of trimmed shrubbery. Still, there was plenty in my office to make me pensive about my life in politics. My staff and I packed up more than 1,600 boxes of official papers and memorabilia, each filled with hundreds of stories, all destined for cataloging at the University of Georgia library.

There were some special mementos, however, I kept for myself. Like this letter dated September 30, 1954:

Dear Herman,

Thanks for yours of September 27. We are looking forward to the ham. We think of you continually and wish that our paths would cross more often.

When you are out of office, perhaps I can come down and spend a couple of days with you on the farm. I would like nothing better.

Please give my regards to Betty.

God bless you,
Billy

What a difference twenty-six years had made. By the mid-seventies both Betty and the ham business were gone—casualties of a disintegrating marriage that ended in a bitter and highly publicized divorce. Perhaps I should have taken the time to write Billy Graham and tell him how faith in the Lord helped me overcome an addiction to alcohol.

I saved the box full of letters my colleagues wrote me shortly after my younger son drowned on Memorial Day, 1975. That's the way the Senate was. One minute they'd be rawhiding you on some "issue," and the next they'd be closing ranks to help you through a difficult spot in your personal life. That made it hurt all the more when in 1979 eighty-one of them voted to denounce me because of financial irregularities in my office. There was a lot more to that story than ever made the press.

There was another letter I'll always treasure:

4

April 1978

Dear Senator Talmadge:

As President, I want to express my admiration for your support of the Panama Canal treaties. Rarely is a national leader called upon to act on such an important issue fraught with so much potential political sacrifice.

On behalf of the people of the United States, I thank you for your personal demonstration of statesmanship and political courage.

Sincerely,
Jimmy Carter

Jimmy and I and every other politician who supported those treaties took an awful lot of abuse, but on that issue we were right. President Carter was voted out of office because his concern for our hostages caused him to make concessions to Iran. His successor said he would never let America be humiliated again. But, six years later, he made a similar mistake.

I kept my autographed picture of Sam Ervin. I'd served with more than four hundred senators, but Sam was one of the best. He and I manned many a filibuster on behalf of states' rights. And then, in the summer of 1973, we came into millions of American living rooms during that whole sorry Watergate mess. To this day it's hard to believe that a politician as smart as Dick Nixon could have allowed something that stupid to happen. He had the most ability of any of the presidents I knew. Sam and I took no pleasure in becoming famous at his expense.

I saved an old plow from the corner of my office. It had been given to me by the agriculture minister of Israel and was like the kind of plow I had used as a boy sixty years earlier. Farming had come a long way in that time—perhaps in part because of my efforts as Governor of Georgia and later as chairman of the senate Agriculture Committee. The farmers had supported me in every race I ever ran, including the last one, but there just weren't enough of them left anymore.

Two personal photos were among the memorabilia I saved for myself. One showed me and my son Gene sitting on a John Deere tractor on our farm in Lovejoy, Georgia. It was taken in 1948, when I was thirty-five and Gene was six. I'm sitting there with a Panama hat on my head and my hands on the steering wheel. Little Gene is in my lap with his eyes closed. The photo originally ran in the *Atlanta Journal* as part of a story on "Georgia's New First Family." The article quoted me as saying that the Brahmin bull "doesn't ever have to switch his tail when flies are bothering him. He just shakes his skin." That's pretty much the way I've tried to live my life.

The other photo was of old Charley Worrill—the pistol-packing judge—swearing me in as Governor of Georgia in the early morning of January 15, 1947. The legislature had elected me when the governor-elect (who happened to be my daddy) died before he could take office. Thousands of my supporters stayed all night to see me installed in the governor's office, and tens of thousands of others listened to my inaugural address on a nationwide radio hookup. There were even war correspondents from foreign countries in attendance, ready to cover the bloodshed that never occurred. Ordinary people loved me back then, but to the cartoonists and editorial writers, I was the Crown Prince, the Pretender, or just "Young Hummon." Maybe that's when I picked up the habit of shaking my skin.

I hadn't planned on being governor or even entering politics, but back in those days events sometimes had a mind of their own. I had a promising law career in 1941 when the war came along and changed the world forever. I hadn't been married long when I was called to active duty and sent to the South Pacific. My sons were conceived on shore leave and born while I was on the other side of the world. I came home to a wife and two children I scarcely knew and to a dying father planning one last run for public office. By the time I took the oath as governor, the unexpected no longer came as much of a surprise.

If you go back far enough, however, you won't find my name or picture in the newspapers. The cheering isn't for me. The editorial writers aren't denouncing me. They're all focusing their attention on a fellow with horn-rimmed glasses and red galluses who mesmerizes huge crowds. His hair keeps falling down over his forehead as he paces around waving his arms to make a point. The man the folks are listening to never left anyone permanently neutral. To some he was a savior, to others the Devil Incarnate. To me he was a special man named Papa. And it is with him that my story begins.

1

Growing Up

My first memory is of the sandy road in front of our farm in McRae, Georgia. Back then we had a beautiful grey mare named Maude. She was fast and reliable, and one day my father hitched her up to his buggy and drove down the road. I remember following after him until my legs were so tired I couldn't go any farther. I lay down in the middle of the road and went to sleep. My father came back later that day, put me in the buggy, and took me home. I couldn't have been more than two or three at the time.

MY FATHER WAS EUGENE TALMADGE, one of the most colorful and controversial figures of his era and the greatest political orator I have ever known. He was elected three times agriculture commissioner and four times Governor of Georgia. In his hey-day one third of the people of his state would have followed him to the Gates of Hell. Another third wanted to see him in Hell. And the remaining third never could make up their minds what they thought of him. It was this last group that always determined his political fate. In his life he ran ten statewide races and won seven. He was headed to a political meeting that day I tried to follow him, over seventy years ago. It is a road I've traveled ever since.

Just about anybody who knows anything about my daddy

knows of two statements he's supposed to have made. The first was: "The poor dirt farmer ain't got but three friends on this earth: God Almighty, Sears Roebuck, and Gene Talmadge." The other is: "I don't want to carry any counties with streetcars running in them." Well, he never said either of those things. The first statement was made by a man introducing him at a political rally. No politician with half a brain in his head wants to sound pompous and self-important, and I've known few politicians smarter than my daddy. As for the second statement, I've yet to meet a candidate who didn't want to carry one hundred percent of the vote if he could get it. What my daddy actually said was that in one election "we *didn't* carry any counties with streetcars running in them." A different matter, as you can see. But then, what is history but a lot of stories—some true, some untrue—that are recorded, read, and reread until they're eventually accepted as absolute fact? (God knows, in my time people have accused me of everything except being good looking.) You might say that this book is an attempt to set the record straight.

My daddy's people came to England from Normandy with William the Conqueror in 1066. After fighting in the Battle of Hastings, they anglicized the family name from "Talmache" to "Talmadge." Then in 1631 the first Talmadges in America arrived on the ship *Plough* and settled on Long Island, New York. My ancestor Benjamin Talmadge was aide-de-camp to George Washington and started the first secret service in this country. He's credited with having captured Andre the Spy, and to this day his sword hangs in Frances Tavern in Brooklyn, New York. My great-grandfather Aaron Talmadge fought with Andrew Jackson in Florida and eventually settled in Forsyth, Georgia, in 1822. Our family has been here ever since.

Although my mother's maiden name was Mattie Thurmond, I can't remember anyone ever calling her anything but "Miss Mitt." She was born in Edgefield County, South Carolina, of the South Carolina Thurmonds. They're a serious and hardworking people, those Thurmonds. They don't smoke, they don't drink, they don't cut up, and they live forever. I'll never forget an incident involving my mother's distant cousin Senator Strom Thurmond. This was back in 1964, when the senate Commerce Committee was considering the nomination of one of Strom's enemies—former Florida Governor Leroy Collins—to be director of some bureaucracy called the Community Relations Service. Strom knew that he didn't have enough votes to block the nomination, but he figured he might keep it from coming to a vote by staying out of the committee room and preventing a quorum. Well, Strom was standing just outside the committee room when this populist senator demagogue from Texas by the name of Ralph Yarborough decided he would force a quorum by shoving Strom into the room. Strom was a good deal older and weighed considerably less than Yarborough, but he ran and did pushups and generally kept himself in excellent shape. Before Yarborough knew what hit him, Strom had him flipped on his back on the marble floor of what is now the Russell Office Building. They shook hands and parted friends, but no one ever again tried to push Strom around. My mother was too much of a lady to wrestle with a senator or anyone else, but she was tough just like that. She died at the age of 101, and if she hadn't broken her hip she'd probably be alive today.

After my mother's first husband John A. Peterson died, she got a job as telegrapher over in Ailey, Georgia. (That was back when they'd put an empty can of Prince Albert tobacco behind some of the keys to enhance the sound.) Mama was one of the youngest telegraphers around and one of the best. I never really appreciated her ability until I tried to learn Morse Code in the Navy and couldn't. And the amazing thing is she never forgot anything she learned. When she was eighty-five years old they had a convention of old telegraphers at the Women's Club on Peachtree and Sixteenth Streets in Atlanta. They set up a male telegrapher at one end of the table and my mother at the opposite end. There they sat clicking messages back and forth at each other, never missing a beat. It had been over sixty years since Mama had last operated a telegraph. She was one remarkable lady.

When Papa arrived in Ailey, Mama was already a young widow with an infant son—my half-brother John A. Peterson, Jr. Papa had found work fresh out of law school with the Atlanta firm of Dorsey, Brewster, and Howell, but he didn't like taking orders

11

and was eager to become his own boss. So when William Peterson, a friend of my grandfather's, suggested that Papa go into practice for himself down in Ailey, he didn't have to ask twice. "Mr. Bill," as he was known, even arranged for my father to room in a house owned by his sister Maggie and her husband. The other boarder in that house was Maggie's sister-in-law, Mattie Thurmond Peterson.

If my parents ever told me anything about their courtship, I'm sure I've forgotten it. But I do know that Mama was a capable and attractive woman, and there wasn't a person alive Papa couldn't charm if he put his mind to it. I guess it was only natural for two eligible young people in a small town like Ailey to start seeing each other. I've heard from other sources that they'd go horseback riding along the cotton fields outside of town and picnic under the pine trees. It must have done the trick, because on September 12, 1909, my mama and daddy got married.

Not too long after that they moved to a farm my mother owned along Sugar Creek in Telfair County outside of McRae, Georgia. It was called a twelve-horse farm, but it should have been a twelve-mule farm, because those were our beasts of burden. There was no shrewder businesswoman than Mama and no better judge of mule flesh than Papa, so things worked out pretty well. That marriage eventually produced three children—daughters named Vera and Margaret and, in between, a son. He came along on August 9, 1913, and was named Herman Eugene Talmadge.

I'd be lying if I said I was eager to go to school. I was seven before I started, and by then I'd gotten used to fishing, playing in the woods, and doing chores around the farm. But then, no one asked me if I wanted to go. They just sent me off to the I.J. Davis School, a mile and a half from home. It was a two-room schoolhouse heated by a stove, and you had to go out back to a two-hole privy to go to the bathroom. My lunches, brought from home, consisted of a cold biscuit, a little bottle of syrup, some fat meat covered with lard, and a sweet potato—all wrapped in paper. Newspaper in my case, because our family was the only one in the community to take a daily paper. For everyone else, the prime means of communication was the party line telephone. The first two things I learned in school, long before I learned how to read and write, were that there was no Santa Claus and that the stork didn't bring babies. I had discovered only the Christmas before that Santa didn't come down the chimney on Christmas Eve, but hid his presents in my parents' bedroom closet for several weeks before Christmas. Even after I learned the truth, I went along with the Christmas tradition for some time. The apples and oranges and occasional pocket knives were nice no matter where they came from. I figured out the stork ruse as I started working (and watching) around the farm.

One of my favorite pastimes as a boy was swimming in Sugar Creek. You might say that we did it for hygiene as well as sport. Sometimes swimming in the nude on the weekend was all the bath a country boy would get. My half-brother John A. taught me to swim by throwing me in the water and making me fend for myself. Years later when I was executive officer on an attack transport ship in the United States Navy, I asked my men how many of them knew how to swim. They were from the urban areas of New York, New Jersey, and Pennsylvania, and eighty percent of them couldn't swim. I figured that if they were out in the middle of the Pacific Ocean under hostile fire, they damn well better learn. That was the first order I gave them.

There were several black families working on the farm, and I mingled freely with them. When we were out there swimming and playing as youngsters, we never noticed any difference in color. We were just children having fun and raising hell. A black boy named Thad and I were particularly close. I couldn't count the number of meals I had at his house. But when it came time to go to school, we went our separate ways. We were still friends, but on a different social standing. I never thought to question the practice of segregation, and I doubt that he did either. Up North, where segregation didn't exist, there were fewer close friendships between black and white. I'm not talking about cause and effect, just social reality. If we are just now beginning to understand the War Between the States, it may take a hundred years for us to understand the way race relations have changed in my lifetime.

I remember less fondly those all-day Sunday trips to visit some relatives of my mama's over in Uvalda, Georgia. Today it wouldn't take any time at all to make the trip from McRae to Uvalda, but back then it would take us three or four hours to drive there in our Grant-6 automobile. We'd have to go across the river on a ferry at Mount Vernon, and we usually had several flat tires along the way. That would require taking the tire off the car, patching it up, and putting it back on. We'd get to Uvalda in time to eat lunch and visit for an hour. Then we'd have to drive another three or four hours home. The trip was all of thirty miles.

One day when I was eleven or twelve Papa went to Atlanta and brought back a carload of mules. I met the caravan at the Oconee River just outside Mount Vernon. Papa had brought with him a Tennessee Welsh pony for me. I got on the pony there at the river bridge and rode her twenty-five miles back to the farm. She was a good pony, and I'd use her to round up the cows at milking time. She was supposed to be with colt, but I'd almost given up hope of that when one morning I came out and saw a little colt lying beside her. The pony's name was Nell, and I called the colt George after a friend of mine. The colt was killed by a car, but Nell lived to a ripe old age.

Santa Claus visited me for the last time when I was thirteen. He brought me a double-barrel sixteen-gauge shotgun, a box of shells, and a dollar bill. That gun was a godsend. The one I had been using had a single thirty-two inch barrel. I'd fire it, be knocked on my rear end, and then have to wait for the black powder smoke to clear to see if I'd killed anything. I don't have to tell you that that's no way to be hunting the beasts of the southern wild. And contrary to what my detractors would have you believe, I don't still have that dollar bill.

Times were hard in the country even before the Depression came along. I remember at age thirteen plowing fourteen hours a day for fifty cents. I worked only half a day on Saturday, so that was $2.75 a week. When I got older I worked in what is now the Piggly Wiggly supermarket and could make that same $2.75 in just thirteen hours on Saturday. We never thought of ourselves as poor because we didn't know any rich folks to compare ourselves with. Today people think they're poor if they don't have a color television set with a satellite dish and a VCR. When I was young our greatest entertainment was eating barbecue on the Fourth of July. They even brought the prisoners out in their chains and stripes to join in the festivities.

It was quite an occasion when movies first came to McRae. I'd steal eggs from my mother's hens to get the money to go see my favorite westerns. I remember that William S. Hart could shoot two guns equally well. Tom Mix was a one-gun man. Years later Leeman Anderson, who worked for my daddy before he became Dick Russell's secretary in the Senate, took me to my first talking picture. I thought it was the most marvelous thing in the world to see people actually talking on the screen. Radio was strictly a novelty. The first one I ever saw was a headphone model that my aunt owned. When we listened to it, it was not so much for entertainment as to see who could pick up the farthest station. I recall getting a station in the Midwest one night. If you'd tried to tell me about television back then I wouldn't have believed it. And yet, nearly fifty years later that medium and a third-rate burglary called Watergate would put Herman Talmadge into millions of American homes for an entire summer.

My granddaddy Tom Talmadge was surprised when his son decided to run for agriculture commissioner in 1926. But he shouldn't have been. Old Tom was something of a politician in his own right. Although he never ran for public office, he was a trustee of Tift College (a Baptist college in Forsyth, Georgia) for many years and was fondly remembered by the girls who went there. He was like a father away from home for them. When I first ran for governor in 1948 people would come up to me from all over and say, "I don't know anything about you, boy, but I'm voting for you because of your granddaddy." In this century only a half a dozen families have dominated the politics of their state for more than a generation: the Byrds of Virginia, the Tafts of Ohio, the La Follettes of Wisconsin, the Kennedys of Massachusetts, the Longs of Louisiana, and the Talmadges of Georgia.

In 1926 my daddy seemed an unlikely man to begin a political dynasty. He was a forty-two year old farmer and lawyer who had never even won a local election. The closest he came was in 1922 when he ran for the state senate from the three-county district around McRae. Papa carried one county and lost two, which meant he lost the election. You see, back in those days we had something called the county-unit vote. That was sort of like the Electoral College, and it controlled elections in Georgia until the courts ruled it unconstitutional in 1962. My father was a maverick who wouldn't kow-tow to the courthouse gang, so they set out to destroy him. Accused him of everything under the sun, including having sexual relations with one of his mules. I endured a lot of taunts from the children in town, being a country boy and the son of a losing politician. But all that would change in 1926.

The incumbent agriculture commissioner was J.J. Brown, a distinguished looking man with a statewide reputation and a well-oiled political machine. I was only thirteen at the time, but I knew that Papa would have himself an uphill fight. Then Brown made his big mistake—he challenged Gene Talmadge to debate. One of the debates would be on Brown's turf, another in my daddy's territory, and the third on neutral ground. Those were real three-hour debates, not the glorified press conferences that pass for debates in this day and age. Each man would speak for thirty minutes and then have a chance for interrogation and rejoinder. Brown was a lackluster speaker and my daddy a real spellbinder. They called him the "Wild Man from Sugar Creek" and a whole lot of less complimentary things.

I remember clearly their debate in McRae. We had big piles of watermelon for everybody. My daddy, being a gracious host, said, "Son, get Mr. Brown a watermelon." I went out and got him the biggest and best I could find. Mr. Brown said, "Leave it there, boy, my chauffeur will get it." Well, the Wild Man from Sugar Creek whipped the pants off that city slicker in his chauffeur-driven limousine. My daddy won the popular vote by almost two-to-one and the county unit vote by almost seven-to-one. I later became close friends with J. J. Brown and even appointed him to the Game and Fish Department when I was governor. I've always felt that the best way to get rid of an enemy is to make a friend of him. It's a policy that has stood me well in my years in public life.

The people who rode in the streetcars and the chauffeur-driven limousines were always underestimating my father. They thought he was an ignorant redneck because he wore red galluses and would come to political rallies sitting on a bale of cotton in an ox-drawn cart. (What they forgot was that he was a Phi Beta Kappa and a graduate of the University of Georgia Law School.) It didn't make any difference, though, because the common people loved him, and there were a lot more wool hats than silk hats in those days. In lots of small communities he'd get every vote. In a rural district south of Atlanta Papa carried one election 106-0. And he never forgot those people once he got in office.

When my daddy got to be commissioner of agriculture, he saw that the seed and fertilizer laws were enforced. The seed laws provided for a germination guarantee by the seller, and the fertilizer laws for a guaranteed analysis. The agriculture commissioner had a chemistry laboratory to check the products and was authorized to issue penalties when they were below what was guaranteed. Under Papa nearly every farmer in Georgia got a refund check, because the analysis or germination didn't measure up to the lab tests. Another duty of the agriculture commissioner was to assist in marketing farm products. At that time the hog packers in Georgia were bidding several cents below the Chicago market. So, Papa used some state money to bid up the price to near the Chicago market value and lost nearly $30,000 in the process. He was accused of misappropriating state funds, but nothing came of it. If anything, it made him more popular than ever. Out in the country he'd get up on the stump and shout, "They say I stole." Then he'd pause just enough for the crowd to get uncomfortable and maybe a little indignant. Then he'd bellow at the top of his lungs, "Yeah, I stole!" After a shorter pause he came right back almost as loud: "But I stole for you. You men in overalls. You dirt farmers!" They loved it.

There were few things my father loved more than outraging the high hat city folks. When he moved into the old Georgia governor's mansion over in Ansley Park, he turned the garage into a barn and brought up some chickens and his favorite milk cow from the farm. It was bad enough when the cow grazed on the lawn of the governor's mansion, but that was only the beginning. We had an old black man who worked for us at the time. Called him the Mahatma because he was the spitting image of the

Mahatma Gandhi. Well, the Mahatma thought it was a crime for all that green grass at the adjacent Ansley Park golf course to go to waste, so he led the cow over to the golf course and had him grazing on the fairway. When the groundskeepers saw what was happening they said, "You can't do that." And the Mahatma just rared back and said: "This is the guvnuh's cow. He can graze anywhere he wants to."

People who don't like my daddy will tell you he was a racist. That's not exactly true. He was a staunch believer in segregation and defended it a bit too vigorously at times. But he never had any truck with the Ku Klux Klan. He once told me, "Hummon, I'd never join an organization where they're afraid to show their faces." (When I was governor we passed a bill unmasking the Klan—they still can march, the first amendment guarantees them that, but they've got to show their faces.) The head of the Klan in Georgia back in my daddy's time was a dentist by the name of Dr. Hiram Wesley Evans. I remember he got so enraged at Huey Long once that he was going to go to Louisiana and straighten Huey out. (I forget what the issue was but I do know that once when Roy Wilkins asked Huey what he was doing for "the Negroes of Louisiana," Huey said: "My motto's 'every man a king,' and that includes the niggers"—which is not the sort of sentiment to warm the cockles of a Klansman's heart.) Well Huey, who had no compunction about taking on the likes of Standard Oil and the President of the United States, was not about to be intimidated by the likes of Dr. Hiram Wesley Evans. So he said, "You tell that tooth-pulling son of a bitch if he comes to Louisiana, I'll run him out of the state." And he would have, too. As I recall, though, it *was* a doctor who finally assassinated Huey.

One thing I learned early in my own political career was to control my temper. When Papa was running for governor for the first time and I was a student at the University of Georgia, I had the job of passing out handbills announcing when and where he would speak. Well, one day I went into this butchershop in Cedartown. As I recall, it had sawdust on the floor and a big chopping block for cutting up meat. I marched in there very pleased with myself and handed the butcher one of my handbills. He took one look at it and said, "I wouldn't vote for that goddamn son of a bitch for nuthin.'" Now I didn't think of my father as a son of a bitch, much less a *goddamn* son of a bitch. I didn't know whether to hit the butcher, call him one, or just get the hell out of there. I knew it was no use arguing with him—he was too big to fight and he had a meat cleaver in his hand. So I just smiled and walked out. I suppose I've had to do that hundreds of times over the years. One thing a politician can't afford is a short fuse. Take Ed Muskie. He was a bright man and a capable senator. He would probably have made a good president. But he was just too thin-skinned. And it finally did him in politically.

Probably the most important lesson I ever learned, however, was not to judge people by outward appearance. I remember right before he announced for governor in 1932 Papa gave a speech in Franklin County, Georgia. He was introduced by this man who had tobacco stains on his mouth, stubble on his chin, and overalls on his back. I said, "Papa, couldn't you find someone else to introduce you?" And he said, "Son, that man is a large landowner and one of the most respected citizens of the community." A couple of years later when I was in college and spending the weekend at the governor's mansion, he dressed me down for making derogatory comments about some of my classmates. And shortly thereafter he wrote me the longest letter I ever received from him. He told me something he had learned from Mrs. Lydia Crews, a very wise and prominent lady who was known as the Queen of the Okefenokee Swamp: "Remember to whom you speak, of whom you speak, when, where, and how you speak. Treat your enemy of today as your friend of tomorrow and your friend of today as your enemy of tomorrow." It's the best advice I've ever received, and I've always tried to live my life accordingly.

I learned many valuable lessons from my daddy, but I also was blessed with some fine teachers in my time. In college I learned a great deal from a superb history teacher by the name of W.O. Payne. In law school Harry A. Shinn could teach you more law accidentally than most teachers could on purpose. But if there is one mentor who stands out above the rest, it would have to be my high school history teacher and debate coach, Enda Ballard Duggan.

She was a maiden lady when she came to McRae but later married a postmaster in Laurens County. She was assistant principal when I started high school and ran the place with an iron fist. Mrs. Duggan wasn't much to look at. In fact you might say she was downright homely. She had a long nose, a receding chin, dark eyes, and an olive complexion. She wore her hair in a bun on top of her head like your typical schoolmarm. And she was a real autocrat. You didn't cut up in Mrs. Duggan's class, and you did exactly what she said. At the time I was no ball of fire as a student. My main interests in life were hunting and fishing and doing just enough to get by. I'll never forget one morning in chapel when she was taking volunteers for the debate team. About five or six hands shot up. Mine was not one of them. By that age I knew enough not to volunteer for anything. Well, after Mrs. Duggan called out the names of the students who had raised their hands, she added, "and Herman Talmadge." That was the beginning of my career as a public speaker.

The first debate I can remember our team winning was when I was in the ninth grade. My partner was a little tenth grade girl named Marjorie. We were up against a team from Hawkinsville High School—big six-foot football players in the eleventh grade. They made Marjorie and me look like midgets. We took the affirmative side on the proposition—"Resolved: Georgia Should Vote $100,000,000 in Road Bonds." And we won. Although it meant nothing to me at the time, the other team was coached by M.E. Thompson. Who in that room would have thought that twenty years later Thompson and I would be involved in a bitter struggle for the governorship of Georgia?

I was voted into all sorts of offices in high school and made quite a schoolboy politician. I remember once running for office against a boy named Jason Jerrard. He was new in town and talked kind of funny. I said, "Here's a boy who has moved twelve miles north from Lumber City to McRae and has picked up a northern brogue in the process." Yes, we used to sling mud even back then. But at least it was more productive than playing hooky. Being on the debate team and studying history got me interested in politics. And it was largely Mrs. Duggan's doing. Her enthusiasm was contagious. The woman had an amazing sense for latent ability. She could really light a fire under loafers and make them work to their full potential. I'm living proof of that.

I remembered my training under Mrs. Duggan and put it to good use when I made my first political speech in 1934. I was about twenty at the time, and Papa was running for reelection as governor. A friend of mine named Aubrey Evans wanted to get some political experience, so he arranged for me to come speak on my daddy's behalf over in his hometown of Rebecca, Georgia. It was a town of about five hundred people, and he had several hundred of them out in the town square to hear me deliver my maiden political speech. But what I remember best was a big banner across the town square saying, "Welcome Herman Talmadge." In huge letters. I really thought I was something that day.

Mrs. Duggan took great pride in the accomplishments of her former students. When I ran for governor in 1948, she introduced me on a statewide radio hookup. Then when I was in the Senate, she came up to Washington and stayed with me for several days. In the Senate dining hall, she enjoyed meeting a headwaiter who had worked there for fifty years and knew many of the famous people she had read about in history. After her husband died, she lived with an old maid sister of hers in Dublin, Georgia. I used to visit them whenever I was in town. One day in the late sixties I heard that she was seriously ill, so I went to see her in the hospital there in Dublin. She couldn't have weighed more than eighty pounds, but that little shriveled up woman still had an alert mind and a commanding presence. She knew who I was, and we talked for the last time. She died two days later. Those who say that the good we do dies with us never met Enda Ballard Duggan.

One of the saddest and most frightening experiences of my early life occurred in November 1930. I was a senior in high school at the time, and we were out milking the cows. I'm not sure who noticed it first, but we looked over and saw that the roof of the house was burning. We went in to try to put the fire out, but it was a wood frame house, and on a windy day the fire was far too advanced for us to do anything but watch it burn. The house and everything in it were a total loss. We had a German shepherd we called Al, after

Al Smith. He was very devoted to my mother and followed her everywhere. Al went into the burning house, looking for Mama, and never came out. Well, Papa had just been elected to his third term as commissioner of agriculture, so we all moved for a time to Atlanta. The house on the farm was eventually rehabilitated, and a new one was built in 1936. But my childhood as a country boy was over and a new chapter of my life just beginning.

2

My Apprenticeship

I've gotta Eugene dog, I gotta Eugene cat
I'm a Talmadge man from ma shoes to ma hat.
Farmer in the cawnfield hollerin' whoa gee haw,
Kain't put no thirty-dollar tag on a three-dollar car.

THAT WAS ONE of my daddy's campaign songs when he ran for reelection as Governor of Georgia in 1934. It was played by Fiddlin' John Carson and his daughter Moonshine Kate. Old Fiddlin' John was your original country music star, before Jimmie Rodgers, the Carter family, or even Uncle Dave Macon. He was signed by Ralph Peer for OKeh records back in 1923, and his rendition of "The Preacher and the Bear" was the first phonograph recording I ever heard. Of course, country music wasn't the big business then that it is today. (Fiddlin' John never made much money at his music, so I gave him a job running the elevator in the Georgia Capitol when I became governor in 1948.) They didn't even call it country music in Fiddlin' John's day. It was "hillbilly" music, and some folks looked down their noses at it. But the folks who came to a Eugene Talmadge rally couldn't have cared less. I doubt that we would have packed them in as well with Wolfgang Amadeus Mozart.

Fiddlin' John was with Tom Watson back before World War I, signed on with Papa in 1932, and became an integral part of the reelection campaign in 1934. He and Moonshine Kate would get the crowd warmed up with favorites like "Turkey in the Straw," "The Hen Cackled and the Rooster's Gonna Crow," and "The Saints Go Marchin' In." We'd give the people a chance to stuff themselves with barbecued pork and socialize a little with their neighbors before off in the distance they'd see an ox-drawn cart carrying the man of the hour. They'd go wild as he came in, got out, and climbed up to the podium. He'd stand there with a little shock of hair falling over his forehead, snap his red galluses, and begin to *orate*. Not some canned speech read off an idiot card, but a real honest-to-God stemwinder that would last for an hour or more. All extemporaneous. And the men in the crowd would snap their red galluses and yell questions at him. I particularly remember some brothers from over in Madison County who would always come to Papa's rallies and sit in a tree. We called them the Tree Climbing Haggards. They'd holler, "Tell us about so-and-so, Gene." And he'd either answer them right off or, if it was something he wanted to deal with later, he'd just say, "I'm a-comin' ta that!"

In 1932 Papa was one of ten candidates for governor. To him, that meant Eugene Talmadge and nine others. He said they had the baseball team running against him, and he gave those boys unshirted hell. Worked out a speech in which every one of them had a position on the team. As I recall, he had John N. Holder pitching and Tom Hardwick catching. There would be a little patter back and forth. Holder takes the mound and Hardwick yells at him, "Honest John, throw me that crooked ball." It was funnier than an Abbott and Costello routine. Well, everyone knew that Papa would come in first in the primary. The only question was which of the other nine would get in the runoff with him. It was inconceivable that anyone would get a majority in a field that crowded. But that's exactly what happened. Gene Talmadge whipped the whole damn baseball team single-handed, waltzed off to Atlanta, and put his favorite milk cow out to pasture on the lawn of the governor's mansion.

It was a strange series of events that opened up the governorship in 1932. First, on April 18 one of our U.S. Senators, William

J. Harris, died. Dick Russell, who was governor, appointed Major John S. Cohen, the editor of the *Atlanta Journal*, to keep the seat warm until they could have a special election to fill the vacancy. Dick then ran for the Senate himself (where he served with distinction for thirty-eight years). That left the governorship open for just about every ambitious politician in the state. Papa had been agriculture commissioner for six years and was restless to move up. (It would have taken an elephant tranquilizer to keep him out of that gubernatorial race.) Although we weren't surprised that he won, the size of his victory was absolutely amazing. After all, John N. Holder was highway commissioner, which gave him the biggest pork barrel in the state. It's a funny thing about roads, though. You can hardly ever make them pay off. Say you've got ten roads that need paving, and you can only pave nine. The folks on the nine that you pave aren't grateful because they figure they've got it coming. But those on the one you don't will never forgive you. As usual, Papa put it best. "Hummon," he'd say, "if road politics was worth a damn, John N. Holder would have been the Czar of Russia."

That song that Fiddlin' John wrote for Papa was about the main accomplishment of his first administration. Before Papa came in, the tags for your car and truck were downright expensive, sometimes more than the cost of the vehicle itself. So when farmers came into town on Saturday afternoon to buy supplies and socialize, they'd often park in the woods to hide from the tag catcher. This was what economists call a regressive tax, because it took a bigger chunk out of the poor man's pocket. With so many people out of work during the Depression, that just didn't seem fair. So Papa promised to lower the cost of tags to three dollars. And he did it, too, but not without a first-class row.

Even though the voters were overwhelmingly in favor of the three-dollar tag, the highway department wasn't about to get off the public tit without putting up a fight. And it had bought enough influence in the legislature to keep those boys from going along with what Papa and the people wanted. So as soon as the legislature was out of session, Papa used his executive authority to suspend all but three dollars of the cost of license tags. Those tags were for identification, he said, not for gouging the poor farmer.

When the director of motor vehicles wouldn't go along, Papa up and fired him, even though he was an old college friend. And when the highway commission wouldn't accept the budget he set for them, he had them removed from office for dereliction of duty. My father believed, as Jefferson did, that the least government was the best government. He reduced *ad valorem* taxes, utility rates, and everything else he could. In fact, he was the last Governor of Georgia to reduce taxes.

My daddy's second administration was even wilder than the first. The legislature fought Papa tooth and nail on a whole range of issues. Ed Rivers, who was Speaker of the House, was bound and determined to create a little New Deal in Georgia, whether or not he had the money to pay for it. (He got his chance when he succeeded Papa as governor in 1936 and bankrupted the state.) What Ed did back in '35 was allow the legislative session to end without appropriating any money. The thing most governors would have done under those circumstances would have been to call a special session of the legislature. But Eugene Talmadge wasn't most governors. He figured that if he called a special session, the legislature would pass a bunch of pork barrel bills that he didn't want, and his enemies might even try to impeach him over one thing or another. So he contended that the last appropriation bill remained in effect until amended by a new one, and he proceeded to try to run the state himself with those funds and the constant revenues from licenses and the taxes on gasoline, cigarettes, and the like.

Now, the state treasurer and the comptroller knew that Papa would try to remove them if they opposed him. So they cleared out their safes and set the locks with eighty-hour time switches. Since they were elected officials the same as Papa, they figured that they could continue functioning in their positions if they could get themselves and the state's money away from the Capitol and let the courts decide who was right. Papa didn't realize the safes were empty until he had the locks burned off with an acetylene torch. There was a big row with the banks and courts, but Papa stood his ground and won the day. When the state supreme court upheld him, he had the Atlanta banks bring the money to the governor's office, with the principal in one bag and the interest in the other.

You can imagine how all of that went over with the ultra-liberals in the press. They called my daddy a "wool hat dictator," a "hill-billy Hitler," and a whole bunch of other names I'd just as soon not repeat in print. Funny thing about dictators, though—they're not supposed to like elections. But Papa absolutely thrived on them. When he opened his campaign for reelection in 1934, there were acres and acres of people there in Bainbridge, Georgia, to greet him. You didn't see many briefcases or fancy suits, but there were a hell of a lot of wool hats and overalls and red suspenders. Thirty thousand folks at one rally alone. They'd sing, "Talmadge red, Talmadge blue, I wish my name was Talmadge too." And they'd carry Papa out on their shoulders when he had finished speaking. Back then it was the people, not the media, that ruled. To this day I have Papa's red galluses framed and hanging proudly in the den of my home in Hampton, Georgia. When I see some over-dressed yuppie wearing suspenders today, I just smile and think that in some things Papa was ahead of his time.

When the farm house in McRae burned in 1930, Papa had just been elected to his third term as agriculture commissioner, and I was in the middle of my senior year in high school. I don't mind telling you I was a little apprehensive about transferring to Druid Hills High School in Atlanta. I figured the city kids would be light years ahead of me in learning. But it didn't take more than two or three weeks before I realized what a good job Mrs. Duggan and the other teachers in McRae had done. In history and govern-ment, I didn't have to take a back seat to anyone. However, math and science were a different story. I never could get those subjects, so when Papa insisted I go to Georgia Tech and enroll in the co-op program there, I had to tell him I wasn't qualified. Instead, I fol-lowed in his footsteps and enrolled at the University of Georgia, in the fall of 1931.

The French have a saying that translates something like this: "The more things change, the more they remain the same." I suspect that's true of college life. Even back in 1931 football was just about the biggest thing on the Georgia campus. They say that football is corrupt today, and maybe it is, but things are a lot better regulated than they used to be. When Papa was manager of the University of Georgia football team back around the turn of the century, there used to be drifters who would go from school to school and play for whatever team would offer them the most money. They were called "ringers." A number of years ago I was at a brunch sponsored by Chip Robert, the great Georgia Tech star from years past. Judge Frank Foley walked up to me and said, "Herman, I got something in my lock box I want you to see." It was a paper showing that Eugene Talmadge and Frank Foley had borrowed fifty dollars from the bank to pay a ringer to play against Chip Robert's Georgia Tech team. They may buy victory more discreetly in this day and age, but then the ante is a hell of a lot higher.

I also followed in my father's footsteps by pledging the Sigma Nu fraternity. My freshman year I was elected pledge chairman and helped to build the fraternity up until it was the best one on campus. My senior year we had the captain of the football team, the president of the interfraternity council, the editor of the school paper, and quite a few scholars. Back then, you'd get a key from each of the organizations you belonged to. So the big men on campus (myself included) would get them a watch and chain and string up all their keys so everyone could see how important they were. (I understand that the Phi Beta Kappas don't even do that anymore.) But times were generally hard. In our entire fraternity we had one car amongst thirty-five or forty members. I remember owning one-third interest in a thirty-dollar Ford. And I was considered well dressed because my parents could afford to buy me a new suit of clothes every year.

One of the things that students would do to preserve their shoe leather would be to put cleats on the soles of their shoes. It preserved the shoes all right, but it made a godawful racket. Especially at times you'd just as soon have been inconspicuous. I'll never forget the time my friend J. Hassel Porter got tired of listening to Senator J. Ham Lewis read a speech on foreign policy in chapel. Porter got up to sneak out, and those cleats went BAM! BAM! BAM! Just like a mule kicking the side of a barn. The authorities read him the riot act for being disrespectful to our distinguished speaker.

Like many students whose parents lived within a few hours' drive of the university, I would often go home on weekends and take a few friends with me. Only for me, home was the Georgia governor's mansion out in the Ansley Park section of Atlanta. It was an imposing granite building that looked like a medieval Spanish fortress. Had fifteen rooms and a leaky roof. The roof leaked when Papa was governor in 1932, and it still leaked when I moved in as governor in 1948. We had to put out washtubs and pots and pans to catch the water. Finally in 1966, Carl Sanders built a lavish new mansion out near Buckhead. I guess it was easier than getting the damn roof fixed.

Back in my college days you could pursue a course of study that would completely bypass the baccalaureate degree and take you to the LL.B. in five years. Since I was a young man in a hurry, that's exactly what I did. When I came up to my senior year in law school, I figured I had the world by the tail. That was before Judge E. W. Maynard of Macon, Georgia, said, "Herman, what are you doing to prepare for the bar exam?" When I told him, "nothing," he just looked at me and said: "You get you a copy of the *Georgia Code* and study it from cover to cover. Then you get you a subscription to the *Southeastern Advance Sheet* and memorize every decision of the Appeals Court and the Supreme Court. You do both of those things, and you might just have a chance of squeaking through." Well, you can bet that scared the bejesus out of me. For the next few weeks, I didn't even go to the bathroom without that code. Even enrolled in a crash course in Atlanta run by one Tillo Von Nunes. I don't remember much about the course, but I do recall that old Tillo had a daughter named Irma who was the first woman I ever saw with a man's haircut. My class at the university was the first to have to take the bar exam. Out of a class of twenty-seven, I was one of only seven who passed it the first time through. An honor graduate flunked the exam twice, and one of our better students flunked it seven times.

Around that time I remember going to a dance one night at the Kappa Sigma fraternity house and seeing a beautiful girl in a red evening dress. Her name was Kathryn Williamson, and she was from Jamesport on Long Island, New York. We danced that night and began dating shortly thereafter. In April, 1937, we were married. There's an old saying that, "When food goes off the table, love goes out the window." I don't think that's always true, but financial difficulties did put a strain on our marriage. It was the depth of the Depression, and young lawyers weren't snapped up at big salaries. I had "hanging around" privileges at the firm of Hewlett and Dennis. That meant I could share offices there and was welcome to any business I could pick up. Kathryn was a sophisticated girl from the Northeast, and I was a country boy. Things just didn't work out as we had planned. In her divorce petition, she complained about my smoking black offensive cigars and going to political meetings she didn't enjoy. The courts called it "incompatability." I guess we were two kids trying to move too fast. Our divorce became final in January, 1941.

Given the conservative mores of the time and region, you would think that my opponents would have tried to use the divorce against me. It was an issue that plagued Adlai Stevenson and ruined Nelson Rockefeller. But those two were already in public life when their difficulties occurred. My sole claim to fame was being Eugene Talmadge's son. The one time that my first marriage ever became an issue was when I ran for governor in 1948. Some crazy fellow who worked for the state put out a libelous pamphlet accusing me of having murdered Kathryn. She would have been surprised to see it, since she was working as a model in New York at the time. But I doubt my accuser was surprised at all when he got a telegram from the newly inaugurated governor returning him to the private sector.

Papa was first elected governor in 1932, the year Franklin D. Roosevelt was elected president. It was three years after the stock market had crashed in October of '29, and millions of people were out of work across the nation. You could walk down Peachtree Street in Atlanta and see men who had once been very prosperous in the business world selling apples or pencils or anything to keep from starving. They'd shiver in the cold because they'd already sold their warm clothes. Out in the country, folks wore overalls year round. That's *if* they were well off. There were many who made their clothes from old fertilizer sacks. Some families would go for an entire year without seeing a five-dollar bill.

I never really went hungry, but I didn't live very high off the hog either. My memories of the Depression are mostly of what it did to people I knew. I was foolish enough to co-sign a few banknotes for friends I was sure would succeed once they got back on their feet. Unfortunately some stayed down for good, and I was stuck with their debts. Andy Jackson once told his son never to sue a man for libel or sign another man's paper. At least the second part of that advice was sound, as I learned the hard way. I'd sooner give a man money than co-sign for what a bank wouldn't lend him on his own. I suppose the other lesson I learned from that era was never to spend more in a political campaign than you can afford to lose. In 1930 George Carswell was the odds-on favorite to be elected governor of Georgia, but he lost in a runoff to Dick Russell. A few years later, he was so destitute that he couldn't even afford a pack of tailor-made cigarettes. He was reduced to rolling his own from a five-cent pouch of Bull Durham tobacco. We called it "Hoover Dust" at the time.

That may have been unfair to Herbert Hoover, who did the best he could under adverse circumstances. But those were desperate times, and the people needed someone to blame. They also needed someone to trust. So they blamed Hoover and trusted Roosevelt. What most people forget is that in 1932 Franklin Roosevelt offered a conservative alternative to Hoover. He was for reduced expenditures, lower taxes, and smaller government. Those were also things my father was for, so he supported Roosevelt in '32. He continued supporting the Roosevelt platform and was shocked to see FDR take a 180-degree turn to the left just as soon as he got in office. There's no question that the New Deal brought temporary relief to millions. And Roosevelt was able to inspire hope in people who might otherwise have given up on our system of government. For those reasons, he will probably go down as the greatest politician in our nation's history. But he was *not* the greatest president. If you think that the New Deal got us out of the Depression, compare the unemployment figures for

1933 and 1939. It was war abroad, not socialism at home, that kept the American economy from going under.

People accused Papa of being power hungry. But the things he did that got them saying that were almost always things designed to reduce the cost and power of government. To his way of thinking, ninety percent of government was bluff and red tape anyway. There are a few people who get into government and grow with the office. But most simply swell with it. One of my daddy's biographers, Judge Al Henson, tells about seeing a man hanging around the governor's office one day. "What's wrong, Jim?" he said. "Don't you have a job yet?" And Jim said, "Yeah, but I ain't got no one under me." That's how bureaucrats think. I'm convinced that Papa was right when he said, "The only way to have an honest government is to keep it poor."

Although Papa was one of the first major Democrats to break with the New Deal, he wouldn't be the last. There was Al Smith in New York and Governor Joseph Ely in Massachusetts. And Huey Long. There has never been another politician like Huey in the history of this country, and I doubt there ever will be. When he was at the height of his power, he had control of all three branches of government in Louisiana. In that sense, he really was a dictator, but he derived his power from the will of the people. He was a spellbinding orator who could move the masses—rural and urban, south and north, even black and white. No one who ever heard him speak ever went away unimpressed. I remember when Huey addressed the Georgia legislature in 1935. Within a very few minutes he had the entire audience eating out of his hand. And after he finished, the first man to come up and ask for his autograph was an Atlanta industrialist worth several million dollars. Here Huey had just been talking about sharing that man's wealth. I don't know whether the tycoon didn't understand or just didn't care. Papa and Smith and Ely thought that the New Deal had gone too far. Huey didn't think it had gone far enough.

At various times both Papa and Huey were mentioned as possible candidates to run against Roosevelt in 1936. Huey was a lot more serious about it and had made a good start on his campaign when he was shot and killed in September of 1935. He had Share the Wealth clubs all across the nation and was a big hit on the radio. He knew that he had no chance of winning the Democratic nomination away from Roosevelt or beating him in the general election. The idea was to run as an independent and draw enough votes away from FDR to elect a Republican in 1936. That would eliminate Roosevelt from public life and put the country in such a fix that the people would practically elect Long by acclamation in 1940. In fact, Huey was so confident about this that he called his autobiography *My First Days in the White House.*

If it's true that politics makes strange bedfellows, it's doubly true of opposition politics. It was one thing for Huey P. Long and Eugene Talmadge to go all over the country rawhiding Franklin Delano Roosevelt about one thing and the other. It would have been quite a different matter for them to agree on a platform for governing the country. You'll remember that Bobby Kennedy and George Wallace made life miserable for Lyndon Johnson back in the mid to late sixties. But could you imagine those two joining forces to run against him? Of course, there was no chance of that ever happening, but in 1935 Huey and Papa got right friendly before Huey was shot. They had planned to launch their movement at a meeting in Macon, Georgia, in January of 1936. They called it the Grass Roots Convention.

Huey's death sort of knocked the wind out of the anti-Roosevelt movement, but the plans for the convention went ahead anyway. It was sponsored by the Southern Committee to Uphold the Constitution. In addition to Papa, the people who helped put it together were a Texas oilman named John Henry Kirby, Huey's old lieutenant Gerald L.K. Smith, and the great Southern novelist Thomas Dixon, Jr. We also got money from some of Al Smith's backers in New York. There were several good speeches— especially by Gerald L.K. Smith, who was a real chest-thumping orator. But the convention was poorly attended and didn't lead to much of anything. By now Papa could see that the best way to fight the New Deal was to serve out his term as governor and try to run the state according to sound financial principles. In the general election Roosevelt won every state but Maine and Vermont. There used to be a saying: "As Maine goes, so goes the nation." Ever since 1936 it's been: "As Maine goes, so goes Vermont."

Papa spoke on a nationwide radio hookup at that Grass Roots

Convention and surprised quite a few people with his intellect. Because Papa and Huey Long had made it a habit to speak to the common people in language they could understand, a lot of reporters simply forgot how well-read those two men were. (When Papa was Phi Beta Kappa at the University of Georgia, very few poor country boys even went to college, and Huey probably had a genius I.Q.) Historians who read my father's official papers are constantly amazed by the elegance of his prose style. Here is some of what he said to that crowd at Macon:

> Every true democrat hangs his head in shame when he realizes that, under the name of a democratic administration, boards and bureaus and the President himself say that the way to bring back prosperity in this country is through scarcity—have less to eat and less to wear.
>
> To carry out this crazy, infamous plan, they ordered millions of hogs and cattle killed and thrown into the rivers or buried. Millions more of little suckling pigs were shipped off to Chicago. On top of this, they paid a premium price to get to cut a good brood sow's throat. It took a little time for this travesty but when they struck the sheep and goats, they drove them on top of the mountains, forcing them to jump the cliffs and kill themselves in the valleys below.
>
> And when the starving people went there to retrieve some of these carcasses that were not too badly mangled by the rocks, the trained welfare workers ran them off, leaving them as food only for the coyotes and wolves. They burned up wheat and oats and plowed under cotton here in the South. Yet in Washington, with their faces wreathed in smiles, they were telling the people that they were bringing back "the abundant life."

☆ ☆ ☆

When Papa decided not to run for president in 1936, that left few options open to him. He was constitutionally barred from running for governor again until 1940. So the only major office he could shoot for was Dick Russell's seat in the United States Senate. We knew from the beginning that that would be an awkward race. Our family and the Russell family were personally close, and both Papa and Dick drew their support from the same group of voters. (If politics can produce strange allies, it can make enemies just as strange.) At that time, the struggle was to see if those voters would maintain their conservative Jeffersonian principles or buy the political snake oil that was being peddled in the name of economic recovery. The longer Dick Russell stayed in government the more conservative he got. But back in '36 he was strong for Roosevelt and the New Deal, and consequently to the left of Papa. The liberal faction in Georgia that year was running on a ticket of the "four R's": Roosevelt, Russell, Rivers, and Roberts. (That would be Ed Rivers and Columbus Roberts, but, as Papa would say, I'll be a-comin' to them.)

I later became warm friends with Dick Russell when we served together for fourteen years in the United States Senate, but the first time I ever met him was when I was a page in the Georgia legislature and he was Speaker of the House. Back then most of the pages hung around in the capitol rotunda trying to get out of as much work as possible. The exceptions were Jack Flynt and myself. We were interested in government, and we stayed on the floor as much as we could. But every once in a while we'd do something to make life interesting. At that time there was a fellow in the legislature by the name of Stokes. He wore a red rose in his lapel every day, and he considered himself quite an orator. Well, Jack and I wrote him a letter saying: "I am the lady in the red dress in the gallery. I admire your oratory very much. Would you please make a speech just for me?" Sure enough, old Stokes swallowed the bait. He looked up to the gallery, saw the red dress, and yelled, "Mr. Speaker..." I don't think he ever caught on to what we were doing, but I wouldn't be a bit surprised if Dick Russell knew what was going on.

Dick had many fine qualities that I came to revere over the years, but the first thing that impressed me about him was his remarkable memory. I recall he was coming through McRae when he was running for governor in 1930. It had been three years since he had seen me, and then I had been a lowly page. I'd also probably grown several inches in the interim. Well, without the least hesitation he walked up, stuck out his hand, and said, "Hello, Talmadge, how are you?" There are few greater assets a politician can have than a good memory for names and faces. I mean, you have to know what to say when some fellow you met in a crowd of five thousand twenty years ago comes up and says, "Herman, I don't suppose you remember me." Now that I'm out of politics I can say, "Hell no, and I don't have to anymore." But when you're asking for people's votes, you can't afford that luxury.

I was a senior in law school during that 1936 senate campaign and had virtually no say in the way things were run. I made a few speeches for Papa, but otherwise I was pretty much a bystander. Without question, my daddy was the most popular politician in Georgia at the time, and in a simple one-on-one contest he could have beaten Dick Russell. But the race was not Talmadge versus Russell so much as Talmadge versus Roosevelt. In Georgia in 1936, it probably would have been easier to run against Jesus Christ than against Franklin D. Roosevelt. The same people who thought that Papa was a pretty good governor didn't want him to go to Washington to vote against the New Deal. So the three little R's in Georgia were swept to victory on the coattails of the big R from Hyde Park, New York.

That was one of the bitterest campaigns in the history of Georgia politics. You had families split right down the middle, and many a campaign rally ended in fist fights. It was also the first time I ever saw an opponent get the best of my father in a public forum. It was a campaign appearance in Griffin, Georgia, on August 26. The principal candidates for governor and senator were to speak throughout the morning and early afternoon with Papa going last. You couldn't ask for a better set up, except that Dick simply had Papa out-foxed.

When he got up to speak, Dick talked about "Old Republican Gene." That was a sore spot right there, because there had been some idle talk earlier that year that the Republicans might want to run Papa against Roosevelt. And the overwhelming majority of Georgians at that time would have voted for an Abyssinian goat before they would a Republican. Then Dick got out a list of questions about Papa's record in public life and his stand on the issues.

He read those questions and nailed them to the podium so Papa couldn't easily duck them. But he did ignore them. He later admitted that was the biggest mistake he made in the campaign and that Dick was right smart to box him in like that. We probably should have seen the handwriting on the wall when word started coming in that farmers at Dick's rallies were taking off their red galluses and laying them at his feet. That was Papa's sixth statewide race and his first loss.

As usual, the press was mostly against Papa. That had never bothered him in the past. He'd just go out, put his message directly to the people, and thumb his nose at "those lying Atlanta newspapers." But this time he started off overconfident, making just one speech a week at first. By the time he hit his stride, things were just going too fast in the other direction. That was the first Talmadge campaign to generate much national interest. *Time* magazine got the worst picture of Papa they could find and put it on the cover. He had a cigar clenched in his teeth, and he looked mean as hell. The story inside the magazine treated Papa and the whole campaign as if they were one big joke. But that was par for the course. For years *Time* never printed anything about the South that wasn't derogatory. I used to buy the magazine every Thursday for its entertainment value. There was no finer satire written anywhere in America. But as far as hard news was concerned, you'd be better off talking to the grease monkey down at the corner filling station.

☆ ☆ ☆

Although Papa lost to the four R's, he wasn't about to tuck his tail between his legs and go back to being a dirt farmer and country lawyer. But he was out of public office for the first time in ten years and couldn't run for governor again for another four. Fortunately, he did have a means of keeping himself before the public. Back in 1934 he paid $1,000 for fifty-one percent of a newspaper called *The Statesman*. Frank Lawson had started the paper in 1930, and it looked to be the perfect vehicle for Papa to get his message across to the people of Georgia. After all, Tom Watson had done right well with his paper *The Jeffersonian* a generation earlier. Under

Papa *The Statesman* took a populist line, defending the little man against big business, big government, and big everything else that took no mind of the individual. Papa even listed "The People" as the editor of the paper. He always considered himself a man of the people. (Other than attacking the New Deal, the only other time he had gone against the Democrats was in 1924 when he ran as an elector for Fighting Bob La Follette on the Progressive Party ticket.) In the mid 1930's the one man in Georgia who seemed to represent everything Papa was fighting against was our stuffed-shirt United States Senator, Walter George. And he was up for reelection in 1938.

Papa took a different approach this time than he had against Dick Russell. He had learned his lesson, but good, about attacking Roosevelt. Figured if he could keep it a race between Gene Talmadge and Walter George, he could win. You see, George was highly respected in Washington, but he had neglected his constituency back home. Made about one speech a year, and that was before the Georgia Baptist Convention. There were quite a few people in the state who felt that George was taking his reelection for granted. And for a politician to let that impression get around can be the absolute kiss of death. I remember once Jimmy Bentley's daddy Lynwood was in a tough race for the State Senate. He won, but just narrowly, and after the election he found out that his own uncle had voted against him. "Uncle," he said, "why'd you do that for?" And the uncle said, "Because you didn't ask me to hep ya." Walter George seemed ripe for the plucking.

That was the first of my daddy's campaigns that I managed. We got us a second-hand sound truck and went around the state drawing huge and enthusiastic crowds. FDR wasn't on the ticket to drag Papa down this time, and everything seemed to be going our way. Even George's motorcades seemed to play into our hands. He had one that was supposed to begin in two parts—in the northeast of Georgia and in the northwest. They were to come together in Hapeville and drive to Griffin. It came out all right, except that as I recall the smallest car of the bunch was an Oldsmobile, and most were Cadillacs. The three-dollar tag crowd was still solid for Papa.

One of our biggest assets was old Walter George himself. He

was a distinguished gentleman who looked like he had reached full maturity back when God was still a boy, but he was a real cold fish of a campaigner. I remember the rally at the end of that motorcade to Griffin. There were about two hundred people there, which was small for those days. What's more, they were just about all wearing suits—corporation lawyers, business executives, and the like. And George even managed to put those boys to sleep. Stood up there reading a speech on foreign policy. Then after the speech some fellow in overalls tried to approach the senator. What he didn't know was that George had bad eyesight. He stuck his hand out, and George turned away. He went around to the other side to try to get George's attention, and the same damn thing happened. Finally, on the third pass he got the senator's hand. When I saw that, I thought, "My God, this is gonna to be duck soup."

And then a funny thing happened. FDR decided it was time to purge a few politicians who had been less than one hundred percent favorable to his policies. He went after Guy Gillette in Iowa, and that failed. He went after Cotton Ed Smith in South Carolina, and that failed. About his only success was in New York, where he got the Tammany organization to help him get rid of John O'Connor, who had chaired the House Rules Committee. Walter George was on that same hit list. The only problem was that if he got rid of George, Roosevelt would have Gene Talmadge to put up with, which was sort of like trading in a fever blister for skin cancer. So Roosevelt had to find him a third candidate who was foolish enough to take on *both* George and Talmadge and strong enough that he stood a chance of getting elected with the president's help. When he offered the assignment to Chip Robert, Chip acted as if he had just been asked to get up and praise General Sherman's efforts on behalf of urban renewal. They finally settled on backing a U.S. attorney by the name of Lawrence Camp.

When Franklin D. Roosevelt's train rolled into Barnesville, Georgia, on August 11, 1938, the president was one of the most popular men in the state. When he left later that same day, he was one of the least popular. Understand why that happened and you've gone a long way toward understanding the South. The minute Roosevelt attacked Senator George, he ceased to be the great white father in Washington and became just another Yankee carpetbagger. The South has a long memory, and there were plenty of people alive in 1938 who had lived through Reconstruction. Lawrence Camp's candidacy was never going anywhere anyway, but what Roosevelt succeeded in doing was turning Walter George into some kind of martyr. Here Papa had been trying to portray George as a Washington insider who had lost touch with the people, and the No. 1 insider had just got done denouncing him.

Well, the people of Georgia circled the wagons to defend one of their own. Telegrams started arriving at our headquarters virtually every hour of the day asking Papa to withdraw in favor of Senator George. And these were from our own people. They thought that this would be the best way to show old Roosevelt that Georgians were a free and independent people who couldn't be bossed like that Tammany bunch. Papa was fit to be tied. The race was close enough that he actually tried to challenge the results at the state Democratic convention, but all that did was make him look like a sore loser. The voters had now kept Papa out of the Senate twice. Once because the other fellow was backing Roosevelt and once because Roosevelt was opposing the other fellow. Any way you slice it, that damn Roosevelt was Papa's nemesis. Fortunately for us, my daddy's successor as governor, Ed Rivers, was busy bankrupting the state, and it was only two years before the people of Georgia would be constitutionally eligible to call on the Wild Man from Sugar Creek to set things right. But I'm getting ahead of the story.

As I mentioned earlier, when I got out of law school I was given hanging around privileges at the firm of Hewlett and Dennis. That was great experience, but it meant that I had to get out and find clients on my own. I remember one day Mr. Hewlett saying to me, "Herman, go over and get Judge Dorsey to put you on some cases." That was Judge Hugh Dorsey, former governor of the state (and the man who prosecuted Leo Frank). So I did and immediately got three murder cases thrown at me. The defendant in the first case had robbed a streetcar and killed the conductor. As you can imagine, Georgia Power, which was in charge of the streetcars, took a special interest in the case. They even got Solicitor General John Boykin to come over and head up the prosecution. Under the circumstances, I doubt that Clarence Darrow could have saved that man's life. I took it on appeal all the way up to the Georgia Supreme Court and even got a dissent from Dick Russell's father, who was chief justice at the time. But the other judges voted against me, and my client was executed.

After fifty years the details of my next case are a little hazy in my mind, but it proved to be the start of an unusual friendship that would last for the next thirty years. I was defending a young black man who had slit a white boy's throat in a fracas down on Marietta Street in Atlanta. When the white boy had bled to death, my client was charged with murder. There was no question about the facts of the case, so our only hope was to get the charges reduced to manslaughter. I certainly didn't want to lose another client to the electric chair. It was at that point that a black gentleman about my father's age introduced himself to me. He said that the National Association for the Advancement of Colored People was interested in this case, and he wanted to know if I needed any help trying it. The man's name was Austin T. Walden.

We made quite a pair—a white segregationist and a civil rights activist joining forces to see that justice was done to a black man on trial for his life in a Southern court. We argued that the killing was an unfortunate result of the fight, not premeditated murder. The jury agreed and turned in a conviction for manslaughter. Austin and I never tried another case together, and we were never political allies. I'm sure that he supported my opponents in every race I ever ran. At least, I accused him of that from the stump. Called him the "black boss," which is what he was. ("Boss," you see, is just another name for an effective leader.) He was an early spokesman for the black people of Atlanta and, for that matter, all of Georgia. When the black vote got to be significant, he became a valued advisor to Mayor William B. Hartsfield. In that day and age, our philosophies were too different for Austin and me ever to become close politically. But our personal friendship endured. I remember when I was governor he came in and told me he was trying a case down in Miller County, and the racial feeling was so high he was fearful for his life. I sent him down there in a state patrol car and dispatched a trooper to protect him for the duration of the trial. Today we have many dynamic and articulate black leaders in Georgia. But long before Andy Young or John Lewis or even Martin Luther King arrived on the scene, there was only my friend and co-counsel Austin T. Walden.

About that time my friend Alex McLennan and I started eating at a Japanese restaurant in Atlanta run by a fellow named Sada Yoshimura. They served excellent food there, and the prices were quite reasonable. As I recall, Yoshimura had some kind of connection with the Japanese government. They were trying to enhance public relations by giving away free trips to Japan to selected Americans. Since I was not widely traveled at the time, I jumped at the chance to go overseas at someone else's expense. I left America in December of 1939 on the *Assama Maru* and returned in January of 1940 on the *Tatsuta Maru*. That second ship (and probably the first one too) was sunk by the United States Navy in World War II. There was a martial atmosphere everywhere I went. Japan was engaged in a declared war with China and an undeclared one with Russia. (Between Japan and Korea, I even shared a stateroom with a Japanese general heading for China.) That trip helped to open my eyes to a world wider than Georgia. When I left to go back to America, we pulled out of Pier 32 in the Tokyo Harbor. I knew then that when I returned to Japan it would be with the American army of occupation.

3

Off to War

August 1945. We drop anchor in Tokyo Bay, begin unloading equipment, and send the troops ashore in attack waves. A few weeks ago the United States dropped atomic bombs on Hiroshima and Nagasaki, and just a few days ago the Emperor Hirohito went on radio to inform his people of Japan's unconditional surrender to the Allies. When I go down to inspect the mooring lines of our ship, I look ashore and see that everything that is not destroyed has been blackened by fire. We are at Pier 33, on the other side of the bay from where I had departed for America five years and eight months ago. The world will never be the same again.

ONE DAY, ABOUT A YEAR AFTER I got back from my pleasure trip to Japan, I was over at my daddy's office in the Capitol. As I was leaving I noticed Miss Nina Cox sitting in the reception area waiting to see Papa. Miss Nina was school superintendent over in Turner County, secretary of the Democratic Party, and a great friend of my father's. When I went over to speak to her, Miss Nina introduced me to her landlady's daughter, a student at the University of Georgia by the name of Betty Shingler. Betty and I began seeing each other shortly thereafter and very quickly fell in love. We were going to marry in the spring of '42, but with the war on the horizon we accelerated our plans and tied the knot in December of 1941.

I had been commissioned an ensign in the United States Navy in April 1941 and was called to active duty in Atlanta that September. Although we didn't know it at the time, Roosevelt was ordering American destroyers to escort the British ships sinking German submarines. Charles Lindbergh and vast numbers of other Americans may have opposed intervention, but I could see that the United States would be dragged into that war sooner or later. Hitler was running roughshod over Europe; Mussolini had invaded Ethiopia; and finally, on December 7, 1941, the Japanese struck Pearl Harbor. Overnight, we were at war with the Japanese Empire abroad and with Japanese American citizens at home.

In the mid-1980's, it's difficult to recall how strong the anti-Japanese sentiment was in America right after Pearl Harbor. The "Japs," as we called them, were pictured as buck-toothed people who were all spying for the Emperor. They were rounded up and put in detention camps, even if their families had been here for generations. Like most Americans at the time I thought this was something we had to do. Since then, I have come to see it as ranking right behind the massacre of the Indians as the greatest perversion of justice in American history. And the action was engineered by two great liberal folk heroes—Franklin D. Roosevelt in Washington and Earl Warren in California.

It's fairly easy to hate a racial or ethnic group in the abstract, but it's a different story when you start dealing with individuals. My friend Sada Yoshimura was an Atlanta businessman, a graduate of Oglethorpe University, and the husband of a native Georgia girl, but he was put in a detention camp and lost everything he had. After the war, he started a hot dog stand and eventually acquired a pretty good restaurant, but he was never able to work his way back up to where he was before. During my years in Washington I served with three Japanese Americans in the United States Congress. Senator Danny Inouye from Hawaii, who became a very good friend of mine, fought heroically for the United States on the Italian front. In fact, his unit (which consisted entirely of Japanese Americans) was the most decorated one in the entire U.S. Army. He lost an arm in the service of his country, but when he got back home, some barber told him that he didn't cut "Jap hair." Blacks who fought in the war received much the same treatment, which was certainly one of the major causes of the civil rights movement.

Shortly after Pearl Harbor, I reported to my mobilization billet at the cable censor's office in New York City. It was pretty boring work. Our job was to monitor cables going in and out of the country to see if anyone might be transmitting information detrimental to the interests of the United States. About all I can remember reading was cable after cable from people in Lebanon telling their relations in America to "please send money." And living in New York City was worse than being in combat. People were herded about like cattle and always seemed in a godawful rush to get on the subway. I think pushing old ladies out of the way was the most fun those people had during the course of an average day.

I remember that we worked across the street from Manufacturer's Bank (it's Manufacturer's-Hanover today). How convenient, I thought. I can go over there and do some light banking while I'm here in New York. So I walked across the street in my ensign's uniform with my two-weeks' paycheck of $62.50. That seemed a bit modest, so I wrote a check for $500 on my Atlanta bank. I stepped right up to some official of the bank and said, "My name is Talmadge. I'm from Atlanta, Georgia, but I'm temporarily stationed here in New York, and I'd like to open an account in your bank." When he asked me how much I wanted to open it for, I said "$562.50," which seemed like a pretty large sum to me at the time. Well, that fellow just laughed and told me that they didn't open accounts for less than $10,000. I guess you could say that was my introduction to the world of high finance. Fortunately for me, the man was either patriotic or softhearted and made an exception in my case. Years later I got to know the chief executive officer of that bank, and he was right amused by my experience.

One day when I got plenty fed up with the idea of living in a place where you didn't know your next door neighbors, I told Betty that we were going to go over and call on the lady who lived in the apartment next to ours. As it turned out, that lady was a recluse and a semi-invalid. She had no friends or family to speak of and was delighted to have someone call on her. We had a car at the time, and Betty used to take that woman driving up in Connecticut. I was pleased that we could spread a little Southern hospitality that far north. But there was a war going on, and I figured my place was where the action was. I was glad to be in the Navy, however. It seemed a whole lot safer to be shot at from a ship than from a foxhole.

When I left the Intelligence division of the Navy to volunteer for combat duty, I was sent to midshipman's school at Northwestern University for intensive training. I remember the hot Chicago summer and the grueling mental ordeal of trying to learn in a few months what it took naval cadets at Annapolis four years to learn. Trigonometry still made as much sense to me as Sanskrit, and for the next four years I was scared to death that I might be called on to navigate a ship. (That that never happened I take as proof positive that God was on the side of the Allies.) I also recall serving as junior officer of the day on one occasion. The senior officer of the day was a young fellow I didn't see again for another twenty years or so. In the early 1960's, I was walking across the grounds at the Capitol in Washington when I heard someone say, "Hello, Herman." I looked around and said, "Take off your glasses so I can see if you're who I think you are." And, sure enough, it was the newly elected congressman from Ohio—Bob Taft, Jr.

When my training at Northwestern was finished, I was assigned to the USS *Tryon*, a disguised hospital ship that was heavily armed. Its function was to carry troops into battle and bring casualties out. You might ask why we didn't just make this a hospital ship, paint a red cross on the side, and seek safe passage into the battle zone. Well, the U.S. had tried that with other ships, and the Japs had blown the hell out of them. So we quickly adjusted to the oriental rules of warfare. Before heading for the South Pacific, however, we docked in San Diego to pick up some Marines. Many of these were young boys who were leaving home for the first time. Some of them would buy fake medals in little shops along the waterfront and try to impress the girls they'd meet in local bars. One night when I was officer of the deck, my bosun mate of the watch said, "My God, Mr. Talmadge, look at that battle-scarred veteran coming up the gangway." It was a kid of about seventeen, wearing the Medal of Honor, America's highest decoration. Lee, the bosun mate, had survived the sinking of the carrier *Yorktown*. We proceeded to have us a little stripping-down ceremony.

It was on ship that my freak habit of getting up before dawn was really set in concrete. Of course, that habit had begun years earlier. When I was a boy on the farm, I had to get up to bring firewood into the house, and I can't ever remember eating breakfast except by lamplight. Then when I was a law student, the only way I could make sure of getting the books I needed to study was to show up at the law library when it opened at 7 A.M. First as a student and later as a campaign manager for Papa, I found that the only time when there was enough quiet and leisure to think was early in the morning before everyone else was up. That also proved true aboard ship, where I had to stand watch twelve hours a day, seven days a week, and later perform all the other duties of an executive officer. By the time I got to the Senate, I was going to bed with the chickens and beating them up. I know some people have a hard time getting used to that. Once when Carl Sanders was staying at my house, he got right testy when I went to his bedroom and said, "Y'up yet, Carl?" As I recall, it was already 4 A.M.

I served twenty-two and a half months in the South Pacific, mostly as flag secretary to Commodore Stanley Jupp in Auckland, New Zealand. We made several trips in and out of Guadalcanal, taking torpedoes and troops up and bringing casualties out. I suppose my most hair-raising experience during that time occurred one night when I was officer of the deck. I noticed a phosphorous wake headed toward the ship off the starboard bow and knew at once that it was a torpedo. Remembering my training, I aimed our boat at the torpedo and watched it pass forty yards off our stern. I immediately sounded general quarters, summoned the captain and the executive officer, and waited to be praised for having saved the ship—not to mention the five hundred-man crew and 1,800 troops it was carrying. Well, the captain didn't say a word, and all the executive officer did was ask me for the recognition signal. Not only did I not know the recognition signal, I couldn't even read Morse Code. So he chewed me out but good. That was your perfect bureaucratic mentality. And no wonder. Before the war that man had been a timekeeper for Roosevelt's Works Progress Administration.

In the military you run into all kinds of extremes. There were fellows like that executive officer who had their heads buried so deep in the rule book that they couldn't see what was going on around them. Their idea of leadership was plenty of profanity and abuse. Then you would run into other situations where no one seemed to be in control at all. I remember once when we were anchored at an atoll near the island of Ulithee in the South Pacific. An officer by the name of George Hart had gone ashore to get the mail and was just coming back on board. He handed me a document and said, "Mr. Talmadge, I thought you might like to see this." I didn't have to look at it very long to see that what he had was Admiral Halsey's secret battle plans. "Where'd you get this?" I asked. And he told me that some ensign on shore was handing them out. The first order I gave him was to lock that document in our safe, and if we ran into danger, to put a weight on the orders and drop them in the ocean. You wonder sometimes if military intelligence isn't a contradiction in terms. I was almost court martialed once for temporarily misplacing a restricted book of naval etiquette.

Other than that incident with the torpedo, there were only two other times during my naval years when I felt my life was in peril. Once was when my ship was caught in a typhoon around New Caledonia. We were tossed about by huge waves for several days. The bow of the ship would go straight up, then the wave would crest and we'd go straight down. Sometimes the propellors would be out of the water just churning air. It's the most helpless feeling in the world. You're at the mercy of the elements, and about all you can do is hang on and wait it out.

The other time when I came near to seeing my life flash in front of my eyes was when we were in Buckner Bay in Okinawa. I had to lend my boats to some other ships to help carry their dead ashore. We had a machine that made a kind of artificial fog to hide the ships. Well, that machine caught fire, and the ship swung out from under the fog, exposing itself to the full view of the enemy. I was busy trying to get the fire put out when I noticed a kamikaze plane heading directly toward us. It kept coming, eluding the fire of ships all around the harbor, until it fell in the sea about twenty yards from us. Political wars can be vicious, but they're nothing compared to the real thing.

People back home in America and military personnel stationed elsewhere in the world probably envied those of us who were in the South Pacific. Here we were in an island paradise with nothing to do but sit on the beach all day eating exotic tropical fruit, soaking up the sun, and frolicking with beautiful native girls in grass skirts. Unfortunately, that's not the way it was. For one thing, most of our time was devoted to fighting the Japs. We went over there thinking we'd whip them in one big naval battle, only to get the stuffings kicked out of us again and again. And when we did have leave out in the islands, the terrain was usually so godforsaken that most of the men wouldn't even get off the ship. We never saw Bob Hope out there, just reruns of old movies. Our greatest fun was hooting at South Pacific travelogues.

As you can imagine, getting to a civilized port like Australia or New Zealand turned us into the proverbial sailors on shore leave. At times, we'd have to throw out cargo nets to gather up all the intoxicated crew members and bring them back on board. But the men I served with were patriots before they were playboys. This was never more evident than when I was personnel officer in New Zealand. A Navy C. B. battalion was sent down from Guadalcanal for rest and recreation. They were granted leave and scattered all over the North and South Island, like a bunch of kiwis in heat. Immediately thereafter, Admiral Halsey sent us a message to ship them out within forty-eight hours. We had no way to get in touch with those men except by sending messages through the newspapers and over the radio. But it worked. Of the several hundred men on leave we rounded up all but one, and he might not have gotten the message. There were many times when those men made me proud to be an officer in the United States Navy, but never more so than on that day.

The man who gave that order was the one commanding presence in the South Pacific during those years. Admiral William F. Halsey, Jr., was called "Bull Halsey," and for good reason. He was a colorful and aggressive sailor of the old school. He probably wouldn't go over today, when military officers need to be politicians and diplomats. But Bull Halsey was an old salt who said and did what came naturally to him. He had no doubt about what the Navy was out in the South Pacific to do. It was to "Kill Japs, Kill Japs, Kill more Japs...Attack-Repeat-Attack...Keep 'em Dying... Strike-Repeat-Strike." And the man looked like a warrior. He was a strutting little bantam cock with the face of a bulldog, but occasionally he could be outmaneuvered by a brighter adversary. On one occasion, he left his post protecting MacArthur's Philippine landing to pursue a decoy Japanese fleet. He also got caught in typhoons a couple of times and was subjected to a board of inquiry both times. However, for sheer flamboyance his only equal was General Patton. At a time when we were losing practically every battle to the Japs, Halsey would talk about riding the Emperor's white horse through the streets of Tokyo. For better or for worse, they don't make 'em like Bull Halsey anymore.

I never had any direct contact with Halsey, but I did meet the other legendary naval officer in the South Pacific, Admiral Raymond Spruance. That was when I was in New Zealand serving as flag secretary to Commodore Jupp. I went with Jupp to meet Spruance's plane shortly after the Battle of Midway. Being naturally curious, I asked the Commodore, "What the hell is Spruance doing in New Zealand?" Jupp said that he didn't rightly know. "But I'll tell you one thing, Talmadge. Anywhere Spruance goes, things happen." Shortly thereafter, we were having drinks in the Admiral's quarters. I recall that Spruance was a pensive fellow who nursed a glass of beer for the better part of an hour. Then when he got ready to ship out for Wellington, New Zealand, I noticed four or five of his officers carrying big piles of documents. They must have been plans for the bloody engagement of Tarawa, which took place a few days later.

After twenty-two months in the South Pacific, I was sent back to the United States and given twenty days leave so I could visit with my wife and my first-born son, Herman Eugene Talmadge, Jr. whom I had not seen. When that leave was up I was assigned to a ship called the *Dauphin*, where I was responsible for training men who were going to sea for the first time. Once out at sea, we joined the Seventh Fleet around the Philippines. I remember when I was at Ulithee atoll one day I could see for a diameter of thirty miles with my binoculars. It was enough to take my breath away. For as far as I could see there was nothing but aircraft carriers, battleships, cruisers, destroyers, transports, and supply ships. That was probably the most visually awesome display of military might in the history of warfare. And now that we have moved irrevocably into the nuclear age, I doubt that we will see its like again.

Throughout my years in politics, I've had ample opportunity to observe various styles of leadership. However, more often than not, the most successful politicians are those capable of projecting a concern for other people. Papa had that ability, and it's what made folks so loyal to him even when the newspapers and other politicians were all down on him. This same quality can also make the difference between an effective and an ineffective military leader. This is particularly true the closer that leader is to dealing with large numbers of subordinates on a day-to-day basis. I was in just such a position as an executive officer aboard ship in the Navy. It was excellent training for politics. The good role models taught me what to do, and the bad ones (who were far more numerous) taught me what to avoid.

I remember one night early in my career standing watch on the USS *Tryon* in the South Pacific when the bosun mate of the watch came up to me and complained about that ship's executive officer. "Mr. Talmadge," he said, "if you'll get the executive officer up here, I'll throw him overboard." That was precisely the sentiment I tried not to inspire in my men when I assumed a position of leadership. You have to be firm and maintain discipline, but your men need to feel that they're being treated fairly. That sometimes requires flexibility and a willingness to bend the rules when the situation warrants it. When I was involved in reviewing court martial cases in New Zealand, I tried whenever I could to overrule this one commander who took sadistic pleasure in court martialing men for minor infractions. The best way to lead is by example, by showing not just telling. Robert E. Lee realized this, and by the end of the War Between the States his men were fighting more for him than for the Confederacy (which was already a lost cause). I can't claim to have been that popular, but when I left my last ship, there was a starboard list from men waving good-bye to me.

If a good officer is flexible, it stands to reason that an inflexible one is bad. Just about everyone has seen or read *The Caine Mutiny*. In that book Captain Queeg went so much by the book that it drove him insane. The skipper aboard the *Dauphin* was a milder version of Captain Queeg. His name was B. Connolly, and he hadn't been to the South Pacific in war time. I tried to be helpful and told him that we needed to take some paint along or the ship would rust. Well, he got real officious and said, "Talmadge, don't you know that you don't carry paint into a war zone?" I just said, "Aye aye, sir." By the time we got to the Panama Canal Zone, that ship looked like a five-year-old syrup can that somebody had left out in the rain. So as soon as we arrived in port, Connolly sent the supply officer ashore to get paint. He later got into a silly row with the ship's doctor about the number of bottles of alcohol in sick bay. And he was so compulsive about how things looked that he actually had the crew standing watch in dress whites two thousand miles west of Pearl Harbor. There were plenty of times that I would have liked to have thrown him overboard.

Now, I don't mean to exaggerate the importance of the human touch. At the top of the military hierarchy you had officers who helped lead us to victory because of abilities that didn't have anything at all to do with human relations. Take our chief naval commander in the South Pacific. Admiral Chester W. Nimitz was a brilliant strategist and theoretician. He could draw up battle plans, which men like Halsey and Spruance would go on to execute. Things wouldn't have worked nearly so well had Nimitz and his field commanders switched roles. We saw that when Halsey took it upon himself to follow that Japanese fleet when he should have been protecting MacArthur. Most of the time, however, each man played to his own strength. And they complemented each other right well.

If you're looking for a warrior who could both plan and execute, you'd have to go with Douglas MacArthur. At the time I couldn't stand the man personally, and I still don't think he was a very likable human being. He was an egomaniac and a prima donna. He loved publicity, and he probably harbored political ambitions. When I think of him with his nose up in the air and that corncob pipe clenched in his teeth, I'm reminded of what Churchill said of one of his uppity political opponents: "There but for the grace of God, goes God." Where I have changed my mind, however, is in my assessment of MacArthur as a soldier.

Back then, my Navy colleagues and I didn't think much of MacArthur's little hit-and-run forays against the Japs. Especially since the Navy was in the thick of the fighting and absorbing heavy casualties. We thought he was a pansy, and we called him "Dugout Doug." Which showed how much we knew. His strategy of hitting the Japanese where they were weak and avoiding them where they were strong brought us to victory. (He lost fewer men in his entire Pacific campaign than Eisenhower did in the Battle of the Bulge alone.) Thank God, MacArthur never became President of the United States. But if he had not been there in the South Pacific during World War II, the Emperor's white horse might have been carrying old Hirohito himself through the streets of Washington, D.C.

There is no doubt about it—we needed strategists like Nimitz, daredevils like Halsey and Spruance, and even preening aristocrats like MacArthur and Patton (though if all our commanders were like those two, we probably would have had a mutiny in the ranks). But as a politician I guess I'm still drawn to the sort of leaders who were respected for who they were as people as much as what they could do as warriors. The American soldiers may have feared George Patton, but they loved Omar Bradley. They called him the "G.I.'s general." And, of course, there was Eisenhower, whose popularity carried him right to the White House. Only now are we beginning to realize what a capable president he actually was. But we've always known that when people said "I like Ike," they were talking from the heart, not just parroting a Madison Avenue slogan.

I served under a man who, at a lower level, inspired that same kind of confidence. Commodore Jupp was a professional officer right to the bone, but he was also a warm human being. He was one commander who was more concerned with his men than with his press clippings. I'll never forget the time his son came by to visit him. The boy was a lowly private in the Army, serving under Lightning Joe Collins. They were at different ranks, in different services, and of different generations; but father and son were each doing his part to defend this country from its foes. Men like the Jupps don't dominate the history books, but their example meant more to me than anything else I saw in the entire South Pacific.

In the summer of 1945, my ship was included in the plans for the imminent invasion of Japan. When the U.S. forces took over Okinawa, the Japanese on the island engaged in mass suicide, even throwing their babies over the cliffs. And from that point on, we were under almost constant attack from kamikazes. We assumed that the invasion of the Japanese mainland would be a bloody affair, costing hundreds of thousands of lives—both American and Japanese. Some estimates went as high as a million dead. There was no question in our minds that every man, woman, and child in Japan would fight to the death with rifles, sticks, rocks, whatever they could get their hands on. Our fondest hope was to see "The Golden Gate by '48."

The dropping of the atomic bomb on Hiroshima and Nagasaki changed all of that. Within a week the Japanese announced their intention to surrender, and I was in Tokyo Bay to help occupy a defeated country, not invade a hostile one. We had been at peace with Japan when I had been in that harbor in January of 1940, and we were at peace again. But the cost of restoring that peace had been immense. The United States had burned up everything it could in the major cities of Japan and had unleashed a weapon that threatened to change the nature of warfare. Even though the Emperor had told his people to lay down their arms, we couldn't be sure what the civilians and some of the military personnel might do. So when we were carrying the first cavalry division into Tokyo Bay, someone asked Halsey what we should do if a Japanese aircraft approached the ship. "Shoot him down," Bull Halsey said, "in a friendly sort of way."

Over forty years later some people find it easy to criticize Harry

Truman for dropping that bomb on Hiroshima and Nagasaki. It certainly would have been terrible to have lived in either of those towns and to have suffered the agonies those people went through. But a person who is killed by a conventional weapon is just as dead as one who dies in a nuclear attack. The only difference between our using the bomb and not using it is in the latter case many hundreds of thousands of additional Americans *and Japanese* would have lost their lives. At least at the time we had every reason to believe that's what would have happened. There are some folks who believe that war is always wrong, and I suppose there are others who believe that the U.S. was in the wrong in World War II. But if you believe that we were in a just and necessary war and that an Allied victory was essential, you can hardly fault Truman for doing what had to be done. Given the perverse calculus of warfare, dropping the bomb was really a humane act. A bumper sticker I saw not too long ago sums it up right well: "There will be no more Hiroshimas when there are no more Pearl Harbors."

Our ship was at Leyte in the Philippines when we got our orders for discharge of personnel. As the executive officer, I figured that I would probably be the last man discharged before the captain was allowed to leave. Now, with the war over, I wasn't too eager to spend another six to eight months in the service waiting for some military bureaucrat to say that it was all right for me to go home. So I went to the captain and told him that I had more than enough time to qualify for discharge and I sure would be obliged if he'd sign my papers. He went ahead and did so, even though—strictly speaking—it was against regulations. When I got to Manila, a hard-boiled four-striper looked at my orders and said, "What the hell are you doing here?" I stood at attention and responded, "Complying with orders, sir." At that he looked up and said, "I'm not going to give you a new set of orders. I'm just going to put a first endorsement on these." (When I got to the U.S. a Wave who was on duty told me that I had a highly irregular set of orders. But since she couldn't very well send me back to the South Pacific, she just wrote me up new ones.) There at Manila I got on an army troop transport ship headed to Seattle. That was such a horrible ride that two soldiers who made it through the entire war jumped overboard and were never heard from again. Still, it brought me back to civilian life in the good old U.S. of A.

I had a lot of time to think as I sat on the train taking me home from Seattle. I'm sure that most of that thinking must have occurred in Montana, which at the time seemed to me to be the largest, most endless state in the union. At the age of thirty-two, I was a veteran with a wife and two little boys (my second son, Robert Shingler Talmadge, had just been born). Times had been hard for a young lawyer during the Depression, and I had taken a good bit of time away from my law practice to work in my daddy's political campaigns. But things were going to be different now. The economy was picking up. I knew that I had at least average intelligence and a damn fine legal education. There was no doubt in my mind that I would be successful in the post-war world. I promised myself, however, that it would be in a profession other than politics.

4

Papa's Last Hurrah

In December of 1946 I went to visit my father, who was lying gravely ill in a hospital in Atlanta. "Son," he said, "there was a fellow in here the other day. He told me, 'Gene, you know every man, woman, and child in the state of Georgia is praying for you. Even folks who never prayed before in their lives.'" I said, "I know, Papa." And he just cracked a smile and said, "Half of them are praying I'll recover and half of them that I won't."

THAT WAS PRETTY MUCH HOW people felt about Papa. Contrary to what you might hear, Georgia was not a one-party state. It's true that the only Republicans were what we called "post office Republicans," folks who would say they were Republicans so they could get some kind of federal job when the GOP was in power in Washington. No, the two parties in Georgia from the late twenties to the late forties were the Talmadgites and the anti-Talmadgites, both of whom called themselves Democrats. They fought their battles mostly in the Democratic Primary and the state legislature, but sometimes they'd spill over into the courts and even into the streets. By the time I was elected senator in 1956, we had pretty much absorbed or routed the anti-Talmadge forces. But in Papa's heyday the main personality and the main issue in Georgia politics was Eugene Talmadge. This was particularly true during the last ten years of his life.

Throughout the latter half of the 1930's, Papa's major opponent in Georgia politics was an ultra-liberal country lawyer by the name of Eurith Dickinson Rivers. As you can imagine, Eurith Dickinson wasn't too partial to his given name. So he asked that people call him Ed. By the time he was finished in politics his wild spending and social welfare policies had practically turned Georgia into a banana republic, but E.D. Rivers got his start in public life— surprisingly enough—as a champion of the Ku Klux Klan.

It may come as a shock to a lot of "historians" and others who should know better, but the Klan wasn't all that powerful in Georgia after about the 1920's. (For some reason, a lot of folks seem to think that until very recently every Southern politician would go home at night, wait for it to get dark, take a white sheet out of his closet, and then go tearing around the countryside, burning crosses and raising hell.) The Klan was formed back during Reconstruction, when there was no self-government in the South. We weren't even recognized as states back then—just occupied "military districts." The Klan was a vigilante group that saw itself as battling that situation. But by the time Papa came on the scene, Georgia had regained self-government and was bound and determined to keep it, despite the best efforts of Yankee imperialists who liked nothing better than to tell other folks how to live their lives. As a bunch of marauders, the Klan did a lot of damage. But as a political force it was an anachronism and a joke. In fact, the *only* major politician I knew who took that white-sheeted bunch seriously was Ed Rivers.

Now, I doubt that Ed was any stronger for white supremacy than your average Georgian of Caucasian descent. It was just that he liked to be popular and curry favor with every group that he could. For that reason, it was a pretty easy transition for Ed, once he saw that the Klan was a thing of the past, to switch his emphasis to the New Deal. In Georgia during the Depression that was an even more popular platform than states' rights, as Papa found out when he lost to Dick Russell in 1936—the year Ed Rivers (the third of the three "R's") was elected governor. Lamar Murdaugh, an old political hand who at various times had worked for both Papa and Ed, told one of Papa's biographers, William Anderson, how he came to see Ed in his room at the Ansley Hotel right after that 1936 election. Ed was lying there shaving with an electric razor and puzzling over some book entitled *Call of the Aged*. He said, "Lamar, I got elected because I was going to provide for old age pensions and a lot of other welfare programs, but I don't know a damned thing about it. How about fixing me up a welfare program?" I'm reminded of a fellow Ben Franklin talks about in his *Autobiography*. "He wished to please everybody," Ben says, "and having little to give he gave expectations." That was Ed all over.

Whoever said "the road to Hell is paved with good intentions" must have had someone like Ed Rivers in mind. Ed wanted to set him up a little New Deal in Georgia and be as well loved as Franklin D. Roosevelt himself. The only problem is that, unlike the federal government, a state has to pay its debts. Georgia just didn't have the wherewithal to support the kinds of programs Ed Rivers promised. But back then the people were so desperate they were willing to buy just about any magic elixir that promised to cure the ailing economy. And God knows, Ed had plenty of time to dream about what he might do as governor. He had been elected to the legislature in 1924 and became President Pro Tem of the State Senate in '26. Then in 1928, he ran for governor against Lamartine Hardman and lost. In 1930 he ran against Dick Russell and George Carswell and lost. And if it hadn't been for Roosevelt's coattails, he probably would have lost to our man Charley Redwine in 1936. But those coattails proved strong enough to win Ed a sizeable victory.

Ed had laid into Papa pretty heavy about not calling a special session of the legislature back in the spring of '35 and then trying to run the state government all by himself. But when the shoe was on the other foot, Ed saw just how frustrating it can be to push for what you think is right when the lawmakers and bureaucrats are pulling in the other direction. He tried to take money out of the highway fund to pay the teachers and got into a big row with W.L. Miller, who was running the highway commission. He'd send the National Guard over to toss Miller out of his office, and then Miller would go to court, get reinstated, and wait for the newspapers to give Ed hell for dictatorial practices. In fact, the *Savannah Morning News* got so indignant that it started comparing Ed to Hitler and Stalin, though I don't think what he did compares with Auschwitz and the Gulag Archipelago.

By the time that Ed Rivers had finished his second two-year term, the state was in bankruptcy. Our credit rating was shot to hell, and the people who were owed money by the state got something called script instead of money. It was a kind of promissory note that folks would try to discount wherever they could. Rich's department store allowed school teachers to buy clothes with their script, but in most other places it was worth about as much as one of Ed's black bow ties. Also, a lot of eyebrows were raised when Ed pardoned a whole truck-load of criminals just before going out of office. I doubt that there was a pardons racket, as some folks claimed, but the timing was bad. Besides, it's hard to know what might have been going on at the lower levels of the administration. Ed didn't exactly run a tight ship. I understand that Warren G. Harding's father once said, "Thank God my son wasn't born female. He'd always be in a family way. The boy just doesn't know how to say 'no.'" Ed Rivers was a likable fellow, and I always got on well with him personally. But his fatal flaw as governor was that he didn't know how to say "no."

Things were looking up for Papa in 1940. The anti-Talmadge forces were putting some distance between themselves and Ed Rivers, and they didn't have anyone else to rally behind. Abit Nix was in the race. So was Papa's old crony Hugh Howell, who had never forgiven Papa for not backing him for governor in 1936. Then there was the state agriculture commissioner, a Baptist philanthropist by the name of Columbus Roberts. Those boys proved easier pickings than the baseball team. I was running the campaign this time, and we had a platform that was just liberal enough to placate the old New Dealers, who had been embarrassed by the fracas over Walter George, but a hell of a lot more realistic than the Ed Rivers boondoggles. The papers even thought that the Wild Man from Sugar Creek was mellowing and starting to get respectable. But that perception didn't last long. When Papa began his third term as governor, the biggest row of his political career was just around the corner.

☆ ☆ ☆

Walk up to ten historians and say, "Other than the Dean Cocking affair, what did you think of the third Eugene Talmadge administration?" and at least nine of them will look at you as if you'd said, "Other than that, Mrs. Lincoln, what did you think of the play?" No question about it, that Dean Cocking purge was the greatest political mistake Papa ever made, and he made a few in his time. But he paid dearly for it. It cost him reelection in '42, and for a long time the Phi Kappa literary society at the University of Georgia took his picture off the wall. But maybe the saddest thing of all is that that row completely overshadowed the fact that in a very short time my father had returned the state of Georgia to financial solvency. The legislature made Papa what amounted to a receiver in bankruptcy. He took in the revenue and paid it out as he saw fit. Before too long the state was back on its feet. Unfortunately, with the Dean Cocking affair it also got up on its hind legs and kicked Papa right out of office.

Walter Dewey Cocking was the Dean of the School of Education at the University of Georgia, and he wasn't very sensitive to our traditions and mores. Today that wouldn't make much difference, but back in the early forties we were still a little touchy about Yankees coming in and trying to change our way of doing things. Cocking was from Iowa, and Papa never was too partial to Iowans. It may have had something to do with Henry Wallace, whom Papa thought was an ignoramus and a near Communist. (He wasn't the only one who thought that, either; Clare Booth Luce called Wallace "Stalin's Mortimer Snerd.") For decades after Reconstruction, whenever an outsider would come in and try to tell us Southerners we were living all wrong, we kept seeing carpetbags and bayonets. I mean, if the most popular president in the South since Jefferson Davis could become a pariah just because he suggested we vote for one Georgian over another, you can imagine what someone of my father's generation thought about a pointy-head from Iowa coming down and trying to mix the races.

You see, Cocking was tied up with some do-gooder outfit called the Rosenwald Fund, which was trying to destroy segregation in the South. If that wasn't bad enough, he up and fired a native-

61

born Georgia woman by the name of Sylla Hamilton. Mrs. Hamilton was teaching in the practice school at the university, and when Dean Cocking terminated her contract, she went to Papa and gave him an earful. As chief executive of the state Papa was sworn to uphold a constitution that mandated segregation. Also, he saw himself as the philosophical spokesman for traditionalists who thought that both races were more likely to prosper if their schools remained separate but equal. He wasn't about to ignore either his oath of office or his principles, so when Papa got wind of what was happening, he decided that Cocking must go.

One of my father's staunchest allies in the Dean Cocking affair was the black educator Joseph Winthrop Holley, president of what was then Georgia Normal College and what is now Albany State College. By the early 1940's Dr. Holley was a legend in Georgia education. He had helped found the college he was running and had started the Georgia Teachers and Education Association, the first state-wide group of black educators to amount to anything. He thought that black colleges ought to be run by blacks, not by the white Board of Regents that ran the university system. Papa was sympathetic with this view and always got on well with Dr. Holley. The same was not true of Steadman V. Sanford, who was chancellor of the university system and was fixing to purge Dr. Holley. Academic freedom, you see, is for white liberals and those blacks who are willing to parrot the liberal line. Rather than paying some thought to what my father and Dr. Holley were saying, the *Atlanta Journal* talked about the "young master and Uncle Holley show."

Because I had been to the university a few years earlier, I knew that Papa would only hurt himself if he tried to treat that academic crowd the way he did log-rolling legislators and bureaucrats. Sure, Cocking was a state employee who had come in under Ed Rivers. And sure, Papa had the political muscle to get rid of him if he wanted to. But why bother? Our social customs were not about to be altered because some outside foundation and a few college professors decided to get a little self righteous at the expense of the wicked old South. Making this into an issue would just divert us from the many progressive things we wanted to do for Georgia. When Papa had been governor before, the Depression kept us from doing much more than keep our heads above water. Now the Depression was starting to lift; Papa had run on a progressive platform, which I had helped draft; and for the first time in his career he had the politicians as well as the people on his side. I could just see those academics getting their tail feathers ruffled about political interference in the classroom and the national media salivating to poke some more fun at "Old Gene" and his red galluses. Mama and I did everything we could to get Papa to forget about that damn Cocking. But once Eugene Talmadge made up his mind about something, mere reason couldn't change it. He knew only one method of attack. The frontal assault.

When the Board of Regents refused to do what Papa wanted, he treated them the way he would the highway commission or any other agency of government that wouldn't do his bidding. He replaced enough of the members until he got a working majority who either agreed with him or were too cowed to cross him. Then he called a public hearing on the Cocking matter and put his main man on the Regents, Jim Peters, in charge. Now, Jim wasn't a rip-roaring orator like Papa, so whenever things got a little dull Papa would lean over and whisper, "Hit the chair and holler, Jim!" It was downright embarrassing.

Well, Papa carried the day hands down. But it was a battle he would have been better off losing. Or, if he had listened to Mama and me, never fighting in the first place. That Southern Accrediting Commission over in Louisville really hit the roof about all these political shenanigans and threatened to withdraw accreditation from the whole Georgia system. To Papa that just smacked of more outside interference. Louisville may have been technically in the South, but it might just as well have been Scarsdale, New York, as far as Papa was concerned. "We credit our own schools down here," he said. And he meant it. There was a brief period when one of Papa's friends on the Regents, Sandy Beaver, seemed to have a compromise worked out. But Papa got his back up and decided to go down with the ship. On December 4, 1941, the Southern Accrediting Commission met in Louisville and withdrew its approval from the Georgia system. From the public reaction you would have thought that they had ordered all the students in Georgia to be lined up, have holes drilled in their

63

heads, and their brains drained out. The students hanged Papa in effigy, the *Saint Louis Post-Dispatch* called him "a prize specimen of full-blown American fascism," and the people of Georgia voted him out of office. If it hadn't been for the Dean Cocking affair, he probably would have been reelected without serious opposition.

You know, time can do funny things. At some point in the late seventies Ellis Arnall was introducing me at a function, and his remarks were so glowing that I could hardly believe my ears. When I got up to speak, I said, "As you all know, Governor Arnall and I haven't always seen eye-to-eye over the years. But I do believe that the older he's gotten, the wiser he's become." How different things were in 1942! Ellis was still a young man, and he would have come out against God, motherhood, and apple pie sooner than say a kind word about the Talmadges. Anyone could see that Papa had shot himself in the foot on the education issue. (Blew himself up is more like it.) But it was Ellis Arnall who had the initiative and the foresight to ride that issue right up to the front door of the Georgia governor's mansion.

Ellis came from Newnan, Georgia, which was the wealthiest town in the state and one of the wealthiest in the country. He was hardly a year out of law school when he was elected to the state legislature in 1932, the year Papa was first elected governor. Originally, Ellis was a strong Talmadge man, but he didn't remain one for long. By the end of Papa's second term, Ellis was carrying water for Ed Rivers, Roy Harris, and the rest of the "Little New Deal" crowd. It sort of made sense politically, given Roosevelt's popularity and the fact that Papa couldn't run to succeed himself in '36. Ed Rivers showed his appreciation by appointing Ellis assistant attorney general in '37. Then at the start of his second term in '39, Ed got the elected attorney general, Judge Manning J. Yeomans, to step down so he could appoint Ellis to the top spot. (You see, Judge Yeomans was giving Ed the same kind of fits the Supreme Court was giving Roosevelt at the national level.) So at age thirty-one, Ellis became the youngest attorney general in the history of the state. Getting elected to the office in his own right in 1940 made him the great hope of the anti-Talmadge camp.

What Ellis figured he'd do was ride Papa hard on the education issue without appearing soft on segregation. I doubt that any of the Yankee liberals who made Ellis such a folk hero and couldn't find things vile enough to say about my father knew what Ellis really thought about race. To this day it makes my flesh crawl to read some of the statements he made, which I'm sure he couldn't have meant. At one point Ellis said, "Over in west Georgia where I live, we don't need any governor to keep Negroes out of white schools. We know how to handle a thing like that without any help. Why, if a Negro ever tried to get into a white school in the section where I live, the sun would not set on his head. And we wouldn't call on the governor or the State Guard either." That was too much for Papa. He said he was sure "the people of West Georgia would not lynch a Negro for seeking admission to a white school, but the sun wouldn't set on the job of a teacher who encouraged [integration]."

Both Papa and Ellis started their campaigns on July 4, 1942. Ellis had him a big crowd on what turned out to be a sunny day over in Newnan. Those folks made short work of twelve thousand pounds of barbecue, twelve hundred gallons of Brunswick stew, six thousand loaves of bread, twenty-five barrels of pickles, and three thousand gallons of lemonade. Then they heard Ellis tear into Papa as a red-gallused dictator. There's no surviving record of the speech he gave that day, but I suspect that it was pretty much in the same vein as the one he gave when he announced his candidacy back in November of '41. At that time Ellis said, "The dictator seeks to control the schools. He would sacrifice the birthright of your child and my child in order that his selfish ends might be achieved. The slimy hands of dictatorial governors must be removed from the throats of Georgia's most priceless possession—the children of our state." It was a pretty raw campaign.

Papa wasn't so lucky with his opener, which was in the town of Moultrie. On the way over that morning he had stopped at a country store to use the outdoor privy. The only problem is that under such circumstances you leave yourself open to the vicissitudes of nature. On this particular occasion Papa was brutally attacked by a black widow spider. The doctor in town gave Papa some medication and told him to forget about the speech. That, of course, made him more determined than ever to go on. If the pain and the medication weren't enough to set Papa back, he was hardly into his speech before a big gulley washer of a rainstorm started. That lost him most of the crowd, but still Papa wouldn't quit. The rain soaked everything—the red, white, and blue bunting, the pine floor of the speaker's platform, the few die-hard supporters who had not retreated to their cars, and Papa himself. His suit was drenched, his hair was drenched, and his body was bent over in pain from the spider bite. Off in the distance, the car horns would honk whenever Papa made a point that the folks agreed with. The speech was scheduled for an hour, but after twenty-five minutes Papa couldn't go on any longer. He had to leave the stage, and veteran legislator H.B. ("Hellbent") Edwards took over for him. Most of the twenty-five thousand fish and fifty thousand hushpuppies prepared for the crowd were soaked in the rain.

Things sort of went downhill from there. Papa never had much of a political organization. He didn't like dealing with the courthouse boys in the various counties around the state. (It may have had something to do with the way he was treated by that courthouse gang in McRae when he was trying to break into politics back in the 1920's.) And, of course, the papers were always against him. The only chance he ever had of winning an election was by going directly to the people and moving them. Unfortunately, in 1942, the issues (or should I say THE ISSUE?) were running against him. I could see that it would be impossible for him to run the kind of race that got him elected in 1940. But I wouldn't be around to help make those decisions for him. On December 7, 1941, the Japanese put my career as a political strategist on hold, so I wound up following that 1942 race from the other side of the world. Which was just as well. I suspect that watching it up close would have been more painful than having a black widow spider light into you with your galluses down.

Ellis Arnall was true to his word on the education issue. He removed the governor from the Board of Regents and made it a more independent body. Not that the outfit was "depoliticized."

It would have been impossible to do that to any government entity and still have a democracy. All that happened was that the politics became more covert and less open to public scrutiny. (Had that been the case when Papa was in office, he wouldn't have had such an easy time getting rid of Dean Cocking, but that in itself would have saved him some embarrassment and probably would have kept him from losing the governorship.) Because Ellis was the first Governor of Georgia to serve a full four-year term, he also had time to do a lot of other things. He reformed the pardons and parole system that had been such a scandal under Ed Rivers, took the railroads to court to get them to stop discriminating against the South in freight rates, and generally pursued a liberal line on social welfare and state services. He was a better administrator than Ed Rivers and had a more cooperative legislature and a stronger economy to work with. All of this made him right popular for a time. But Ellis had his eye on a larger audience, and that eventually did him in politically.

Somehow Ellis got the notion he had been ordained to play the role of leading Southern liberal for the rest of the country. He got a pretty good start at that at the 1944 Democratic National Convention in Chicago. The New Deal wasn't quite as popular as it had been when people were standing in breadlines. Not that Roosevelt was in any danger of being dumped. Talk about a third party or slates of unpledged electors was just that—talk. And short of resurrecting Robert E. Lee, the Republicans stood no chance of cracking the Solid South. But Vice President Henry Wallace was another matter. Wallace had been unpopular in our neck of the woods since the time he was Secretary of Agriculture. Everyone from Huey Long on the left to Papa on the right thought he was a damn fool, and we expected our governor to let Roosevelt know it. But when old FDR told Ellis he would like to see Wallace renominated, Ellis just wagged his tail and barked the entire Georgia delegation into line. Because the rest of the party wasn't that craven, it soon became clear that another term for Wallace wouldn't wash. So Roosevelt said, in effect, "Hell, you fellows fight it out amongst yourselves, just so long as I get my fourth term." And he let it be known that Harry Truman or William O. Douglas would also be just dandy running mates. You might say that Roosevelt double-crossed Ellis, but back home it looked as if the governor of this sovereign state was nothing but a lap dog for the left-wing element in the national party.

If that Wallace debacle wasn't bad enough, Ellis went and published a book called *The Shore Dimly Seen* in 1946. All about how the South needed to rejoin the union. It got real good notices in the Yankee press and made him quite a celebrity. Whether he had national political ambitions is anyone's guess, but he was trying damned hard to be a "good Southerner." You know how you felt as a kid when your parents would say, "Why can't you be like Johnny? He cleans up his room, never talks back, and is first in his class at dancing school?" Well, Ellis was playing Johnny for the rest of the country. Went on lecture tours talking about poverty and ignorance in the South. Sure there was poverty and ignorance in the South, but we didn't need to be reminded of it. And we sure as hell didn't need our governor traipsing around the nation bad-mouthing us to the very people who were responsible for our plight. Ellis might have told them that General Sherman destroyed our civilization and perpetrated some of the worst civilian atrocities in the history of warfare. He might have told them that Reconstruction crushed our economy and made a mockery of our political system. He might have told them that far from being separated from the union, we had given our sons in disproportionate numbers in two world wars. He might have told them all of this. But instead, he portrayed us as a bunch of ignorant peckerwoods living on Tobacco Road. It sort of hurt his base of support back home.

Of course, the irony of Ellis's situation was that without a strong home base from which to run, he couldn't hope to do anything nationally. In 1946 there were no senatorial seats open in Georgia, and Ellis was constitutionally barred from succeeding himself as governor. The only way he could extend his career without interruption was to pass a constitutional amendment that would let him run for a second term. Ellis tried that but only succeeded in generating opposition from everybody who wanted to follow him as governor, especially from two men who up to that point had been among his strongest allies—Ed Rivers and Roy Harris.

Ed Rivers was more of a nuisance than a real threat. He had

gone out of office under such a cloud that people weren't standing in line to elect him to another term as governor, but any votes he pulled would have split the anti-Talmadge forces and just made it that much easier for Papa to return to office. Roy Harris, however, was a different matter. Roy was an extremely powerful legislator from Augusta, who had been with Ed Rivers when Ed was governor, switched to Papa in 1940, and then backed Arnall in '42. He was Speaker of the House and was probably owed more favors at that time than any other politician in Georgia. Roy figured that it was time for him to come out from the smoke-filled room and get a little public adulation to go with the power he had always wielded. "Goddamnit! I've been kingmaker for three governors," he'd say. "Now it's my turn to be king." Ellis was afraid of Roy because he knew he couldn't control him. Also, they were on opposite sides of the race issue.

For years blacks had been allowed to vote in the general elections in Georgia, but they were barred from participating in the Democratic primary. That tradition seemed in jeopardy when the United States Supreme Court declared that the white primary in Texas violated the fourteenth amendment to the Constitution. Shortly thereafter, a black barber from Columbus, Georgia, by the name of Primus King, filed suit against the Muscogee County Democratic Committee for denying him the right to vote in the Georgia primary. He won his suit in the federal district court and was upheld in the Fifth Circuit Court of Appeals. When the U.S. Supreme Court refused to review the case, the Democratic White Primary effectively became a thing of the past. Both Ellis Arnall and Ed Rivers were for accepting the court ruling. But not Roy Harris. He was finally fixing to run for governor, and the Supreme Court had dropped a potent issue right in his lap.

When Ellis couldn't get the required two-thirds vote in the legislature to pass the succession amendment, he was eliminated from the 1946 race. He blamed Ed Rivers and, especially, Roy Harris for working against the amendment, and he wasn't about to support Papa. That meant that Arnall and what was left of his organization had to find themselves a new standardbearer. That honor went to an attractive young businessman by the name of James V. Carmichael. Jimmie Carmichael had been general manager of the Bell Bomber Plant in Marietta, Georgia. He was such a crackerjack administrator that he cut the cost of B-29's in half. The Army even said that Jimmie's plant shortened the war by six months. (It was a real comfort to those of us being shot at overseas to know that ablebodied men like Ellis Arnall and Jimmie Carmichael were doing their part on the home front.) Jimmie had served in the legislature for two terms and had been in charge of reorganizing the state revenue department under Arnall. It's lucky for Ellis that he talked Carmichael into running. Things were getting so desperate that one group over in Randolph County was getting ready to draft Ellis's wife.

What looked to be an eye-gouging, four-man race got reduced to three when the liberal forces in Augusta got together with the returning veterans and defeated Roy Harris for renomination to the state legislature. (The legislative primary was held a few months before the one for governor and the other statewide executive offices.) Roy had been so busy wheeling and dealing up in Atlanta that he had forgotten to protect his home base. With the people in his home district voting him out of the legislature, there was no point in Roy's running for higher office. That meant that he would once again be kingmaker instead of king. Since the only candidate speaking Roy's language in the primary was Papa, he became the heir apparent.

As I mentioned earlier, I came back from the Navy determined not to become a professional politician. Of course, as Gene Talmadge's son, I would always be interested in government, but the last thing I wanted was to get the political bug. Politics is an all-consuming mistress that can destroy your family life, warp your personality, and wreck your health. This was never more apparent to me than in 1943 when I returned to the United States from having spent twenty-two months overseas in the Navy. I remember my ship was in Norfolk, Virginia, getting ready to be transferred to the Pacific fleet, when the officer of the deck reported to me that my mother and father and wife were down on the quarter deck. When I rushed down to meet them, I was in for a shock. Papa's color had changed, and he must have lost fifteen pounds since the last time I had seen him. "Papa," I said, "when was the last time you had a physical examination?" Well, he said it hadn't been for a while. So I told him he ought to have one because he didn't look too good. We dropped the subject there, but I'm sure that was the beginning of his liver problem.

Cirrhosis of the liver, which is what Papa eventually died of, usually affects heavy drinkers. But Papa was always a moderate drinker. His rule was never to drink before sundown or after his evening meal. It was the irregular hours and the bad diet of the political life that killed him. When you're campaigning, you're on the move eighty to a hundred hours a week. You might get one or two hours sleep a night. You're rushing from one place to the next, eating whatever you can grab on the run, which is usually junk food, and even that you don't digest properly. Papa said that his last campaign for governor would take ten years off his life. As it turned out, he didn't even live to take office.

The problem with trying to leave politics behind is that once it gets in your blood, it can be like a narcotic. You know that it's no good for you, even that it's killing you, but you just can't leave it alone. That is not true of *all* politicians. When Georgia governor Ernie Vandiver developed a heart condition, he returned to private life and adjusted quite well. But there are far too many others who keep running for office like an old fire horse chasing smoke. Once Papa got the bug, he was never happy unless he was in office or running for office. Between 1942 and '46 he bought and sold cattle and made a little money from his law practice, just waiting for his chance to get back on the stump and snap his galluses and have the people carry him out on their shoulders. What if he had lost three of his last four statewide races? What if his arch-enemy Ellis Arnall and the rest of that anti-Talmadge bunch were in control of state government? Papa had wooed the people for too long and had been lifted too often by their love for him to believe that he couldn't win them back. Mama knew he was a sick man and tried to talk him out of running again. But she probably knew deep down that it was no use. Even if that last race would kill him, he was going to do his damnedest to go out on top. Out of politics, Gene Talmadge was already as good as dead.

☆ ☆ ☆

There's a story that's been going around for years that I wrote Papa's platform in 1946 and released it without showing it to him. That's not true. I did write the platform, but Papa approved it before it ever went out for public consumption. We were heading into an era of post-war prosperity, and I knew that if Georgia was to keep pace with the rest of the nation, the state government would have to take on responsibilities that Papa never dreamed of back when he was fighting the New Deal. We called for a fifty percent hike in teachers' salaries, more money for old age pensions, a million dollars a year to aid counties in building rural medical facilities, the paving of every road on which a mail truck ran, and a host of benefits for veterans—free business licenses, a five-year exemption from *ad valorem* taxes, and a lifetime driver's license. When Papa looked at that platform he said, "You're carrying me pretty fast, aren't you, son?" And I had to tell him, "You've got to travel fast if you're going to win this one."

That was probably the most uphill race my daddy had run since he had announced for agriculture commissioner against J.J. Brown twenty years earlier. Virtually every daily newspaper in the state was against him. Most of the major politicians in state government were against him. The newly enfranchised voters (blacks and those eighteen to twenty-one years old) were against him. I had him giving two and three speeches a day in various parts of the state. Sometimes he would have to travel half the night to get to the next stop. The crowds still responded, but they were in the hundreds not the thousands. Folks had radios now, they could more easily afford to go to the movies, and politics itself was no longer as much fun as when Papa was running against the baseball team. We had music over loudspeakers, but no more Fiddlin' John and no more Moonshine Kate. Also, with the federal courts crushing the white primary, this was the first race since Reconstruction where self-government and states' rights, not local issues, would dominate the campaign. Things were getting downright nasty.

When the votes were finally counted, the country folks had again carried Papa to victory. With the repeal of the poll tax, many more poor people were able to vote than ever before. There were

114 counties in Georgia where the population was seventy-five percent or more rural. Papa carried ninety of them. Of the twenty-two counties that were between fifty and seventy-five percent rural, Papa carried twelve. But of the thirteen streetcar counties, where the population was less than fifty percent rural, he carried only two. Ralph McGill, the great liberal journalist, who was our personal friend and political foe, caught Papa's appeal pretty well in an article he did for *The New Republic*: "'They talk about the state,' [Talmadge] would tell them. 'You are the state as much as the sweet-talking big shots in the town, as much as the newspaper columnists talking about democracy and good government. You can't feed your kids democracy and you can't buy pig and chicken feed with it. The newspapers talk like you can put all that fine talk in your kid's lunch box and let him get fat on it. They ain't done nothing for you.' And the sad fact was that no one had."

Right after that primary election in June, Papa started acting funny. He had never been much of a traveler in his life, and you would think that after a strenuous campaign all he would want to do was sit at home and get some rest. But that wasn't the case. He just couldn't stay put. First he went down to Mexico for a visit, then up to Yellowstone Park in Wyoming. He wasn't back in McRae but a short time when he up and left for Jacksonville, Florida. We all thought it would be good for him to relax on the beach before having to come back and officially accept his nomination at the state Democratic convention in Macon. Then three or four days before the convention, I got a call from a friend who was with Papa. He said, "Herman, you better come down here. Your daddy's in the hospital."

I caught the next plane from Atlanta to Jacksonville and rushed over to Saint Vincent's Hospital, where my father was recovering from a ruptured blood vessel in his stomach. Papa seemed feisty as ever, and I really didn't think his condition was very serious. He wasn't scheduled to take office until the following January. There was a little matter of the general election, but he was running unopposed, so that figured to be pretty much of a legal formality. The real campaign had been in the primary. Still, as the Democratic candidate, he was expected to appear at the state convention. When his doctor told him that would be impossible,

I wrote a speech for him, got his approval on it, and hired a public stenographer to come over to the hospital and type it up. I delivered that speech on his behalf, little knowing that in a few short months I would be assuming the office for which Papa had been nominated for a record fourth time.

This is the way it happened. A short while before the general election, Gibson Greer Ezell, the school superintendent from over in Jasper County, called me up and said, "Herman, have you ever thought about what would happen if your daddy died before he was able to take office?" Now, you might say that was a real icebreaker, but the truth is I hadn't given the matter much thought. Obviously, Gibson Greer Ezell had. He sat around reading history all the time, and he pointed out a provision in the state constitution that seemed to answer the question. It said that the state legislature was to "open and publish the returns,...and the person having the majority of the whole number of votes shall be declared duly elected Governor of the State." So far, no problem. But it went on to say, "If no person shall have such majority, then from the two persons having the highest number of votes, who shall be in life and shall not decline an election at the time appointed for the General Assembly to elect, the General Assembly shall immediately elect a Governor viva voce."

Well, I studied that provision and had other lawyers study it, and we all reached the conclusion that if Papa died, the legislature would have to elect a governor from the two candidates getting the most write-in votes in the November general election. Since Papa was the only candidate whose name was on the ballot, he would obviously get the majority of votes. But if he died before the General Assembly counted those votes in January, he would no longer be a legal person. We knew that some die-hard Jimmie Carmichael supporters would write in Jimmie's name in the general election and that there would be some scattered write-in votes for all kinds of crank candidates. If we allowed that to happen without devising a counter-strategy, then we would be letting down the tens of thousands of people who had supported Papa and the things he stood for. So I passed the word to a few reliable friends to arrange some write-in votes for me. You might call it an insurance policy. If I couldn't keep Papa from dying, at least I could keep him from dying in vain.

One thing that people outside of politics have a hard time understanding are the personal ties that sometimes develop between men who don't agree on a damn thing philosophically. I've seen it happen time and again in the U. S. Senate, which has come to be known as the most exclusive club in the world. And it was certainly true in my daddy's career. His relationship with the press was a case in point. The vast majority of newspapers never had anything good to say about Papa, and he was always able to give back as good as he took. His attacks on the press went over well with Papa's constituency, who thought that reporters were a bunch of urban smart alecks who looked down their noses at country folks. But off the record, the reporters liked Papa and he liked them. A reporter assigned to cover "Old Gene" knew that, whatever else his job might be, it would never be dull. And when Papa wasn't actually on the stump, he was pleasant company and could get along with just about anybody. He and the reporters would give each other hell because that was their job. But like a couple of veteran prizefighters, they could go out for a drink afterwards. That was how it was between Papa and Ralph McGill.

Although I wasn't there, I've read that Papa went to see McGill after that 1946 primary. Ralph was sitting in his office at the *Constitution* with Ellis Arnall when a copyboy stuck his head in the door and warned them that Governor Talmadge was coming down the hall. Ralph's biographer Harold Martin describes Papa as standing there in a rumpled seersucker suit, "his black forelock dangling over one eye, his steeltrap jaw snapped shut around a cold cigar." According to the story, he took the cigar out of his mouth and said, "Ralph, I give you a good whuppin' this time, didn't I?" Papa and Ralph sat there talking over old times, with Ellis probably feeling about as out of place as a college sophomore who'd stumbled into a fifty-year class reunion. That was until Papa finally took a look over at Ellis, pointed his cigar at him, and said, "This little fellow here wouldna beat me the last time if that black widow spider hadna bit me on the balls."

The last interview Papa gave before he died in the Piedmont

Hospital in Atlanta was to Ralph McGill. And Ralph summed up Papa's career right well in an obituary he wrote shortly thereafter. "Eugene Talmadge had no middle name," Ralph wrote. "Yet it might have been Ishmael. Certainly there were times when, like Ishmael, his hand was against every man and every man's hand was against him. And he took pleasure in the phrase 'Wild Man From Sugar Creek.'" Then Ralph went on to say:

> In the past there were legendary giants, John B. Gordon, the handsome Galahad who had covered Marse Robert E. Lee's pitiful retreat to Appomattox; Bob Toombs, whose organ-like voice and masterful rhetoric made him one of the political gods of the War Between the States...; Alex Stephens, the small sickly little man who perhaps was the greatest and soundest political mind of the period; the great Ben Hill, Howell Cobb, and, finally, Tom Watson, an Ishmaelite indeed, whose speeches a young student at the University of Georgia used to recite, tromping up and down a room while his senior roommate, John Monaghan, admonished him, saying, "Listen, Gene, don't get so excited."

Of course, John Monaghan might just as well have saved his breath. When Gene Talmadge got excited about something, no force in heaven or on earth, short of death itself, could quiet him down. And he even gave death a run for the money.

In our family there were two times during the year when we'd all get together—Thanksgiving and Christmas. We didn't have any special traditions or customs, but for a politician simply to be alone with his family was something pretty special. Papa took sick for the last time right after Thanksgiving, and we knew that he wouldn't make it to Christmas. On Sunday, December 15, he suffered a gastro-intestinal upset. On Wednesday he developed a temperature, and early Thursday morning the hemorrhaging began. When the word went out that he needed a blood transfusion, virtually the entire police and fire departments of Atlanta volunteered as donors. The transfusion helped him rally, but complications set in. At 11 P.M. Friday his physician, Dr. J. Edgar Palling, announced that Papa had lapsed into a coma. All I remember about that night is that it seemed to last forever. I'd talk about one thing or another with the family, friends, and reporters who were all there waiting for the end. Then along about seven Saturday morning I went out on the hospital lawn to watch the winter sun rise. In the distance I could hear a newborn baby cry. And then the news came that Papa was gone. It was probably the saddest moment of my life, but I didn't have time to grieve. There was too much yet to be done.

5

The Two-Governor Row

"He rode in a great bronze coffin under banked red roses. He wore the blue serge double-breasted suit he would have worn at the inauguration, and in its lapel was a white narcissus put there by his sister because he had always put one there when he stood up to take his oath as Governor. He had his red suspenders on, and the horn-rimmed specs, and on his forehead the famed unruly forelock that was his trademark and his badge. They had tried to slick it down at the funeral home, but they could not quite make it stay. And Lindley Camp rode with him, as he always used to do, along the route as familiar as the palms of his own hands."

That was part of Harold Martin's account of Papa's "Last Ride Home," from the *Atlanta Constitution* of December 24, 1946. Papa died at 7 A.M. on Saturday, December 21. Within hours we received a message of sympathy from President Harry Truman. Ellis Arnall ordered that the flags at the Capitol be lowered to half staff and that the Christmas lights which were burning for the first time in five years be turned back off. Now that the war was over, the rest of the nation felt free to celebrate Christmas, but in Georgia the festivities would have to pause as the state buried its most controversial son. There were quite a few registered voters who had no memory of Georgia without him.

On Sunday they laid Papa's body in the rotunda of the state Capitol, and thousands came to pay their last respects. The honor guard of highway patrolmen brought him in shortly before 1 P.M. I remember the winter sunlight shining through the windows of the dome and across the blue ceiling above the casket. Shortly thereafter the mourners started filing in, mostly two abreast, sometimes in larger groups, at the rate of more than two thousand an hour. They were from all walks of life, but most were the rural poor, people like the Tree Climbing Haggards, who had followed Papa for years. Hundreds were from Atlanta, but many were from places like Tucker and Greensboro, Alpharetta and Hapeville, from Dahlonega, East Point, and Winder. There were folks from Forsyth and Thomasville, Jackson and Franklin, from Lawrenceville and Powder Springs. More than ten thousand people passed by his body that afternoon. Many were on crutches, and most had tears in their eyes.

There were formal tributes from the high and mighty, some of whom had never had a good word to say about Papa when he was alive. But I think he would have preferred what his own people, the simple dirt farmers, had to say. One ex-con told a reporter, "You know why I was for him? Cause he done me a favor one time. Thirty of them hemmed me in and I had to cut my way out. Old Gene got me out and it didn't cost me a nickel. Got the pardon out at my uncle's now. That State Seal and Old Gene's signature on it." And there was another fellow who allowed that Gene Talmadge was always "for the poor sons-of-guns like we is."

The funeral was held on Monday, December 23, at the Baptist Church in McRae, Georgia. The Reverend A.D. Woodle, who was pastor of the church and a great friend of my father's, delivered a moving eulogy to Papa. I remember his reading from the eleventh chapter of Hebrews that marvelous tribute to the great men of the Old Testament: "By faith Abel offered unto God a more excellent sacrifice than Cain, by which he obtained witness that he was righteous." And they sang all the wonderful old hymns that Papa loved so much: "When They Ring Those Golden Bells," "Beautiful Isle of Somewhere," and "The Old Rugged Cross."

And then the pallbearers (Lindley Camp, Zack Cravey, Dr. J.C. Maloy, W.S. Mann, W.E. Wilburn, Jim Peters, Charley Redwine, and George W. Wilson) lifted the casket and took Papa to his final resting place. As he was lowered into the ground, the Reverend Woodle read a poem by one of Papa's favorite writers, Mark Twain:

> *Warm summer sun, shine kindly here;*
> *Warm southern wind, blow softly here;*
> *Green sod above, lie light, lie light;*
> *Goodnight, dear heart, goodnight, goodnight.*

The floral wreaths made that little Baptist church look like a greenhouse. There were four freight carloads, several truckloads, and hundreds of individual floral offerings. Many were from people Papa never knew but who knew him and couldn't imagine what our state would be like without him. If Papa had polarized the politicians in Georgia during his life, they all came together briefly to mourn his passing. They were all there—the sitting governor, Ellis Arnall, and former governors Ed Rivers, Clifford Walker, Hugh Dorsey, and John M. Slaton. Our two United States Senators, Dick Russell and Walter George, were there. And so was J.J. Brown, the powerful agriculture commissioner, whom no one thought could lose the 1926 election. Especially not to that Wild Man from Sugar Creek.

As impressive as the funeral was, I can't help thinking that the truest memorial to Papa was etched in the faces of the many common people who lined the road and stood in silence as the hearse bearing his body made its slow ride home from Atlanta to McRae. In the *Constitution* the next day Harold Martin wrote that Papa "would have understood all that he saw along the road... the old lady in the sunbonnet before the lonely cabin, waving, waving, waving as he passed... The old men on the corners in the little towns, their hats held on their breasts... He would have noticed that most of the heads were gray... He would have recognized these, his own, the legions of the faithful who believed in him and who would never change."

From the moment Papa entered the hospital for the last time, speculation started to get hot and heavy about who would be governor if he should die. In the general election he had gotten over 140,000 votes, and thirty-two other candidates had gotten a smattering of write-in votes. Of these, the most significant were Jimmie Carmichael, myself, and a tombstone salesman from north Georgia by the name of D. Talmadge Bowers. We had each gotten around 650 votes, and according to the state constitution, the legislature had to elect a governor from the two of us with the most votes, "who shall be in life and shall not decline an election." On the day that Papa died, Jimmie Carmichael announced that he would have no part of such an election. That meant that the legislature would have to choose between me and Mr. Bowers.

From time to time people ask me about D. Talmadge Bowers. I can't remember ever having met the man. I don't think he was any kin to our family, so he was probably named for the great evangelist DeWitt Talmage, who was a distant relation of ours even though he spelled his name differently. As I recall, Bowers could never make up his mind whether he was a Republican or an independent, but he ran as a write-in candidate for some office or another in just about every statewide election. He was a crank, whom the Republicans probably wouldn't have backed, even if there had been Republicans in the state at the time. But with Jimmie Carmichael declining election, despite a lot of armtwisting by Ellis Arnall, it looked as if the next constitutional Governor of Georgia would be Bowers or myself. Since I had inherited my daddy's support and Bowers had no support at all, the anti-Talmadge forces would have to come up with a fancy political maneuver to thwart the will of the people. They did just that by arguing that the next governor should be the lieutenant governor-elect, M.E. Thompson.

The post of lieutenant governor had just been created in the new constitution that had been passed during the Arnall administration, so no one was quite sure what the hell a lieutenant governor was or what he was supposed to do. The constitution prescribed that he would take over in case of the death, resignation, or inability of the governor, but it said nothing at all about the lieutenant governor-elect taking over for the governor-elect. And at first, Ellis Arnall was none too eager to suggest that should happen. For one thing, Ellis was hoping that he could get the legislature to elect

Jimmie Carmichael. For another, Ellis considered Thompson a political lightweight. M.E. was a former schoolteacher and assistant state school superintendent who had served as Ellis's executive secretary. Ellis had tried to talk him out of running for lieutenant governor and, when he couldn't, had backed another candidate in the election. But when Jimmie Carmichael refused to go up against me, Ellis's only hope to keep his crowd in power was to put all his chips on M.E. Thompson.

By the time the legislature convened on January 13, 1947, the Talmadge organization was in the midst of its third campaign inside of a year. The first was the grueling primary race that won Papa the Democratic nomination and cost him his life. The second was the write-in effort for me in the general election. Now we were trying to convince the legislature that the best way to ratify the will of the people who had elected Papa was to support me rather than an anti-Talmadgite like Carmichael or Thompson or a nut like Bowers. On January 13th our candidate Fred Hand was elected Speaker of the House, and Thompson's man Bill Dean was elected President Pro Tem of the State Senate. Both bodies would meet in joint session on January 14 to open and publish the returns from the general election. Since the first amendment to the United States Constitution guarantees freedom of assembly, I invited all of our friends to come up to Atlanta and watch their government in action.

Over the past four decades the events that took place in the Capitol in Atlanta on the evening of January 14 and the early morning of January 15, 1947, have become the stuff of legends. This is how *Newsweek* magazine described the scene at the time:

> The showdown arrived Tuesday, Jan. 14. The Talmadge crowd—the poor white farmers and crossroads grocers and "wool-hat boys" from the sticks—brought a carnival air to Atlanta's staid graystone Capitol... They wanted to tromp in and put their shoes on desks and spit on the floor and break out into Rebel yells now and then. And they made the most of their chance.

The Talmadge faithful came early and stayed late. They milled around the Capitol and whooped it up in the galleries and overflowed onto the floor of the General Assembly. They lived on soda pop and crackers and stale sandwiches, littered the aisles with peanut shells and apple cores, and clogged the toilets with broken whisky bottles. They shucked their coats to flaunt bright red galluses, their dead hero's political trademark. Few of them understood or even cared about the constitutional question which the General Assembly was sweating out—so long as "Hummon won."

Now let me tell you what really happened.

First of all, the state attorney general Eugene Cook tried to keep the legislature from acting at all when he issued an opinion on January 4 denying that it had the authority to do anything other than declare that Papa and M.E. Thompson had been elected governor and lieutenant governor and wait for Ellis Arnall to turn the governor's office over to M.E. Well, Eugene Cook was certainly entitled to an opinion on the matter, but that opinion was in no way binding on the legislature, which was itself a sovereign body. What's more, a majority of the members of that sovereign body were pledged to elect me governor.

Both M.E. and I had established headquarters in the old Henry Grady Hotel. Then on the day of the fourteenth, I moved my base of operation over to Fred Hand's office, and M.E. set up shop with Bill Dean over in the Senate. Ellis stayed down in the governor's office one floor below the legislature. In addition to the elected officials, thousands of ordinary citizens were also on hand. They packed the corriders and the galleries, and old Fiddlin' John was going through the halls playing "Sugar in the Gourd." So many folks were actually on the floor that some legislators had trouble finding their seats. Bill Dean, who had the constitutional responsibility of chairing the joint session of the legislature, rapped his gavel for an hour to try to get order, then declared a two-hour recess, hoping to clear out everyone but members of the legislature and the working press. When Senator Grady Coker of Canton moved that the legislature go into executive session, all you could hear was an angry chorus of boos. His motion didn't even get a second.

Our folks might have been a bit rowdy, but Thompson's crowd wasn't exactly playing by the Marquis of Queensbury Rules. I remember standing there talking to Judge Charley Worrill right before the legislature was ready to vote. Charley was a judge from over in Cuthbert, Georgia, and he was on hand to swear in the new governor. He had spent his younger days out in the Wild West, and he still carried two .45 revolvers in his brief case. If you got into an altercation with Judge Worrill, he let you choose your weapon.

So, anyway, I was shooting the breeze with Charley when one of my lieutenants came up and told me that Thompson's men were serving drinks with knockout drops in them to some of our legislators. We managed to enlist enough public health doctors to foil that bit of tomfoolery. We had people being revived back to consciousness all over the Capitol lawn. Then a couple of our men came in propping up a crucial swing vote by both arms. This fellow had a bad drinking problem and had been missing for several days. The Thompson forces had kidnapped him and kept him drunk the whole time. The man was ready to vote with us, but he looked like hell and was shaking from the D.T.'s. He said, "Herman, I need a drink bad." Well, I took out a ten-dollar bill and turned to Judge Worrill. "Charley," I said, "you get a bottle of whiskey and give our friend here a drink every hour on the hour. But when the time comes to vote, make sure he's out on the floor doing his constitutional duty." Those were right squalid times.

My chief strategist was Roy Harris, and I had Bob Elliot running things down on the floor. M.E. had a couple of state senators, W.D. Trippe of Cedartown and Everett Millican of Atlanta, calling the shots for him. When there was finally enough order for the legislature to begin its business, Bob Elliot moved that the ballots from the general election be counted, with separate reports for each of the nine state house offices. The motion also stipulated that no action be taken on other returns until the election of a governor had been settled. A couple of Thompson supporters, Charles Gowen and Adie Durden, countered with an amendment that would have had all the results of the general election published before any other business was transacted. Had that amendment passed, M.E. would have been officially the lieutenant governor with a much stronger claim to succession. We defeated that amendment 128-126 and passed the original motion by voice vote. At that point, the returns were brought up from the secretary of state's office in a huge laundry basket and two cardboard boxes, and a committee was appointed to tabulate the results.

The initial tabulation commenced about four o'clock in the afternoon and was over five hours later. As expected, the four leading candidates were Papa, Carmichael, Bowers, and myself. It was a little embarrassing, though, that I was bringing up the rear. 143,279 votes had gone to Papa, 699 to Carmichael, 637 to Bowers, and 617 to me. But with Papa dead and Jimmie Carmichael declining election, the legislature would have to choose between Bowers and myself. At that point Ellis Arnall revealed what an opportunist he actually was. He started passing the word, through Representative Pierre Howard, that Jimmie Carmichael was on his way to the Capitol to accept the governorship. Ellis told a reporter from the *Americus Times-Recorder* that, "We are reversing our position and we are going to elect [Carmichael] and I will surrender the office to him." Sorry about that, M.E.

Well, as it turned out, Jimmie Carmichael had no intention of allowing Ellis to use him as a pawn to checkmate me and the people of Georgia. But as Ralph McGill pointed out, this move amounted to an admission by Ellis that the legislature did have the right to elect a governor from the two candidates with the most write-in votes. The official tabulation was completed when the committee doing the counting found fifty-eight additional votes for me that had been placed in the wrong envelope. That gave me 675 votes and put me ahead of Bowers. Adie Durden then proposed a resolution declaring that Eugene Talmadge had been elected governor and that the legislature had no authority to determine his successor. That went down 132-118. In its place the legislature adopted, by a vote of 137-114, Bob Elliot's motion that "no person" had received a majority of votes for governor and that it was therefore the duty of the legislature to go ahead and elect one. Bob then nominated me, and 167 legislators concurred.

Eighty-seven registered their opposition by voting "present."

When I had come home from the Navy a year earlier, I had wanted nothing more than for my daddy to be elected governor again and for me to be set up in a law practice where I could make a living for myself and my family. Now here I was, with my hand on the Bible, being sworn in as the second youngest governor in the history of Georgia. It was two A.M., January 15, 1947, when I took the oath of office. As I stood at the podium to give an impromptu inaugural address, I looked out over both houses of the Georgia legislature and at the galleries packed with folks who had always voted for Papa and who now saw me as their champion. But I was also entering a political arena that went beyond the Georgia legislature and the wool hat boys in red suspenders. My speech went out over a nationwide radio hookup to homes all across America. I had one foot in Papa's world and the other in a strange new world he had never lived to see.

We had two armies in Georgia at that time—the National Guard, which had just returned from active duty in World War II, and the State Guard, which had been created as a temporary replacement for the National Guard and had not yet been deactivated. (The National Guard was loyal to me, and the State Guard to Ellis Arnall.) Moreover, the Capitol was packed with thousands of my civilian supporters, most of whom had been there since early Tuesday morning. Some were drunk and a few were armed. In fact, it was such an explosive situation that there were around fifty war correspondents on hand to cover the proceedings. Some were from as far away as Australia and New Zealand. After I made my brief inaugural remarks, a committee of legislators was formed to escort me downstairs and install me in the governor's office.

Now, I didn't exactly expect Ellis to welcome me with open arms. He had wanted very much to be governor again or at least to determine who his successor would be. But it should have been obvious that I had won the round that day. I fully expected Ellis to say, "Herman, I think this is illegal and I'll see you in court." But I never had any idea that he would try to hold onto the office. Contrary to what my detractors would have you believe, the last thing

I wanted to do was provoke a confrontation that might get some-body hurt. And I hoped that Ellis would see things that way, too.

There's some controversy over what happened next. Ellis claimed that we battered down the door of his outer office. I have no recollection of that occurring, but if it did, I have to wonder why he chose to lock his door against the state legislature, the peo-ple of Georgia, and the constitutionally elected governor. He had no court order backing him up, only the *opinion* of the attorney general, whom he had appointed. Well, I walked into that office with the legislative escort committee. Roy Harris was on one side of me and Mama on the other.

"I presume you have been informed that I've been elected gover-nor by the General Assembly," I said.

"The General Assembly cannot elect a governor," Ellis shot back. "I refuse to yield the office to you, whom I consider a pretender."

"Do you defy the General Assembly?" I asked.

"I do not," he said. "But I uphold the law."

Seeing that he wasn't going to budge, I just turned around and said, "We'll see."

But Ellis managed to get in the last word. As I was walking out, he said, "You were nice to come in." One thing about Ellis was that he had a quick wit. After he left office he made a big hit on the radio up north along with Oscar Levant and the rest of that New York-Hollywood crowd.

It really didn't make a damned bit of difference to me whether I got into the governor's office that night or the next day, but I was fearful for Ellis's safety. Some of my supporters were so mad that they wanted to throw Ellis out bodily. There was a little scuffle between one of my supporters, John Nahara, and Ellis's chauffeur Thad Buchanan. Unfortunately, Buchanan's jaw was broken, but there was no serious bloodshed. It's a wonder nobody was killed. Both that night and the next day I had to quiet the crowd down and plead for order. We had won, and if Ellis wanted to continue hanging around the Capitol, it was his right as a private citizen to do so. I turned to my adjutant general, Marvin Griffin, and said: "Marvin, when Ellis gets ready to leave, see that you have some-one escort him back to his home in Newnan. I don't want any harm to come to him. And while you're at it, change the locks on the governor's office."

I returned to my home in Lovejoy that night and got maybe a couple hours sleep. We had always had guns around the house when I was growing up, but I very rarely went around armed. However, given the tenseness of the situation in Atlanta, I figured it might be a good idea to be prepared for violence. So the next morning, I stuck a .38 Smith and Wesson in my belt and headed to the Capitol for my first full day as Governor of Georgia. We took possession of the governor's office at 7 A.M., before Ellis had a chance to get back in town from Newnan and try to bar us. That day I swore in Zack Cravey as comptroller general, J. Paul Smith as director of public safety, Charley Redwine as commissioner of revenue, and Jim Gillis as highway commissioner. I then dissolved the State Guard, ordered the National Guard to stay mobilized, and asked my followers to return peacefully to their homes.

Things really got interesting on my second day in office. Ellis arrived at the Capitol at about 10:30 in the morning (he never was an early riser) and gathered a whole pack of reporters around him. When that gang got to the governor's office (where I was in complete control), Ellis found my executive secretary Benton Odum waiting to greet him. By that time of the day there were quite a few people in the outer office waiting to see me. When Ellis saw that Benton Odum wasn't going to let him barge right into the governor's office, he started pounding on the door. Then, when there wasn't any answer, he turned to Benton and said, "May I see the pretender?"

"You can wait your turn to see the governor, *Mr.* Arnall," Benton replied. And just to make sure that Ellis got the point, he added, "Like any other citizen."

Well, Ellis was fit to be tied. He said, "Are you denying me the right to my office?"

"I am denying you the right to enter the office of the Governor of Georgia," Benton said.

At that point, Ellis started knocking harder than ever.

"You may wait in the reception room," Benton said.

Ellis continued knocking, and Benton repeated just a bit louder: "You may wait in the reception room, *Mr.* Arnall."

Seeing that he wasn't going to get anywhere at the state Capitol, Ellis decided he'd go out to the mansion (where we had already moved in) and make a stand for the cameras. (We weren't exactly kicking Ellis out of his home, because he had moved out and returned to Newnan before the legislature had even convened.) He invited all of his reporters to the mansion for lunch, figuring he could cut some shines out there. But before he did, he went to the barbershop to get his hair cut, so he'd look nice for the photographers. With Ellis being prematurely bald, that didn't take very long. So, by lunchtime Ellis and his covey of reporters were out at the mansion jawing with the state troopers who had been assigned there.

"Are you refusing me entrance to the mansion?" Ellis asked.

Sergeant J. Frank Jones told him that was about the size of it.

"You mean you will resort to force and violence?" Ellis sputtered.

"Not unless we have to," Jones told him. "We honestly hope that no violence will be caused."

Having got his publicity fix out of that scene, Ellis rounded up his reporters and took them to lunch at a nearby drugstore. (I'm not sure whether he even picked up the tab.) Meanwhile, back at the mansion, a patrol car pulled up with Betty, the two boys, and our maid. Betty got out, posed for pictures, and answered some questions. When someone asked if we had moved in for good, she just smiled and said, "It kind of looks that way." The Talmadges were coming home.

As you can well imagine, with Old Gene gone the national press couldn't wait to start lighting into the "crown prince." As I recall, there was one cartoonist who actually drew a picture of me wearing a crown and lounging around on a throne, which was plopped on the sweating back of some fellow labeled "Georgia." And that damn Herblock, who never was one for originality, had me depicted as a little shrimp who was blinded by a big wool hat. The Georgia legislature was some uncouth redneck telling "The People of Georgia" that "We don't want none of your outside interference." (How Herblock figured he knew "The People of Georgia"

90

better than their elected representatives did is a question that never seemed to bother him.) But the real prize in all of this undoubtedly goes to my old favorite *Time* magazine. It printed a story about some old black fellow who was up on a bigamy charge in a court in Atlanta. Prior to sentencing he said to the judge, "I cain't see where it's wrong for a man to have two wives when it's all right for a state to have two governors."

As Ellis and I were both jockeying for position, I got a little unsolicited help from Jimmy Dykes, a legislator from over in Cochran, Georgia. When Ellis wasn't able to get into his old office by Thursday, he went and set himself up a new office at the information booth in the Capitol rotunda. He remained there for several days, holding press conferences. Just as he was about to sit down at his desk one afternoon, there was a big explosion, just like a gunshot. The echo effect made it sound about two or three times as loud as it actually was, and there was smoke all over the place. One lady reporter had picked herself up off the marble floor and run over to the telephone to report an assassination attempt when someone looked down at the floor and saw fragments of a firecracker. If they'd looked up about a story or so, they probably would have seen the culprit, Jimmy Dykes, leaning over the railing, grinning like the cat that swallowed the canary. And poor Ellis was the canary.

The next day when Ellis came back to take his place at the information booth, Jimmy was sitting there. After they shook hands and exchanged greetings, Jimmy said, "Would you like an appointment with the governor?"

"Jimmy, I am the governor," Ellis said.

"Ellis," Jimmy said, "you remind me of a hawg in the slops. You've got your head in the trough and you just can't stop." (At 237 pounds, Jimmy hadn't missed too many meals himself.)

"Have you taken over my office?" Ellis asked.

"I have," Jimmy replied. "It's my day to play governor."

That was too much for Ellis. He promptly moved his base of operation to his law office down the street, although rumors persisted for awhile that he was holding down the men's bathroom in the basement of the Capitol.

You remember those fifty-eight votes for me that wound up

in the wrong envelope? Well, M.E. Thompson started nosing around when he heard from a Baptist preacher and a county commissioner that those votes were suspicious. And he passed the word to C.E. Gregory, who was political editor of the *Atlanta Journal*. The first I ever heard about it was when Gregory assigned the story to a reporter by the name of George Goodwin, who wrote up a lurid exposé and won himself a Pulitzer Prize. Goodwin is supposed to have said to Secretary of State Ben Fortson, "Do you know that they rose from the dead in Telfair County, marched in alphabetical order to the polls, cast their votes for Herman Talmadge, and went back to their last repose?"

I suspect that is not exactly what G.K. Chesterton had in mind when he talked about the "democracy of the dead." And it sure as hell isn't what I had in mind when I passed the word to my friends to get me some write-in votes. It's absurd to assume that there weren't enough living people in Telfair County who would have voted for me that I had to start voting tombstones. I never told my people to steal votes for me, never intimated that they do so, and wouldn't have condoned it if I had known about it. Not even my opponents have accused me of being personally involved in any electoral chicanery. But even if we throw out every disputed ballot, I was still one of the two top vote getters, in life, who was willing to accept election by the General Assembly. So if the legislature did, in fact, have the constitutional responsibility to elect a governor, it was well within its rights in selecting me. Those fifty-eight votes make a good story, but they never had any material bearing on my claim to the office of governor.

On Saturday, January 18, the plot thickened a bit more. Ellis Arnall resigned as governor in favor of M.E. Thompson, who had been sworn in that same day as lieutenant governor. Thompson was now claiming to be acting governor, and he told reporters that he was going to come around on Monday morning and demand that I turn over the keys to the governor's office and the executive mansion. He also started making appointments to various government offices. As things were shaping up, the state not only had two governors but two of just about everything else. Since the courts had yet to rule, the legislature was the only independent branch of government that had declared itself on the matter, and it was solidly behind me. But you never would have guessed it from reading the Atlanta newspapers.

Georgia was still polarized into Talmadge and anti-Talmadge camps, and the people who hated the Talmadges were just as passionate as those who loved us. The accusations that hurt the most, however, were those that compared me to Adolph Hitler. One fellow named Clark Foreman, who was head of some outfit called the Southern Conference for Human Welfare, said that my election reminded him of Hitler's Munich beer hall *putsch*. And 150 Georgia Tech students wrote a letter to the editor of the *Atlanta Journal* accusing me of acting "in true 'Heil Hitler' fashion." Another letter writer said he would leave the state if "Von Herman" remained governor. I had just spent four years risking my life trying to defeat Hitler so that these folks could retain the right to call me a Nazi or any other damn thing they wanted. Well, like Papa, I was one "dictator" who was never afraid of an election. That seemed to be the only sensible way to determine who really was Governor of Georgia.

So on Tuesday, January 21, I proposed to the Georgia legislature that M.E. Thompson and I both resign and present ourselves before the people in a special election to be held within sixty days. If Ellis and M.E. were right in holding that the Talmadge forces were nothing but redneck stormtroopers who had seized control of the state government through a *coup d'etat*, here was a perfect chance for the people to throw us out on our ears. If, however, I was right in holding that the majority of the people believed as Papa did and wanted me to carry out his program, they would be able to make that clear. I'm not sure what Herblock and *Time* magazine thought about my proposal, but M.E. turned it down flat. He figured that if he could hold on until the courts ruled in his favor, he'd be able to play governor for another two years. I was persuaded that our side could win any court case, but I would have preferred governing with the mandate of the people rather than through a legal technicality.

In the meantime, a few of the anti-Talmadge holdovers were doing their damnedest to keep the state government from functioning properly. For one thing, attorney general Eugene Cook was refusing to bond my revenue commissioner Charley Redwine.

Then the state treasurer, George B. Hamilton, announced that he would simply ignore requests for operating expenses from the revenue and highway departments until he was personally satisfied that all of my appointees had met the legal qualifications for their offices. That meant that the highway department wouldn't receive any state funds, and all federal checks to the department would be held in the treasurer's vaults. Papa, where'd you put that acetylene torch?

Probably the oddest row of all during that period was over something called the Great Seal of Georgia. As governor I was required to sign all sorts of documents. Those documents didn't become law, however, until they were embossed with the seal of the state. The seal was officially in the custody of Secretary of State Ben Fortson, so when I needed it I sent my comptroller Zack Cravey over to fetch it from Ben. Now Ben was a dedicated public servant, despite being confined to a wheel chair, but he could be stubborn as hell when he had his mind made up about something. This was one of those times. He told Zack that he wasn't going to take the seal out of the safe. "We can't use the seal," he said. "I don't know if Herman is governor or not." When Zack came back without the seal, I told him to forget about it. But Ben got the notion that I was going to send someone over to steal the seal from him. So he took it out of the safe and hid it on his person. Years later he told a reporter that he had sat on the seal by day and slept on it by night. "If you don't believe it leaves a lasting impression," Ben allowed, "try doing that for sixty-three days."

I've always believed that the bigger government gets the less efficient it becomes. And that was certainly true during those early months of 1947 when the state of Georgia literally had twice as much government as it needed. I was really looking forward to that definitive court ruling that would leave our administration in charge and allow us to get on with the task of governing. I had no doubt whatsoever about the legal rightness of our position, and when we were supported by two out of three lower court decisions, it seemed that we were home free. Especially when you consider that the judges who had ruled in our favor had both been appointed by Arnall. I held judges in considerable esteem at the time. They always voted according to the law, without regard to personal bias. Or so I thought.

You can imagine how shocked I was when the Supreme Court of Georgia (the majority of whom had been appointed by Arnall and Rivers) held, by a vote of five-to-two, that the state legislature had the right to elect a governor only if no person had received a majority of votes. Since Papa had received a majority in the general election, the legislature was supposed to declare him governor-elect. The court didn't seem to be a bit bothered by the philosophical difficulties of considering a corpse to be a legal person or declaring a dead man governor. Some of my lieutenants might have taken it upon themselves to vote tombstones, but they never tried to elect one. The effect of the decision was that M.E. Thompson would continue as acting governor until a special election could be held in 1948. In a sense, I felt vindicated twenty years later when the Georgia and the United States Supreme Courts both upheld the right of the Georgia legislature to elect a governor in the Lester Maddox-Bo Callaway case. That was also a situation in which no person received a majority of the votes for governor. The reason was a strong write-in effort on behalf of a third candidate—my old friend Ellis Arnall. You might say that I was more than a little surprised when, just a few years ago, Ellis revealed that he had known all along exactly how the Supreme Court of Georgia would vote in our two-governor row.

In the forty years since that bizarre fracas, the wounds have mostly healed. (I get along well with Ellis Arnall today and was warm friends with M.E. Thompson for the balance of that good man's life.) But the controversies continue—among old politicians who remember those days and young historians who weren't even born at the time. Throughout it all there is one phrase you hear again and again—the "will of the people." Well, what was the will of the people? Against tremendous odds and in failing health, Eugene Talmadge took his case to the people in 1946. Because they believed in what he stood for, they gave him the largest vote in his entire career and elected him governor. The will of the people was indeed thwarted, but not by vote fraud or political shenanigans. It was thwarted by death itself. The man the people wanted had been taken from them. All that was left was his program and his platform. It was at this point that the politicians who couldn't defeat Papa while he was alive tried to do it after he was dead. They tried to get Jimmie Carmichael elected by the legislature. Then when Jimmie wouldn't go along with that, they maintained that the legislature had no right to elect a governor. When I proposed a special election to test the "will of the people," they rejected that idea and took the matter to court.

But I do believe that the biggest hypocrites of all were the cartoonists and commentators from outside Georgia who were so strong for the "will of the people." What did they know about the Georgia dirt farmer or even the common people of their own states? I doubt that they'd ever met any common people on purpose, and they probably couldn't stand the ones they ran into by accident. But, thank God, in a democracy the will of the people is more than just fancy talk. It's folks from every stratum of society, even ones in wool hats and red suspenders, making their voices heard. There would be a special election in 1948 to determine the will of the people of Georgia. And I was going to be a candidate in that election. I told Betty we'd be moving out of the mansion for awhile. "We're taking our case to the court of last resort."

6

The Restoration

One day my executive assistant Benton Odum brought in a letter written on tasteful blue stationery. He said, "Governor, this is one you'll have to handle yourself." It was from a woman who was having a little row with her husband. It seems that before they were married she had told him she was a virgin, and now he was beginning to have his doubts. She wanted to use the state's lie detection equipment to prove her veracity. I read that letter without cracking a smile and handed it to my comptroller-general Zack Cravey. "Zack," I said, "read this. I'm appointing you head of a commission to look into this matter." "Oh, good God, Governor," he replied, "don't do that." Well, we wrote a letter to Lieutenant Barney Ragsdale, who was in charge of the polygraphic equipment for the state highway patrol, requesting that he comply with her request. I later learned that this pretty young girl and a big double-jointed fellow drove up in a Cadillac. Barney strapped her up to the polygraph and started asking questions. Then, pretty soon, her husband took over the questioning, specifying names and dates and places. The needle flipped around a good bit at the mention of one name in particular. But Barney pronounced the test negative, and the couple walked off arm in arm. That was but one of the many services I performed for the people of Georgia during my six years and two months as governor.

☆ ☆ ☆

WHEN THE GEORGIA SUPREME COURT ruled against me in 1947, I figured that the state had had just about enough of this two-governor nonsense. I suppose I could have carried the matter to federal court, but that would only have prolonged the confusion. It was time for one administration to take charge and try to govern. So I cleared out in deference to M.E. and the courts. But the very day I vacated the governor's office, I also threw my hat into the ring for that special election in 1948. And for the next twenty months I traveled across the length and breadth of Georgia, leaving my home in Lovejoy on Monday and getting back on Friday afternoon. That special election finally brought to an end a nearly continuous series of campaigns that had begun when Papa announced his candidacy for governor three years earlier.

I gave M.E. Thompson a pretty rough time in that campaign, but, all things considered, he wasn't a bad governor. He had to sign or veto all of the bills that had come to me during my two months in office, work with a hostile legislature, and campaign for vindication in the special election. The most notable thing he did as acting governor was to purchase Jekyll Island, for the sum of $675,000. I thought it was a mistake at the time and gave him hell for it. However, history has proved that M.E. made a wise move. Jekyll Island has been a popular vacation spot with the people of Georgia, and, by the time Thompson died in 1980, it was worth between thirty and forty million dollars.

It's been argued that M.E. Thompson was not the strongest candidate the anti-Talmadge forces could have put up in 1948. But they pretty much had to go with him. Ellis Arnall was not eligible to run for governor again until 1950, Ed Rivers had been discredited by the scandals in his administration, and Jimmie Carmichael had effectively dropped out of politics. Besides, as acting governor, M.E. had squatter's rights. I suppose that the one fatal mistake he and his supporters made in that campaign was underestimating me. They had me pegged as a neophyte trading on my daddy's name. Now that Papa was gone, they figured that Roy Harris was the ventriloquist and young "Hummon" the dummy. When I agreed to debate M.E. on a statewide radio hookup, the Thompson forces were so delighted they actually bought time on radio stations that weren't part of the original broadcast. When the debate was over, they probably wished they had paid radio stations *not* to carry it. Ralph McGill was a fair and impartial moderator of that debate, and the *Atlanta Constitution*, which had never seen eye-to-eye with Papa on anything, decided not to oppose me and remained neutral in the election.

Radio was an important factor in political campaigns at that time, but television was only in its infancy. This was still a time when a candidate would go out and meet people face-to-face and look them in the eye. The folks would listen to him talk and judge his sincerity. I remember that everywhere I went in that campaign people would come up and poke money at me. By the end of the day my pockets would be stuffed with all kinds of bills and coins. Speaking outside as much as I did, I'd also be soaked with sweat. Many a time I would go to a friend's house to take a bath, while my lieutenants spread the money out on the bed and counted it for me. It was then spent, as the need arose, to defray legitimate campaign expenses. As I recall, my 1948 and 1950 campaigns for governor cost about $250,000 each.

After I became an elder statesman, I got a lot more judicious and temperate in my utterances. But back in those days, I was a young Turk on the stump. I knew that to go after M.E. exclusively would have been to make him into a bigger deal than he actually was. If those anti-Talmadge boys had tried to depict me as a political pawn and failed, I figured I could beat them at their own game. So I went around accusing Thompson of being a lackey to Arnall and Rivers. I said that this campaign was a shotgun marriage. I wasn't rightly sure who was the bride and who was the groom, but I did know that the offspring was "M.E. Too." Right before the election, the administration got so desperate that the highway department put out stakes along roads all over the state. The implication was pretty clear: Vote for Thompson and you'll get your road paved. Well, I got up and said, "As soon as this election is over, they're going to come and try to remove those stakes. Don't you let them do that. When I'm governor, we're going to pave every one of those roads."

I won that 1948 election and, with it, vindication of my stance in the two-governor row. Had M.E. consented to the special election I had proposed back in '47, we could have settled the issue then and there. But no matter. The people had spoken, and I was immediately installed to fill the unexpired term to which Papa had been elected in 1946. By that time we had taken to calling his grandson, Herman Eugene Talmadge, Jr., "Gene" after Papa. One day when Betty was in Atlanta with little Gene, they went to an unfamiliar barber shop to get him a haircut. My son was wearing bright red suspenders at the time, and the barber took immediate notice of them. Figuring he'd engage in a little friendly banter, he said, "I thought nobody wore red suspenders but Gene Talmadge." Well, little Gene just rared back and in a voice that would have done his granddaddy proud, he told that barber, "I AM Gene Talmadge!" We were home to stay.

Moving back into the executive mansion really was like coming home. I hadn't exactly lived there when Papa was governor, but Mama had and so had my sisters Margaret and Vera. I had visited there many times during my years as a student at the University of Georgia, and it just didn't seem right that the old fortress should house the likes of Ellis Arnall and M.E. Thompson. When Betty and I moved back in November of 1948, we had what we thought would be a little reception for the few folks who might want to stop by. As I recall, it was to last from 3:00 until 5:00 in the afternoon. Well, people started showing up about 2:00, and by 6:00 there were still long lines. I have no idea how many hands Betty and Mama and I had shaken, but it must have been thousands. I asked to be excused and went up to the living quarters and poured myself a good stiff drink. At thirty-five, I was the nation's youngest governor, but I was plain worn out. When I went back down Mama was still there, fresh as a daisy, smiling and pumping hands. At nearly twice my age, she was Queen of the May.

A lot of politicking went on at that mansion and at the state Capitol in downtown Atlanta. But a good deal of the affairs of government were also conducted at the site of the previous executive mansion. The state still owned the land and leased it to the Henry Grady Hotel. Up until about 1930 the Kimball House had been headquarters for most of the major politicians in the state. Then for the next forty years the Henry Grady was the place to be. From early in the morning until late at night, legislators, bureaucrats, campaign workers, political reporters, and interested bystanders would mill around in the lobby or swap stories and cut deals in the ground-floor coffee shop. (There was also a high-priced restaurant with band and orchestra on one of the upper floors, but I usually ate at the S&W Cafeteria across the street.) That building should have been preserved as a shrine, but instead it was torn down to make way for one of our ultra-modern Sunbelt hotels—the Peachtree Plaza. The Henry Grady didn't have a waterfall in the lobby or a revolving restaurant on top, and you opened the doors of the guest rooms with keys rather than computerized cards. Maybe that's why the Grady seemed more like a home than a shopping mall.

There was probably no place in the old Henry Grady where the cigar smoke and the political intrigue were any thicker than in Roy Harris's room on the fourteenth floor. Roy was not a physically impressive man. He was short and stocky. He had stubby little fingers, and when he wanted to make a point, he'd wave a half-smoked cigar around in the air. He looked like a cardiac case waiting to happen, but he was a very active man and lived to a ripe old age. Roy was one of our most outstanding legislators for over twenty years, but after his defeat in 1946 he never sought elective office again. He wasn't even eager to serve in an appointive post. He declined any number of positions, including a seat on the state supreme court, which I offered him as soon as a vacancy occurred. (He did agree to serve on the state Board of Regents, but that was more because of his interest in education than any political ambition.) Roy was the sort of counselor and adviser who makes history if not the history books. During the fifties and sixties there was no stauncher segregationist in the South, but shortly before his death Roy was appointed city attorney by Ed McIntyre, the black mayor of Augusta, Georgia. In terms of political acumen and knowledge of state government, no man in this century was better qualified to serve as Governor of Georgia than

Roy V. Harris. It's a shame he never made it.

Another capable man who should have been governor but wasn't was Fred Hand. Fred was Speaker of the House during my years as governor, and he was instrumental in getting some of our most important legislation passed. Physically, he was very much the opposite of Roy Harris. Fred was a tall, muscular bear of a man. His family was from Pelham, Georgia, where his father owned a store called the Hand Trading Company. It was five or six stories high and a block long. You could get just about anything there that you could get at Sears Roebuck. They sold everything from coffins to wagons—seed, clothing, fertilizer, you name it. I think they even had a bank. Fred was an extremely capable legislator, and if I could have appointed a man to succeed me as governor, it would have been Fred. Unfortunately, he was not what you would call a hail-fellow-well-met. Fred was a very warm human being, but he gave strangers the impression of being aloof. He just wasn't a good mixer. He lost to Marvin Griffin in the 1954 race for governor and shortly thereafter retired from politics.

The fact that Marvin Griffin beat Fred Hand in 1954 tells you something about the importance of personality in politics. Marvin made some bad appointments as governor, and his administration was plagued with scandal, but he was one of the best campaigners who ever lived. He had a kind of unassuming folksy charm about him, and with the possible exception of Alben Barkley, no one could tell a funny story any better. I don't know whether he made them up or just had a good memory, but he never seemed to tell the same story twice. Marvin could walk into a room and make everyone present, from a banker to a beggar, think that he was the most important person on the face of the earth. If he hadn't gone into politics, Marvin could have made it as a professional comedian. He had that kind of rapport with an audience.

Marvin was originally a newspaper man from Bainbridge, Georgia. He served in the legislature prior to World War II and ran unsuccessfully for Congress against Eugene Cox. He was executive secretary to Ed Rivers and once got sentenced to twenty days in jail and a $200 fine for tossing the highway commissioner out of his office and down a flight of stairs. According to one story, he stayed out of jail by giving himself a pardon over the governor's signature. Marvin was in the Georgia National Guard when war broke out, was called to active duty, and served in New Guinea. When he came back home after the war, Ellis Arnall made him Adjutant General of the Georgia National Guard.

In 1946 Marvin ran for lieutenant governor on the same platform as Papa but lost to M.E. Thompson. As you may recall, Marvin supported me in the two-governor row and served as my adjutant general during the two months that I was in office in early 1947. We ran together as a team in 1948 and '50, and Marvin was lieutenant governor during my six years as governor. In fact, since M.E. Thompson never did serve as lieutenant governor, you might say that Marvin kind of defined the office. Constitutionally, the lieutenant governor's only responsibilities are to preside over the State Senate and wait around for something to happen to the governor. Marvin took to the latter responsibility with considerable relish. He would never fly in the same National Guard plane with me. He figured that if that plane went down, he'd be cheated out of his right of succession. I tried to tell him that the plane was safe. "They work on it all the time," I said. He thought that over for awhile and then said, "Herman, I'm not sure I want to be flying in a plane they got to work on all the time."

When I remember Marvin Griffin, I see a man with a big red nose, a silly grin on his face, and a cigarette close at hand. And I also see anywhere from a tableful to a roomful of folks in stitches. He'd tell a story about an old fellow in new overalls who came to one of his strategy meetings. This old fellow sat there listening to everyone else tell how many votes he could deliver to Marvin. So then they asked the old man how many he could produce. To which he replied, "How in the hell do I know how many votes I'm gonna give him until I know how many he NEEDS?"

Marvin had to sit out for four years after his term was up. When he tried to regain the governorship in 1962, he lost to Carl Sanders, which ended his political career. In that election one black precinct went 2,300 to Sanders and three to Griffin. When Marvin heard those results, he said, "Somebody voted under a misapprehension." Years later, Carl Sanders saw Marvin waiting in line at a crowded restaurant and invited him over to his table.

Well, Marvin kept Carl and his dinner companions entertained for the balance of the evening. After Marvin left, one of Carl's friends leaned over and said, "How'd you ever beat that man?" Of course, Marvin's record is what beat him, but as a human being he was impossible to dislike.

With the state capital being in Atlanta, I naturally had close dealings with the city administration during my years as governor. Although the city has grown and prospered tremendously since the late forties and early fifties, it was pretty impressive even back then. It was a city that had rebuilt itself from virtually nothing after being burned to the ground during the War Between the States. When I was governor, Bill Hartsfield was Mayor of Atlanta. As I recall, he supported Papa from time to time, and I always got on well with Bill. I suppose he will be best remembered for his contributions to aviation. This was brought home to me very forcefully one day when the boys came back to the mansion after school. They were real excited because their class had taken a field trip to what is now Hartsfield Airport to see the planes come in. And little Bobby said, "We even got to meet the Mayor of Atlanta."

Bill Hartsfield was succeeded by my good friend and contemporary Ivan Allen. Ivan had gone to Georgia Tech at the same time that I was a student at the University of Georgia. Years later, he was head of the Tech Alumni Association and I was head of the University Alumni. Now, you don't need to have lived in Georgia for very long to know that on the football field there is no love lost between the Bulldogs and the Rambling Wreck. And when I was an undergraduate, I could yell "To Hell With Tech" along with the best of them. But it seemed to me that Ivan and I could do more for our schools educationally if we cooperated rather than competed in fund raising. So we launched a joint fund raising drive that was so successful that it has been continued to this day. Much of the money raised in these campaigns goes to endow Alumni Professorships. That way if one of our two schools has some crackerjack professor that Harvard or MIT wants to hire away at twice the salary, we can make a good strong effort to keep that teacher in Georgia.

The one issue where I never saw eye-to-eye with Bill Hartsfield and Ivan Allen was the county unit system. Given our different backgrounds and constituencies, that was probably understandable. The county unit system was the means by which candidates were chosen in the Democratic Primary up until the time that it was declared unconstitutional by the U.S. Supreme Court in 1962. In the county unit system the eight most populous counties each had six unit votes, the next thirty each had four, and the 121 least populous counties each had two unit votes. Whichever candidate received a plurality of votes in a given county got all of that county's unit votes. As you can see, this system did not adhere to the formula of one man-one vote. And for that reason, the more populous counties felt that they were underrepresented. Since Papa and I derived much of our support from the rural areas, we thought the system was just fine. Beyond the question of electoral arithmetic, however, there is a philosophical case that can be made for the county unit system.

As members of a society, we do not exist solely as individuals; we are also members of groups. We belong to families, churches, neighborhoods, fraternal organizations, political parties, and the like. A republican form of government (as opposed to a mere plebiscitary democracy) ought to reflect this diversity in its political institutions. The ancient Greeks and Romans believed that every tribe, no matter how small or how remote, deserved representation. The British still adhere to this principle in their parliamentary system. The prime minister is elected by members of parliament, and the districts they represent are very unequal in size. Each state has exactly two United States Senators, regardless of the population of that state, and the U.S. Senate is the most important legislative body in the world. As everybody knows, the Electoral College is the outfit that officially elects the President of the United States. Electoral votes do not exactly reflect the popular vote, and on more than one occasion the candidate with the most popular votes has lost in the Electoral College. And yet, for two hundred years all proposals for reforming this system have been rejected as worse than the Electoral College itself.

The theory of group representation may be a conservative doctrine, but in recent years left wingers have latched onto it with a vengeance. In the Democratic Party today you find all kinds of quotas based on race, sex, and God knows what else. I think the party has gone too far in that direction, and the American people seem to agree with me. But the point is that liberals can't treat one man-one vote as if it were holy writ when it suits them to do so and ignore it otherwise. It would be interesting to see what would happen if some voter challenged this quota system in court on the grounds that it diluted his vote. The courts would probably throw the suit out on the grounds that a political party is a private entity with the right to determine its own rules and procedures. But we couldn't get them to see things that way when the county unit system was on trial.

One of my few unsuccessful initiatives as governor was an attempt to get the county unit system extended to the general election. The people defeated that in a referendum. I still think it's because the supporters of the unit system were disorganized and apathetic, while the other side mobilized its forces a lot better. But, of course, I have no way of proving that. Still, a vote of the people, not a court ruling, is the way that such matters should be decided. I'm told that when judges find some specious constitutional justification for decreeing their own social views to be law, they call that "judicial realism." If you ask me, that label makes about as much sense as referring to a Communist dictatorship as a "people's republic."

When I took over as governor in 1948, we had a long way to go to make Georgia what it claimed to be—the Empire State of the South. We couldn't do it without increasing state revenues, but the existing sources of taxation were already inefficient, inequitable, or nearly exhausted. We got about a third of our revenue at the time from *ad valorem* taxes on property, about a third from highway use taxes, and another third from the state income tax. We also raised a negligible amount from well over a hundred so-called nuisance taxes. I thought we'd be better off allowing the localities to levy and spend *ad valorem* taxes as they saw fit and getting rid of the nuisance taxes altogether. The only problem was that to try to maintain, much less enhance, state services on the basis of an income tax alone would have driven industry from the state and dried up potential sources of revenue. (The highway use taxes were just about at the point of diminishing returns and thus would not have brought in that much additional money even if they had been increased dramatically.) The only alternative appeared to be a state sales tax. That was an option I resisted as long as I could for both philosophical and practical reasons.

The philosophical case against a sales tax is that it is regressive. Everyone, regardless of income, has to spend a certain amount of money on the necessities of life. Consumption will always represent a larger percentage of a poor man's income. An income tax (especially a progressive one) is levied according to the ability to pay. A sales tax is based on the need to consume. For that reason, Papa always opposed a sales tax, and so did I. The practical objection had to do with politics, not policy. I was in office only to serve out the final two years of Papa's term. To reform the tax code and begin to use the new revenue to improve our schools, our highways, and the various social services run by the state would require a full four-year term. If I was defeated for reelection in 1950, I wouldn't be able to do any of this, and premature support for a sales tax might have been just the issue to defeat me. In state after state, governors were supporting a sales tax and going down to defeat at the polls. About the only exception was John W. Bricker in Ohio. Politically, my strategy was to delay consideration of a sales tax until after the 1950 election and hope for the best.

In my State of the State Address before the 1950 session of the general assembly, I asked for the repeal of over one hundred nuisance taxes and a constitutional amendment to repeal the *ad valorem* tax. I also said, "I am not in favor of any increased or additional taxes at this time." I knew I'd have a fight on my hands with that agenda, but I stuck to my guns. We managed to defeat Representative Frank Gross's sales tax bill in the House of Representatives, but we were unable to eliminate the *ad valorem* tax or any of the nuisance taxes. Still, I was able to go into the 1950 election without the millstone of a sales tax hanging around my neck. Justice Oliver Wendell Holmes, Jr., once said that taxes are the price we pay for civilized society. Too often, however, folks feel that they are being gouged on that price or that they simply aren't getting their money's worth of civilization.

After being reelected in 1950, I submitted a tax program to the legislature. This time I was backing a three-percent sales tax, along with an end to *ad valorem* taxation by the state and a repeal of the nuisance taxes. Not surprisingly, there was major opposition to each of these proposals from one quarter or another. This was the most radical tax revision to be proposed in the history of the state, and you don't change entrenched ways of doing things without disturbing some people and frightening quite a few others. Fortunately, we did make progress on the most important items. Although the legislature wouldn't eliminate the *ad valorem* tax altogether, it was reduced from five mills to one-quarter mill. We also passed the sales tax and eliminated 130 nuisance taxes. Economically, it was a sound program, but it was also political dynamite. I figured that it was just as well that I couldn't run for another term as governor in 1954. At that point, I was sure that my political future was worth about as much as a cancelled postage stamp.

I still had reservations about the sales tax, but often politics is a matter of choosing the least objectionable alternative. In 1948 the state was taking in a mere $108,300,000 a year in revenue. *Ad valorem* taxes were discouraging business and industrial expansion (not to mention the fact that it took until 1960 to get the *Ad Valorem Tax Digest*, which assessed property values in the state, back to where it was in 1860), and the nuisance taxes saddled both state government and the private sector with a lot of ridiculous and unproductive bookkeeping. (Some of the nuisance taxes cost almost as much to collect as they produced in revenue.) As a result of years of inadequate funding, our schools, roads, and hospitals were in a deplorable condition. But with tax revision, state revenues more than doubled by 1953. (Approximately ninety-eight million dollars, or an amount slightly in excess of ninety percent of the entire 1948 budget, was brought in by the sales tax alone.) We saw those additional funds as a trust as well as an opportunity and spent them as frugally as possible. One study showed that outside of direct grants and actual services rendered to the people, the cost of administering state government was only 4.5 percent of the total budget. I was so tight with the state's money that I wouldn't even let my department heads have air conditioning in their offices.

When that sales tax passed, folks were mad as hell. They had opposed the idea of a sales tax in a recent referendum and felt, with some justification, that their wishes were being ignored. I believe that the vast majority of the time a public official should do the bidding of the people. But I also agree with Edmund Burke that a statesman owes his constituents his judgment as well as his vote. Over time, when the people could see what we were doing with their tax dollars, they began to realize the wisdom of tax reform. I remember one of my men, who had his ear to the ground, reporting to me right after the sales tax had gone into effect. He said, "Governor, back in my home county Old Jim is pretty put out with you." Old Jim was a farmer whose idea of retirement was to move into town and open himself a general store. He figured the sales tax would be bad for business. A few weeks later, my man came back in and told me that Old Jim wasn't as mad anymore. Apparently, some black people had been in his store buying provisions. When they got ready to pay and he added three percent to their bill, they were right perplexed. You see, they thought the sales tax was just for white folks. Old Jim got a big kick out of telling them otherwise. I went out of office more popular than I went in.

A punitive tax system can stifle economic growth, but inadequate government services can do so as well. A good example of this was the state fire protection in Georgia at the time I took office. In 1946, only 37 of 159 counties had fire protection programs. And because even these few units operated independently, there was very little coordinated effort in fighting forest fires. (Those fires, you see, don't respect county boundaries.) A governor's study commission, chaired by Ivan Allen's daddy, had looked into the matter and recommended that a statewide fire protection system be administered by the state Department of Forestry. Unfortunately, that advice had about as much effect as water on a duck's back. By 1947, only forty-three counties had protection, and that was under the same loose, haphazard, county-by-county system.

Clearly something needed to be done.

The potential for forestry in Georgia was immense. We had no other natural resources to speak of, but two out of every three acres of the state were wooded. Without adequate fire protection and clear-sighted political leadership, the economic potential of our forests was going to waste. When I was a boy growing up in McRae, folks would actually set fires to kill boll weevils and rattlesnakes. And up until the late forties, forest fires were so numerous that roads would be impassable from the thickness of the smoke. I was convinced that the money the state spent on fire protection and forestry services would come back many fold in the economic benefits and increased tax revenues produced by a thriving timber industry. Those benefits have exceeded our wildest expectations.

In terms of sheer numbers the immediate progress we made in forestry was staggering. When I took office in November 1948, Georgia ranked forty-sixth in the nation in forestry. In less than six years we moved up to No. 1. In 1949 we created a five-member state Forestry Commission and appropriated three-quarters of a million dollars to finance our forestry program (that was over six times as much as was appropriated for the same purpose in 1946). Shortly thereafter, we made fire protection available to all of the counties in the state. By 1954, 132 of the counties had signed up, and we brought the remaining twenty-seven on board in due course. In six years we more than quadrupled the number of state forestry employees and more than tripled the number of fire towers. The number of fire fighting vehicles increased from 95 to 459, and the number of radio units used to report fires and to direct fire fighting operations from 20 to 834. When steel became scarce during the Korean War, the commission purchased thirty-five oil derricks and converted them into fire towers. By the time I went out of office, the state appropriation for forestry was over fourteen times what it was in 1946. When you add what the counties and federal government contributed, you have a total appropriation for forestry of nearly three million dollars. Eighty-seven and a half percent of our forested acres were under protection.

We also initiated quite a few forestry services that had nothing to do with fighting or preventing forest fires. But the true measure of what we did does not lie in the amount of money spent or the number of programs started. Instead, one must look at the progress made by forest industries in Georgia during the time that I was in office and in the years since to see what a dividend we have reaped from our investment in forestry. To begin with, between 1948 and 1954, the number of people working in forest related industries increased by a third. When I left office, well over three thousand plants and industries in Georgia depended on forest products for raw materials. Since 1948 Georgia has led the South in the production of pulp wood (nationally, we trail only Oregon in income from total timber resources). By 1954, our naval stores industry had expanded to produce seventy-two percent of the supply for the United States and thirty percent for the entire world. In 1948, forest industries were bringing $300 million a year into Georgia's economy. When I left office that figure had doubled. In 1985 it stood at seven billion dollars. Few states have ever moved so far so fast in developing a basic natural resource.

But I don't have to look up the statistics, as impressive as they are, to know what timber has done for the state of Georgia. All I need to do is get into my four-wheel drive Blazer and ramble around my 2,500 acre farm in Henry County. Back when I was governor, I was too busy running the state to devote much time to making money. I had two dairy farms at the time, and even in good years they would do little better than break even. My friend J. Philip Morgan tried for a long time to get me interested in timber. He kept telling me that it was a renewable resource that did not require constant care and frequent harvesting. But like most Georgians, I was a bit leary about investing in a crop that might be burnt up. When we got the fire protection program in full swing, I changed my mind. I began planting pine trees on the Henry County farm in 1951 and continued planting about two hundred acres a year for the next decade. Since the trees reach their peak in value between thirty and fifty years after planting, I began harvesting them in 1981. Getting into timber was one of the smartest decisions I've ever made.

Of course, like any crop, timber is subject to the caprice of nature. Drought doesn't do it much good, and the Japanese pine beetle can be absolute murder. Another danger that you can't protect against is tornadoes. In March 1986, one touched down on the farm and uprooted about 200,000 board feet of pine quite at random. In one place you might see a tree on its side and not five feet away one standing totally unharmed. That you allow for, because it can't be helped. But recently we've had to face another enemy in the timber business. Although it doesn't touch the trees themselves, it can be just as deadly as drought, twisters, and pesky little insects. I'm talking about subsidized imported timber. Today about half of the timber being used in Georgia is imported from Canada, despite the fact that our state is the second leading producer of timber in this country. The Canadian government owns many of that nation's forests and sells the cutting rights very cheaply. Consequently, Canadian timber is driving our homegrown product out of the market.

Free trade is wonderful in theory, but our national security interests can be severely damaged if we allow ourselves to become dependent on foreign producers who can shut off our supply of some vital product whenever they are politically of a mind to do so. We found that out during the Arab oil embargo. Back around the turn of the century, Teddy Roosevelt wasn't afraid to bust a few trusts in order to assure fair commerce in this country. What we need today are politicians unafraid to go after some of these international trusts that are threatening our domestic commerce. Unilateral free trade is sort of like unilateral disarmament—a noble sentiment with disastrous consequences in the real world.

For the past forty years I've lived on or near that farm in Henry County. When I got out of the Navy in 1946, Papa gave me the deed to a house and a thousand acres of land that he owned down there in Lovejoy, Georgia, about forty miles south of Atlanta. The property had been part of the estate of the late Chuck Crawford, and Papa had purchased it from the C&S Bank. The old antebellum farmhouse was so dilapidated that I came close to tearing it down with the idea of using the salvageable materials to build me a little bungalow. But the more I looked at that house the more I was convinced it was too pretty to tear down. So I hired a carpenter who lived in the area to rehabilitate the place room by room. As I recall, we managed to fix up one of the bedrooms and the kitchen right off and then had to wait for me to make some more money before we could get to the rest of the house.

We dug out minnie balls that had probably been in the walls since the War Between the States. When we peeled off several layers of rotted wallpaper, we found walls of solid pine planks of the sort you couldn't get today. We took those boards down, sanded them, and put them back up. The house had been carefully put together in portions with wooden pegs, probably by slave labor. The sills were hewn by hand and measured eighteen by twenty-four inches. Sherman's right wing went through this area and destroyed all but two of the ante-bellum homes—the old Fitzgerald place (which was the model for Tara in *Gone With the Wind*) and the farmhouse that I owned. As you may recall, the movie version of *Gone With the Wind* begins with a shot of some blacks singing and picking cotton, and then the camera pans to an old, broken down ante-bellum house with weeds growing up around it. That was based on my house.

About the time I was getting into the timber business, we started another enterprise that would make "Talmadge" a household name in thousands of homes that had no interest in or knowledge of Georgia politics. When I was a boy in McRae, we had cured hams on the farm with an old family recipe of my mother's. So when it became obvious that I wasn't going to make any money from dairy products, we started buying up hams about two hundred at a time and curing them in a little plant about the size of a two-car garage (at the time, far too many Georgia hams were being sent out of the state to be cured). Pretty soon the business got so successful that we wanted to expand and get into interstate commerce. I went into the the Trust Company of Georgia one day and walked out with a loan of $100,000. My friend Mose Turman, who was an officer of the bank, had given me that loan simply on his knowledge of my character. I didn't even have to present collateral. Which was a good thing. That loan was just about equal to my net worth at the time.

Since I was pretty busy running the state, Betty took over day-to-day management of the ham business. She took to that with a good deal of enthusiasm and got on some national television programs, including "What's My Line." Probably the most publicity came, however, when she got into a row with a Yankee entertainer by the name of Henry Morgan on a TV show called "Leave It to the Girls." I call Henry Morgan an entertainer because he was on radio and television a lot, but I'm not sure what the hell it was he did that was so entertaining. He didn't sing, he didn't dance, he didn't act, and he wasn't nearly as funny as Marvin Griffin. About all he did was sit around and make snide comments about things he didn't understand. When Betty started talking about Southern cooking, old Morgan said it was nothing but "throwing a lot of grits and turnips into pots of water." And then he allowed that he wouldn't eat a Georgia dinner if it were placed before him. That got the folks in Georgia so riled up that Fulton County Solicitor General Paul Webb served a *subpoena duces tecum* on Betty to bring in a country ham dinner with all the fixings to prove that Yankee had libelled the good name of Southern cooking and Southern womanhood. I don't think I need to tell you what the verdict was. Anyway, that TV show was cancelled right afterward, and I understand that Henry Morgan is doing a radio call-in program today.

At the time there was considerable prejudice against the South in the rest of the nation. It seemed that anytime someone would write about the South in the national press, he would be projecting some negative stereotype that had to do with poverty, ignorance, or racism. It got particularly vicious after the United States Supreme Court outlawed segregated schools in the famous Brown decision. So when folks up north got to see a flesh-and-blood Southerner up close, it came as something of a revelation to realize that we didn't have horns, cloven hooves, and a tail. When I appeared on "Meet the Press" during the 1952 Democratic National Convention, I had the opportunity to go into millions of American homes with my own views and my own personality. People could see the real Herman Talmadge, not some media caricature. I got thousands of letters thereafter, many of them from people who previously would have traded me for an alley cat who now wanted me to run for president.

I had had a similar experience on a smaller scale when I ran for governor in 1948. We had a motorcade to Baxley, Georgia, where I was scheduled to give a speech. By the time we got to Baxley, there must have been five or six hundred cars in the motorcade, and traffic was backed up for miles around. Afterwards, I got letters from Northern tourists who had gotten caught up in the traffic jam. They weren't complaints, either. They were testimonials from folks who said they had heard me speak and wished they could vote for me. I would have to wait another twenty years, until the nationally televised Watergate hearings, to regain the popularity I enjoyed in the North during the late forties and early fifties. (Of course, the segregation rows undid many a Southern politician during those intervening years.) But I never harbored ambitions for national office. I was always too busy building support on the home front.

Eugene Talmadge could always stir the passions of a crowd . . .

. . . and Herman Talmadge developed the same oratorical skills

Talmadge's first marriage to Kathryn Williamson

During college at U.Ga.

Naval officer Talmadge

Above: Judge Charley Worrill swears in Herman Talmadge as governor of Georgia on January 15, 1947.

Left: Rival M.E. Thompson offers congratulations as Talmadge aide George Wilson looks on.

Below: In November of 1948, Talmadge is sworn in again.

Georgia's first family: (L-R) Bobby, Betty, Herman, Gene

Son Gene on the tractor with Dad in Lovejoy, Georgia

1950 family portrait: (L-R) Sister Margaret Shepherd, mother, sister Vera Smyly

On the campaign trail in middle Georgia, early 1950s

Movers and shakers:(L-R) J.C. Penney, Robert W. Woodruff, John A. Sibley, Herman Talmadge

Singer Kate Smith with Herman and Betty Talmadge

Congratulations from former Senator Walter George

Georgia's famed senators, Richard Russell and Herman Talmadge

7

Building a Legacy

Back when I was Governor of Georgia, that office carried with it a good deal of responsibility and a good deal of power. I assumed the responsibility and wielded the power, just as fully as I possibly could. I was dedicated, hardworking, and—when the situation warranted it—downright mean. I had two special phones on the desk in my office. One was a direct line to Speaker of the House Fred Hand. The other was a direct line to my floor leader in the State Senate, Crawford Pilcher. I kept track of how legislators voted on important bills, and I let them know how I felt. Not too long ago, Fritz Hollings reminded me of the first time we met. He came into my office when I was on the phone giving Fred Hand hell about some legislator who had voted the wrong way on some matter. "You tell that son of a bitch," I said, "that I'm going to come out and personally unpave his road."

I SUSPECT THAT PAPA WAS RIGHT when he said, "If road politics was worth a damn, John N. Holder would have been the Czar of Russia." But he was talking about using roads as a springboard to higher political office. In and of itself, being on the highway commission was better than having your own pork barrel. It was more like owning the whole hog and being able to cut off slices whenever you wanted for whomever you wanted. But what was good politics was bad government. While the boys on the highway commission were carving up the pork, the people of Georgia went without adequate roads. During the war we did virtually nothing to maintain our roads, and even the main arterial highways were filled with potholes. Many rural areas could be reached only by dirt roads, and they became impassable whenever we had a good rain. The situation was a godawful mess.

Folks born since World War II probably think of roadbuilding and maintenance in terms of painting signs on the interstate or installing a traffic light at a busy intersection. But if you try to imagine a situation where farmers and merchants couldn't get their products to market, where some homes were cut off from mail delivery during certain seasons of the year, and where people were literally risking their lives just getting in their cars in some areas of the state, you can see that we were dealing with something more than the convenience of hot rodders and tourists on their way to Florida. Back when our country was founded, Alexander Hamilton told anyone who would listen that adequate roads were essential to civilization itself. Now that the sales tax gave us sufficient revenue to build and maintain decent roads, all that we needed was a political structure for spending money in the interests of the people. The old system simply wouldn't do.

In my first State of the State address, which was delivered to the legislature in January 1949, I said, "It has been common practice in this state for gubernatorial candidates to make the most of their road commitments during the heat of a political campaign. Votes should not be the basis upon which our highways are located." My idea was to establish a five-member constitutional Highway Board, which would be relatively insulated from political pressure. I expected that the entrenched powers would put up a fuss over this but was somewhat surprised that the strongest opposition came from folks who thought I wasn't going far enough. In particular, there was a much more sweeping reform proposal by state senator J.K. Gholston.

The Gholston plan called for a ten-member board appointed solely by the legislature. It would also have established a rigid formula for allocating highway funds. I thought that ten members were too many and that the funding formula didn't allow enough flexibility. Otherwise, I had no real objections to the Gholston plan. It really didn't make a damned bit of difference to me whether the board members were appointed by the governor or the legislature. As long as my supporters were in control of the legislature, I could be fairly certain of getting a board that would not try to undercut me. And if we ever lost control of the legislature, I would have more to worry about than who was on the Highway Board.

The Talmadge-Gholston controversy resulted in an impasse in 1949 and a "compromise" in 1950. The final reform bill, which was enacted into law in 1950, created a three-member Highway Board to be elected by the legislature. There would be one member each from the Southern, Central, and Northern Highway Districts; they would each serve six-year terms; and those terms would be staggered so that a vacancy occurred every two years (this would prevent all three members from being appointed during a single gubernatorial administration—except, of course, for my own). As soon as the bill was passed, the legislators elected three of my staunchest supporters—Jim Gillis, Dixon Oxford, and John Quillian—to the board and eulogized J.K. Gholston for his statesmanship. I'm sure that Gholston thought he had won a great victory.

During my four-year term that commenced in January 1951, we embarked on the greatest road-building program in the history of Georgia. The first thing we did was outlaw the "negotiated" or sweetheart contract and institute competitive bidding. (It's estimated that under the old system the state was paying twice as much as it should have for road work.) The legislature then enacted a constitutional amendment, later ratified by the people, that allocated the revenue from all highway use taxes to the highway department. By the time I went out of office in January 1955, we had provided over 319 million dollars for use in all phases of the highway program. That compared with around sixty-nine million dollars in the Ellis Arnall administration. We put all engineers, draftsmen, laboratory technicians, and accounting and clerical personnel under the state Merit System. We began hiring graduate engineers from Georgia Tech and other first-rate schools. We built thirty million dollars' worth of new bridges. And by October 31, 1953, Georgia was ranked second among southeastern states and eleventh in the nation in the amount of federal-aid highway work planned or under way. Roads had ceased to be a political boondoggle and had become an economic boon.

The road building program was popular throughout Georgia, but it was an absolute godsend in all the counties where the street-cars never ran. Of the nearly $190 million worth of road contracts awarded as of the end of 1953, almost forty-two million went exclusively for the construction of farm-to-market roads. And our direct grants to counties for work on bridges and off-system and farm-to-market roads almost doubled during my years in office. Those grants gave the counties extra money with which to maintain their roads and also allowed them to devote more of their local revenues to schools, health-care facilities, and other public services. In 1950, I promised that by the time I went out of office we would be in the process of paving over ten thousand miles of road. By the end of 1953, we already had contracts on nearly 12,800 miles. I was beginning to feel a little like the British architect Sir Christopher Wren. When Wren died, someone said, "If you would see his monument, look about you." But I got brought down to earth mighty quick.

As I've said, in road politics you'll always get more grief for the one road you don't pave than credit for the nine you do. When I promised to pave over ten thousand miles of road, I also promised that "the last road in Georgia to be paved will be the one beside my farm home." That enabled me to get a dig in at the favoritism of past administrations and to rise above politics. I remained true to my word. It didn't make any difference that we were paving close to thirteen thousand miles of road. The minute I had state workers out to Lovejoy to pave that quarter-mile of road leading to my house, some disgruntled person somewhere would be raising hell because I paved my road before I got to his. Everyone was impressed with this big sacrifice I was making. Everyone, that is, except Betty.

There was no question that our road needed paving, so when we got the contracts let on all those other roads around the state,

Betty started asking when the state would get to our road. I hemmed and hawed and put her off as long as I could. But Betty was never a woman to take "maybe" for an answer, and "no" just wasn't in her vocabulary. When she saw she wasn't getting anywhere with me, she called in the three members of the state Highway Board and fed them a dinner of country ham that would have made even Henry Morgan drool. Then she asked them when they were going to pave her road. Well, those boys didn't want to turn down this charming lady, but they didn't want to catch hell from me either. So like all good politicians, they squirmed and stalled and alibied. Finally, she talked J.C. Chaffin, chairman of the Henry County Board of Commissioners, into paving the road with county funds. After all, the Talmadges did pay taxes in Henry County. I don't know whether a prophet is always without honor in his own country, but that one experience did teach me why I would never become the Czar of Russia.

Not too long ago I was in the office of our current Governor of Georgia, Joe Frank Harris. During the entire three hours I was there only one other person came through, and he was a state employee. I couldn't help thinking how different things were during the Herman Talmadge administration. During those years, I would get up by 5 A.M., have breakfast by six, and be at the office by seven. That would give me about an hour and a half to meet with my staff and plan the day's activities. Then about 8:30, we'd throw open the doors to the governor's office and begin seeing anyone who'd made an appointment. Those who had not made an appointment but wanted to see me could do so if they waited their turn. Back in those days, anyone who had business with the state would start with the governor and work his way down. If his business was with the capitol janitor, he'd want to go with the governor's blessing. Sometimes I'd be in there all day, but most of the time I'd leave for lunch around one o'clock and spend the afternoon and evening giving speeches around the state. (I'd give anywhere from eight to ten speeches a week, every week.) I recall my secretary coming in one afternoon when I had spent the entire day in my office. She told me that during that single day I had seen 532 people—some individually, some in groups.

The day-to-day contact I had with people in my office and out on the stump was absolutely invaluable. It helped me keep in touch with my constituents, and it put me before them without the intervention of a hostile press. The first amendment guarantees freedom of the press, but that doesn't mean a whole lot unless you have several million dollars to start a paper of your own. When I came into office I inherited my daddy's bad press, and the two-governor row only made the situation worse. However, the solid accomplishments of our administration began to turn the tide. First, the newspapers around the state began to come over, then the *Atlanta Constitution* (which had always been fair, if not favorable, in its coverage of the Talmadges) had to concede that I was doing a good job. Ralph McGill even said to *Newsweek* magazine, "I think Governor Talmadge has done a constructive job, that he has contributed greatly to Georgia's progress in every field save race relations." And for Ralph that was high praise, indeed. By the time I ran for the Senate in 1956, even the *Atlanta Journal* had come around. Both Atlanta papers endorsed me in that race.

In general, the national press was harder to win over. To its credit, *Harper's* magazine took a look at the record of what we had done in Georgia and concluded that I was the "Best Southern Governor." *Time*, however, was still taking a smidgen of truth and developing a satire around it. The articles it would publish about the South were entertaining as fiction but generally worthless as informative journalism. One day Jim Linen, who was the publisher of *Time*, was in my office and asked me what I thought of his magazine. Well, I let him have it with both barrels. I said, "Whenever you write something about the South, it usually has to do with somebody lynching somebody or threatening to. The most significant news story in America today is the industrialization of the South, and I haven't read one word about it in your magazine." I don't know whether my little lecture had anything to do with it, but about six weeks later the cover story in *Time* was "The Industrialization of the South."

At that time the most important official on the governor's staff was his executive secretary. As governor, I would decide what needed to be done and then have my executive secretary do it.

Just about all political executives have such an aide. The title may vary from time to time and place to place, but the position always carries with it a good deal of responsibility and power. If you have a strong executive, his principal assistant functions as a chief of staff. If the executive is a mere figurehead, the assistant may actually be running the show. (When Harold Wilson was Prime Minister of England, he had a powerful executive secretary by the name of Marcia Williams. Her receptionist once told a fellow waiting to see her that "Mrs. Williams is busy, but the Prime Minister will help you.") I was always firmly in control as governor, but my executive secretary spoke with my blessing and acted with the authority of the governor's office.

My first executive secretary was Benton Odum. He had been a fraternity brother of mine in college and was a lifelong friend. When I told Benton to do something, I knew that it would be done and done right. I could assign him a task and then move on to the next item on the agenda. I suppose that Benton's first official act as executive secretary was keeping Ellis Arnall from barging into my office at the height of the two-governor row. He was with me during those sixty-seven days when I held the governor's office in 1947 and then again when I was elected by the people in 1948. One of the bills the legislature passed in 1949 would have provided pay for those who had served in my administration during those sixty-seven days. I figured that if the Supreme Court of Georgia regarded our government as illegal, we weren't entitled to any pay, and so I vetoed the bill. As I recall, Benton was quite put out with me for doing that. I later appointed him secretary-treasurer of the Highway Department, where he served with distinction for the balance of my administration.

When Benton Odum left as my executive secretary, I replaced him with my brother-in-law Bill Kimbrough. One of the bright young men on Bill's staff at the time was a fellow who had been a leader of my student supporters at the University of Georgia. I noticed that whenever I spoke within a hundred miles of the university, there would be a busload of students coming to hear me... with Jimmy Bentley leading the way. I saw the quality of Jimmy's work during his student days, and as soon as he was out of college, I appointed him to a position on the executive secretary's staff. Then when Bill Kimbrough stepped down, I named Jimmy Bentley to replace him. At twenty-three, he was the nation's youngest executive secretary. But that was only fitting, since I was still the nation's youngest governor. Jimmy stayed with me for the rest of my term as governor and was later elected comptroller-general of the state. He was one of five state officials to switch from the Democratic to the Republican Party during the Humphrey-Nixon race in 1968. None of those five ever won elective office again. When Jimmy tried to run for governor in 1970, the Republicans wouldn't accept him and the Democrats wouldn't forgive him. Today, he is in business in Atlanta and remains a close personal friend.

When one considers the hundreds, even thousands, of people I would see during a typical week as governor, it's understandable that I wouldn't have vivid recollections of very many of them. On the other hand, individual citizens tend to recall meeting the governor as a special experience. Not too long ago, one such citizen tried to jog my memory about a brief encounter we had in 1954. She was in the ninth grade at the time and was accompanying a friend of hers, her friend's mother, and their county agent to Atlanta to get the governor to sign a safety proclamation they had drawn up as a 4-H project. These folks waited their turn in my outer office and finally got to see me for a few minutes. I signed their proclamation and quickly moved on to weightier matters of state. At the time that ninth grade girl from Twin City, Georgia was named Lynda Cowart. Thirty years later, in September 1984, she became Mrs. Herman E. Talmadge.

Of the many things we were able to do for Georgia as a result of tax revision, none was more essential than improving the quality of our schools. If there was far too much poverty and ignorance in the South from Reconstruction up through the Second World War, the poor quality of our schools was both cause and effect. If we were to enjoy economic progress, we needed a public school system that would turn out educated workers, who would then want to stay in Georgia and help make it a better place in which to live. But in order to have that kind of public school system, we needed sufficient money to support it. As it was, many of our students were attending one-room schools that were so dilapidated they could study astronomy through the roof and geography through the floor. The white schools were bad, and the black schools were even worse. When I took office, a good number of schools were on the verge of shutting their doors and releasing hordes of uneducated children to fend for themselves. We had a plan to turn that situation around. It was called the Minimum Foundation Program, and with the revenue from the sales tax, we finally had enough money to get it started.

Getting the program started and bringing it to fruition were, of course, two different matters. With the children of the post-war baby boom entering school, there was a drastic need for school construction and renovation. Even the revenues from the sales tax would not be enough for us to do as much as we needed to do as fast as we needed to do it. It was at that point that Fred Hand said, "Look, the Minimum Foundation Program guarantees a certain yearly allocation for the School Building Authority over the next twenty years. But we don't have twenty years. The need is now. There ought to be some way of spending that money in advance." Well, Fred and our state auditor, B.E. Thrasher, pursued the idea a bit and came up with a plan for issuing revenue certificates against future appropriations for school construction. The Authority would build the needed schools and lease them to the school systems for the amount of the yearly school-building appropriation. In less than two years (from September 1952 to June 1954) the Authority issued bonds of nearly $128 million to construct new buildings in 123 of the state's 159 county systems and twenty-six of its forty-two independent systems. Supplemental federal and local funds raised the total appropriation for the construction of new schools to nearly $169 million. During that period we either built or renovated over a thousand schools, and we reduced the number of one-room schools by over a thousand between 1948 and 1954. Shortly after I left office, the one-room schools were eliminated altogether. Our building program was so successful that school officials from as far away as Alaska came to study it.

So many educational services that are taken for granted today were unheard of in Georgia before the Minimum Foundation Program was put into effect. We quadrupled allotments for school transportation and increased the number of school buses by more than a third. Before we did this, there were children in sparsely populated rural and mountain areas deprived of an education because the nearest school was too far away for them to walk and they had no way of getting there otherwise. (In fact, before I came in as governor, black school children didn't have any buses at all; we provided them with buses and did everything possible to equalize educational opportunities between the races.) We also expanded the school year to nine months and added a twelfth grade to the curriculum. Our most significant accomplishment, however, was in the area of personnel. Before I came in we were losing teachers to other states. We turned that around and actually added teachers. The pay of white and black teachers was equalized and the pay of all teachers was doubled. In fact, during my six years in office, we spent more on public education than all of the previous administrations combined. All told, fifty-three percent of our state budget went to education, which was a greater commitment than that of any other state in the union.

One day when I was governor, the dean of the state medical school in Augusta called and said that he wanted to see me. I looked at my calendar and invited him to have breakfast with me out at the executive mansion at 6 A.M. one day the following week. I had a pretty good idea what he wanted to talk to me about. From time to time someone would tell me about a son of his who was getting straight A's but couldn't get into medical school. The problem was that we just didn't have enough room in that school for all the highly qualified students who wanted to attend. Considering the condition of health care in Georgia at the time, that was a real tragedy. As with just about everything else, we needed more medical facilities and more doctors. When I was a boy there were a few dedicated country doctors, but hospitals were something you found only in the big cities. People injured in Telfair County had to be taken to Macon or Savannah or Augusta if they needed hospitalization. So the dean came to breakfast and told me what needed to be done to double the enrollment at the state medical school. He talked me out of seven million dollars that morning. And that was back when seven million dollars was a lot of money.

As a general rule I believe that essential public services (and there should be no public services except for essential ones) ought to be performed and financed by the level of government closest to the beneficiary. But that is not always feasible. In Georgia, most of our wealth was concentrated in the cities and much of our need in the rural areas. So in fields such as public education and public health, it was necessary for the state to help the individual counties do what they were unable to do on their own. By the same token, we as a state looked to the federal government for supplemental aid. In the area of hospital construction, we got it when Congress enacted the Hill-Burton Plan in 1947. Shortly thereafter, the state legislature authorized a three-million-dollar-a-year program of hospital construction, to be financed one-third each at the federal, state, and local levels. This enabled us to undertake 141 projects at a cost of over fifty-six million dollars. That included fifty-one hospitals, sixty-eight health centers, fifteen hospital additions, and three nursing homes around the state, and a laboratory at Batty State Hospital in Rome, Georgia. By the time the Hill-Burton Program ended in 1957, a total of eighty-two million dollars was spent for new hospitals and other health care facilities. Over seventy million of that was provided while I was in office. I might add that the 116-bed Hughes-Spalding Pavilion in Atlanta was considered the finest hospital for blacks in the entire nation.

As was true of so many other state services, our financial commitment to health care far exceeded that of any previous administration. Even excluding hospital construction, the state appropriation for health care increased almost six-fold (from $700,000 to nearly $4.2 million) between 1946 and 1954. By 1952, 139 of the state's 159 counties had public health organizations, compared to eighty-seven in 1948 and sixty-six in 1946. We divided the state into thirty-five public health districts, with a physician in charge of each. We also put a nurse in each county under the direction of the public health commissioner for that district.

Today, over thirty years later, that probably sounds right primitive. But until we were able to produce more doctors and nurses, it was the best we could do. And it was a start. For the first time in history, some form of health care was within easy access of every citizen in Georgia.

Back in my daddy's time, life was pretty bleak for the average person growing up in Georgia. More than likely, he would have to walk several miles to a substandard school building that was falling down around him. There he would be taught a little reading, writing, and arithmetic from old worn-out textbooks by a committed but grossly underpaid spinster lady. He would drop out well before high school and enter the work force as an unskilled worker (which was just as well, since we didn't have that many skilled jobs in Georgia, anyway). If he decided to make his living on the farm, he would do backbreaking work from dawn till dusk and then not have adequate roads to take his produce to market to be sold at depressed prices. If he owned the farm, he wouldn't be able to hire many field hands at a decent wage, and if he was a hand himself he wouldn't be able to feed his family on what the farmer paid him. So in either case, he would pull his children out of the same substandard school he had gone to (where they might be using the same textbooks and learning from the same spinster lady) to help supplement the family income by working the land. If he was injured, he could very easily be dead by the time they got him to the nearest hospital a hundred miles away. And if the injuries didn't kill him, he would have his pick of a whole passel of chronic diseases to die from. (The most feared were typhoid fever and tuberculosis.) He stood a good chance of losing his wife in childbirth. Otherwise, they would look forward to growing old together in worsening poverty and ill health.

By the time I went out of office, that old man would see his grandchildren riding to better schools on new schoolbuses and studying from the latest textbooks. That dedicated old spinster lady would be retired with a modest pension, financed in part by the state. She would be replaced by well-educated and better paid university graduates. Those grandkids would probably go on and graduate from high school. From there, they could enter an improving university system or find promising jobs in industry (during five of my six years in office Georgia led the South in industrial expansion). If they stayed on the farm, there would be a whole array of agricultural services to make their lot easier. And they would be able to take their crops to expanded farmers' markets on paved roads. When they were injured, they stood a much better chance of getting to a good hospital in time to recover. Tuberculosis and typhoid were virtually wiped out, and many other chronic diseases had been brought under control. That old man had voted for Eugene Talmadge, and he and his children and grandchildren continued voting for me. But as Georgia prospered on the foundation laid in my administration, millions of people from elsewhere in the country moved in. They knew only the new Georgia, not the old. And they had no idea how we had gotten from the old to the new. One such individual was a typewriter salesman from Indiana who moved to Georgia about the time I was going out as governor. His name was Mack Mattingly, and I'll be a-comin' to him.

The 1950 gubernatorial campaign was the last gasp of the anti-Talmadge forces. I had been in office for only about a year and a half when the campaign started. The sales tax and the dramatic expansion of state services were still in the future. We had begun to sow the seeds of progress, but the harvest had yet to come. What was left of the Arnall and Rivers organization was backing M.E. Thompson again. As usual, the campaign was a series of stump speeches before a large crowd in the hot sun. And it seemed that everywhere we went in those days they served barbecue or Brunswick stew, or both. I remember once in the '48 campaign I had barbecue ten times in one week. It got to the point where I was ashamed to look a shoat in the eye. The popular vote was close in 1950, but I swamped M.E. in the county unit vote and assumed office for a full four-year term.

During my years as governor, I established myself as a man with my own style. I was Herman Talmadge, not just Gene Talmadge's son. I suppose that the biggest difference between my daddy and myself was that I kind of liked peace and quiet, and he couldn't stand it. Papa wasn't happy unless he had two or three major rows and ten or fifteen minor ones going on at all times. I wasn't bashful about attacking the opposition when I had to, but I much preferred to absorb it. After I went out as governor, we elected two more governors from the Talmadge camp—Marvin Griffin in 1954 and Ernest Vandiver in 1958. By the time I ran for reelection to the Senate in 1962, M.E. Thompson, Ellis Arnall, and the rest of the old anti-Talmadge crowd were supporting me. In fact, the first campaign contribution I received in that race was a check for five hundred dollars from Ellis Arnall.

More than in any other profession, success in electoral politics is dependent on popularity. A star athlete can stop talking to the press and shun the public, but as long as he performs on the playing field his position is secure. Some actors and pop singers are even expected to be moody as part of their image. But a politician has to romance the people and hope that they return his love. When they stop loving back, he's finished. The year 1956 proved to be a turning point for both M.E. Thompson and myself. M.E. had lost gubernatorial elections to me in 1948 and '50 and to Marvin Griffin in 1954. When he ran against me for the Senate in 1956, that was his last hurrah. I carried every county in the state and went on to spend twenty-four years in Washington. I was reelected by landslides in 1962, '68, and '74. I became chairman of the senate Agriculture Committee and gained nationwide fame for my service on the Watergate Committee. M.E. returned to Valdosta, Georgia, and went into business. Every once in a while he would call me collect to discuss some matter of public policy or just to talk over old times. On October 3, 1980, I heard that he had died.

At that time my own romance with the electorate had begun to sour. There had been a bitter and highly publicized divorce in 1977, treatment for alcoholism, and a senate investigation into my finances. The newspapers had started a vendetta against me, and I was in a close reelection race against a Republican opponent. In the midst of all this, I paused to pay my last respects to a man who had faded from the limelight so many years earlier that it seemed as if I knew him in another life. In fact, it had been over fifty years since little Marjorie and I had beat M.E. Thompson's high school debate team. I got to the Carson-McLane Funeral Home in Valdosta early on Sunday afternoon, October 5, hoping to get a seat before the crowd arrived. But the crowd never came. There were only two hundred people at the funeral and only about a dozen at the graveside. Marvin Griffin and I were the only political figures who had bothered to show up. I'm convinced that Gray's "Elegy in a Country Churchyard" was right: "The paths of glory lead but to the grave." It's a lesson that those of us in public life would do well to remember.

8

Post-War Dixie

Friday, September 23, 1949. Nearly three years after his death, the family and friends of Eugene Talmadge gather on the lawn of the state Capitol in Atlanta. Shortly before noon everyone's pulse begins to race as the 54th Fighter Wing Band strikes up "Dixie." Little Gene and Bobby pull at a couple of red cords, and a white canopy falls. A new statue takes its place along with those of John B. Gordon, Joseph E. Brown, and Tom Watson. It is the likeness of a man in a rumpled suit with his arm outstretched and his hair falling over his forehead. The sunlight shines through the leaves of the overhanging trees, and if you look at the forehead and left shoulder of the statue in a certain way, you can almost see a halo. At noon the chimes from a nearby church echo against the Capitol dome. And Papa belongs to the ages.

I WAS REMINDED OF THOSE DETAILS recently when I reread Albert Riley's account of them in an old issue of the *Atlanta Constitution*. I had been governor for nearly a year when that statue was dedicated. The project had been initiated by one of Papa's biographers, Judge Al Henson, and it had been seen through to completion by Zack Cravey. The Eugene Talmadge Memorial Fund was supported entirely by small private donations. Throughout his life Papa had always depended on the little people, so it seemed only fitting that this tribute be from them. Thirty-five thousand dollars went to build the statue, which was the work of Georgia's premier sculptor, Steffan Thomas. The balance of the $57,113 raised went to a number of worthy causes, including the 4-H Clubs, the Georgia chapter of the Future Farmers of America, and the Boy's Estate at Brunswick, Georgia. But as much as we cherished these tangible remembrances, we knew that Papa's real legacy lay in the unfinished work he had left behind. The battle for states' rights had just begun when he died. It would continue with growing intensity for another twenty years.

The issue that had carried Papa to victory in 1946 was the Democratic White Primary. Viewed from the perspective of the 1980's, that institution seems downright indefensible. (Before I left the Senate, I was even favoring extension of the federal Voting Rights Act.) So it may take a good deal of memory (or imagination) to envision Georgia as it existed forty years ago. I suppose that Southerners have always looked more to the past than the future. As a result, we have produced more than our share of historians and literary folk. But we have also been slow to change. During Reconstruction, some of the best educated and most responsible white citizens were disenfranchised at bayonet point, and our local and state governments were turned over to Yankee carpetbaggers, white Southern scalawags, and barely literate freed blacks. Our experience with blacks in politics was that they were manipulated by outside forces that wanted to exploit us socially and economically. These forces invariably belonged to the Republican Party. So in the wake of Reconstruction the two political forces most feared by the typical white Southerner were blacks and Republicans. The Democratic White Primary was designed to exclude both.

Ignoring the racial aspect for a moment, it's not hard to see why a political party might want to restrict the sort of people who pick its candidates for the general election. In the mid-forties, and for a long time thereafter, it was common practice in many states for a party's candidates to be picked by a convention consisting only of professional politicians. Even today, quite a few states limit participation in party primaries to registered members of that party.

Where you have a completely open primary, there is no way to prevent Republicans from voting in the Democratic Primary or vice versa. When that happens, there can easily be an organized effort by outsiders to nominate a weak candidate and thus sabotage the general election. In the spring of 1986, a couple of followers of Lyndon LaRouche got on the general election ballot as Democrats in Illinois because the regular Democratic Party was asleep at the switch during the primary. If an invading army had come into Illinois for the express purpose of installing those LaRouchites into public office and throwing the existing office-holders out, and if the situation had existed for over a decade, you might expect the people of Illinois to take precautions against that happening again. That's the way Southerners felt about blacks and Republicans in Georgia. Originally, the Democratic White Primary was simply a means of assuring that the people would have an opportunity to vote for someone who was both white and a Democrat. There was no provision, nor should there have been, to prevent blacks and Republicans from voting in the general election.

In looking at things with the clarity of hindsight, I have to admit that the Democratic White Primary was not only discriminatory but unnecessary. The threat to local self government had passed with Reconstruction. But we just didn't want to take any chances. Moreover, the fact that it was the federal courts that struck down the White Primary sort of stuck in our craw. Maybe they weren't sending the occupying army back in, but the whole business smacked of Yankee imperialism. This sort of intrusion into the affairs of a private organization, which is what the Democratic Primary was, made the vast majority of white Georgians see red. There was no major politician in the state at that time who really wanted to do away with the White Primary. The question was whether we should fight to keep it. The Talmadgites wanted to restore the White Primary in a way that would pass constitutional muster, and the anti-Talmadgites simply wanted to knuckle under to the court's ruling. When the people voted for Papa in 1946 and me in '48, they made it clear that the fight was to continue.

Unfortunately, it wasn't just the courts that were giving us fits. Under Harry Truman the national Democratic Party was fixing to make an unprecedented assault on states' rights. The political logic of this position was pretty sound, even if it was a mite cynical. Ever since Thomas Jefferson's time, the South had been strong for the Democratic Party. After Reconstruction it was a "solid South." It was not uncommon to hear Southerners boast that they would vote for a yellow dog if he was a Democrat. So people like Clark Clifford were telling Truman: Forget about the South. They're yellow dog Democrats. What you need to do is woo the urban liberal constituency, and a radical civil rights program is the way to do it. The South won't like it, but the one thing they'll never do is vote Republican.

Roosevelt had appointed blacks to important positions in government, and his wife had taken a strong personal stand for racial equality. Also, the welfare programs of the New Deal benefited blacks economically. But Roosevelt was very cautious about using the power of the federal government to challenge the customs and mores of the South. Truman, however, was a different story. He was scared to death that Henry Wallace would run as a third-party candidate and drain off enough of the left wing vote to hand the election to the Republicans. The ultra-liberals never would have deserted someone as popular and charismatic as Roosevelt, but Truman was vulnerable. He had to be even more liberal than FDR to keep the New Deal coalition together. Thank God, Wallace and the fellow travelers who supported him couldn't get Truman to deviate from his anti-Communist foreign policy, but they did move him to the left on domestic affairs. Many Southerners began to think that if they went with Truman in '48, they would indeed be voting for a yellow dog.

At the time he was in office, I took a back seat to no one in my dislike for Harry S. Truman. When he returned to private life in January 1953, he had an extremely low rating in the popularity polls, and his presidency was widely regarded as a failure. He didn't have the personal charm and speaking ability of Roosevelt, and he wasn't a national hero like Eisenhower. The people who thought we shouldn't be in the Korean War blamed him for getting us involved, and many who favored the war hated him for sacking

MacArthur. On the home front the Fair Deal seemed like a warmed over version of the New Deal. Conservatives thought it went too far, and liberals didn't think it went far enough. When people weren't cussing Truman out, they were apt to be laughing at him. And I suppose I did a good deal of both.

But what a difference a little historical perspective can make. By the time he died in 1972, Harry Truman was a revered elder statesman (which was a role he hated, since he regarded "statesman" as just a fancy name for a retired politician). When the Republicans held their national convention in Kansas City in 1976, busloads of delegates went to the Truman Library in Independence, Missouri, like pilgrims paying their respects to a saint. And this was a man who never missed a chance to give their party unshirted hell. You'd have to go back to Lincoln and Jefferson to find figures so admired across the political spectrum. People came to see old Harry as an honest man who could make a decision and stick by it. If Eisenhower seemed a figurehead, Truman was always in charge. If Kennedy was too much glitter and not enough substance, Truman was just the opposite. If Johnson and Nixon would say one thing and do another, Truman didn't seem to have a duplicitous bone in his body. I think he was probably the most trustworthy president to serve in my lifetime. But in 1948 my regard for Harry Truman was still a thing of the future.

Southern Democrats, particularly those of us running for public office, were in a bind in 1948. Our national party had turned its back on us to cozy up to the Henry Wallace crowd, and the Republican ticket of Thomas E. Dewey and Earl Warren wasn't calculated to wean us away from our yellow dog loyalties. With our own party taking us for granted and the other one writing us off, we might as well have been disenfranchised. Our only hope seemed to be to make a stand at the Democratic National Convention in Philadelphia and try to keep the party platform from being too antagonistic to the Southern way of life. I didn't attend that convention, but those Southerners who did came away mightily disappointed. And mad as hell.

The big star of that convention was a young fellow I would later come to know very well in the Senate. At the time, Hubert Humphrey was the mayor of Minneapolis, Minnesota, and a real liberal firebrand. As a human being, Hubert was one of the least malicious people you'd ever want to meet. There wasn't anyone who knew him who didn't like him. But when he set out to promote a cause he believed in, he was like Saint George about to slay the dragon. The original draft of the 1948 party platform had reaffirmed a general commitment to civil rights but had held off endorsing specific legislation. Everyone knew that the Southerners would offer a states' rights plank as an alternative and that it would be soundly defeated. But that wasn't enough for Hubert and his fellow liberals. They had their own minority plank that committed the party to a legislative program that was absolute anathema to the South. He managed to get a number of labor bosses and big-city political machines from the North to go along with that plank and gave a right impassioned speech on its behalf before the entire convention. That was enough to carry the day. The South had not just been defeated, it had been humiliated.

Most of the Southern delegates remained at the convention and cast their votes for Dick Russell for president. (It was an empty gesture, because Truman won the nomination by a substantial margin—947 votes to Russell's 263.) But there were thirty-five delegates from various Southern states who chose to walk out when the presidential balloting began. When they left the convention hall, they stepped into a heavy summer rainstorm, which they probably should have taken as an omen. The dissident Southern Democrats met to form the States' Rights Party in Birmingham, Alabama, and then held a formal convention in Houston, Texas. They nominated J. Strom Thurmond of South Carolina for president and Fielding Wright of Mississippi for vice president. In the fall, that ticket picked up thirty-eight electoral votes by carrying the states of South Carolina, Mississippi, Alabama, and Louisiana. (Three major party presidential candidates in this century—Alf Landon in 1936, George McGovern in 1972, and Walter Mondale in 1984—won fewer electoral votes.)

As I've already mentioned, Strom Thurmond was a cousin of my mother's. Our families were not close, however, and I never actually met Strom until we were both governors. Although I did vote for him in 1948, I remained officially neutral in the campaign. The Democrats in Georgia (including the Talmadge forces) were split between Truman and Thurmond, so the only way I could avoid making enemies was to concentrate on my own race for governor and let the presidential election take care of itself. There was no way that a third party running on a single issue with a regional base of support could win the presidency. However, Strom may have figured that if he could win enough electoral votes to prevent either Dewey or Truman from getting a majority, he could serve as a power broker in the Electoral College. He could have offered his electoral votes to Truman in exchange for some concessions on civil rights. According to this scenario, Truman would have had to deal with Strom to keep the election from going into the Republican House of Representatives. But things didn't work out that way. Truman won the majority of electoral votes in his own right (carrying Georgia in the process), and the Democrats even regained control of Congress.

One of the cardinal rules of politics is that if you want to be a power broker, you better be damn sure you have the power. Strom didn't. His Dixiecrat campaign proved two things: (1) that in spite of the attack on states' rights, the majority of Southerners were still yellow dog Democrats; and (2) a Democrat could be elected president without the solid South. In the next three presidential elections, the majority of Southern states voted for the Democratic candidate (Adlai Stevenson in 1952 and '56 and John F. Kennedy in 1960.) When several Southern states finally did go for a Republican (Barry Goldwater in 1964), the Democratic candidate (Lyndon Johnson) managed to win the largest percentage of the popular vote in American history. The lesson seemed to be clear—the South could not elect an unpopular Democrat such as Stevenson or defeat a popular one such as Johnson. So the national Democrats thought they could ignore the South altogether. Then, low and behold, in 1968 Richard Nixon won the presidency by pursuing a "Southern strategy." In that race, as in 1948, there was a third-party candidate (this time, George Wallace) drawing votes away from the national Democratic ticket. It took twenty years, but the chickens of 1948 had finally come home to roost. And it was only fitting that the national Democrat who was defeated by this "Southern strategy" was none other than Hubert Horatio Humphrey.

☆ ☆ ☆

Since the third-party route hadn't led to the White House in 1948, Southerners decided to try to nominate a candidate within the Democratic Party in 1952. Although the twenty-second amendment had been ratified, it could not be applied retroactively to Harry Truman. So he was constitutionally able to run for reelection if he wanted to. We figured that if he chose not to run, he would want to pick his successor. The last thing we wanted was for Truman or someone of his philosophy to be the Democratic standardbearer in 1952. And we didn't think the country wanted that either. The political spectrum in America had swung to the Right since the heyday of the New Deal.

For one thing, a lot of folks were scared that Communist expansion overseas would get us into another world war. And when Truman, Dean Acheson, and the entire Democratic administration came to the defense of Alger Hiss, it looked as if our own government was in danger of being subverted. Alger Hiss, you will recall, was a former high-ranking State Department official who was exposed as a Soviet spy. The Republican politicians, and a good many ordinary Americans, were beginning to wonder how many other Alger Hisses were passing top secrets to the Russians right under Truman's nose. Also, with the post-war economic boom in full swing, the social welfare policies of the ultra-liberals were not nearly as popular as they had been during the Depression. The leading Republican candidate at that time was Robert A. Taft of Ohio. The country seemed ready for someone with his brand of conservative politics. So we argued that if the Democrats wanted to hold on to the White House, they would have to nominate someone just as conservative and just as respectable as Taft. We had such a man in Dick Russell.

Strom Thurmond's candidacy in 1948 had been a hastily organized insurgency, and it suffered from being based in one region and on one issue. We aimed to avoid those drawbacks in the Russell campaign. Dick threw his hat in the ring and started organizing well before the national convention in Chicago. He was seeking office within the regular party channels, not trying to subvert them. Also, because of his twenty years service in the Senate, he had broad national ties and expertise on a wide range of issues, especially in the areas of foreign policy and national defense. Dick Russell was an outstanding statesman, not just a protest candidate. What we had not counted on was the prejudice of Northern Democrats against politicians from the Deep South. Also, the nature of presidential politics was about to be changed forever by two relatively new phenomena—television and preferential primaries. The one man who saw these changes coming and made the most of them was a Southern senator very different from Dick Russell. His name was Estes Kefauver.

I suppose the best way to describe Kefauver is to say that he was a Democrat from the South but not a Southern Democrat. He was elected to Congress from Chattanooga, Tennessee, in 1939 and came to the Senate ten years later. With the seniority system firmly in place, it was unusual for someone to gain enough prominence to become a major presidential candidate after only three years in the Senate. But Estes Kefauver was not an ordinary freshman senator. There was a good deal of concern in the nation at that time about organized crime, so Estes sponsored a resolution for a special Senate investigation. As sponsor of the resolution, he was made chairman of a special investigating committee. Under normal circumstances, that would not have been as important as being chairman of a standing committee. A special committee is called into existence for a specific purpose and goes out of business when its work is done. But Estes took that committee of his around the country. And when they got to New York City, the proceedings were put on television.

That was 1951 and television was just coming into its own. Folks had not yet gotten hooked on the few soap operas that were on the tube, and a lot of daytime programming was downright boring. Then along came Estes with his sensational probe into the underworld. It was like a courtroom drama without most of the procedural red tape. You had shadowy figures coming on and giving lurid testimony. In some cases the cameramen were instructed to photograph nothing but the witness's fidgeting hands. In New York the morning viewing audience increased by seventeen times over normal. One study showed that an average of 86.2 percent of the viewing audience was watching the hearings. (Entire city blocks looked like ghost towns as people stayed home to watch those hearings, and Consolidated Edison even had to add a generator to handle all the additional sets in use.) Now, Estes milked the publicity for all it was worth. He had a kind of laid-back, down-home quality about him that folks liked, and he just exuded sincerity. People were starting to say that if Truman didn't run again, the Democrats ought to nominate Estes. Then, as the president's popularity continued to plummet, they began saying, "To hell with Truman, the party ought to go with Kefauver regardless."

Of course, it's one thing to have people say you ought to be elected president and quite another actually to be elected. Estes was such a maverick that he knew he couldn't get the backing of the regular party people unless he could demonstrate such overwhelming support in the country at large that they wouldn't dare deny him the nomination. He figured he could do that by entering every presidential primary in sight. Back in those days, presidential primaries were largely popularity contests. In many cases, they had no direct connection with the actual selection of convention delegates. For that reason, a major candidate might enter one or two primaries and concentrate the bulk of his efforts on winning the support of party officials who could actually deliver delegates. Estes was the first presidential contender to run in primaries all across the country. As a result, he piled up quite a few victories against mostly token opposition. The win that really got him going was in the first primary of the season, the one in New Hampshire. Although Truman didn't campaign there, he was forced to leave his name on the ballot so it wouldn't look as if he were ducking the race. But when he lost to Kefauver, he did better than duck the race—he pulled out altogether.

Estes experienced only two primary defeats in 1952. One was in the District of Columbia, where Truman managed to orchestrate a victory for Averall Harriman. The other was in Florida, where he lost to Dick Russell. That Florida primary featured a real contrast in personalities and political philosophies. During the time that he had been running for president, Estes had neglected his Senate duties. A freshman senator could do that with relative impunity, because he had very few important responsibilities to begin with. (If he had a good staff, they could help the home folks with their problems, and the senator himself wouldn't even be missed.) Dick Russell didn't have that luxury. As he tried to point out, he *would* be missed in Washington if he went gallivanting around the country in search of votes. He reminded folks that he was chairman of the Armed Services Committee, of which his opponent was a member, and he would have been right pleased to have had Estes back in Washington with him tending to our national security. When I became a senator, I found that my colleagues fell into two categories—show horses and work horses. Dick Russell was a work horse. He won the Florida primary, as expected, and went on to the national convention in Chicago hopeful that his fellow senators could deliver enough delegates for him to be nominated.

Because of my personal and political friendship with Dick Russell, I was probably more involved in that 1952 campaign than with any other presidential race in my lifetime. As Governor of Georgia, I was able to assist Dick's primary campaign in north Florida, where quite a few former Georgians lived and voted. I also went to the national convention as head of the Georgia delegation. It was the first national convention I had been to, and I'm glad to say it was also the last. Truman and the other party bosses had a complicated agenda. First, they wanted to keep Estes from getting the nomination. Second, they wanted to keep the Southern delegates from walking out without having to make any substantive concessions to them. And third, they wanted to pick a candidate they could control. Although no one was willing to admit it publicly, the election in November had already been written off as a lost cause. The only candidate who could have won for the Democrats that year was General Dwight D. Eisenhower. He was the most popular man in America and was regarded as "above politics." Unfortunately, the Republicans had already nominated him. What was at issue in Chicago, then, was control of the Democratic Party.

The one issue that could have prompted a Southern walkout was the effort to require a loyalty oath of all delegations wishing to be seated. That meant agreeing in advance that the nominees of the convention would appear on the state ballot in November under the Democratic heading. The idea was to prevent the Dixiecrat phenomenon from repeating itself. Things got pretty tense when the Virginia delegation refused to take the pledge. At that point, the Kefauver and Harriman forces launched an effort to keep the Virginia delegation from being seated. The vote was going pretty strong against Virginia when, all of a sudden, Illinois switched from an anti to a pro-Virginia stance. It seemed mighty strange at the time, but the strategy was brilliant. Had the hard-core Southern delegations, which were anti-Kefauver anyway, walked out, Estes would have been in an even stronger position. As it was, they stayed in the convention more determined than ever to stop Kefauver.

You might ask why Illinois of all states would be falling over itself to defend the South. Well, the Governor of Illinois was about to enter the presidential contest. He had not run in a single primary, and right up to the time of the convention he was denying any interest whatsoever in the nomination. But Truman and a lot of the party bosses liked him. And the Cook County Democratic organization was willing to go to just about any length to get rid of him. I'm speaking, of course, of Adlai Stevenson. I had met Adlai at a governor's conference and had found him to be a charming and witty fellow. I don't think he would have made a good president, though, because he was too indecisive. (I can't imagine what would have happened had he been in the White House rather than the United Nations during the Cuban Missile Crisis a decade later.) But he was a good man to run in an election you were going to lose anyway.

Adlai was very articulate. The intellectuals liked him, the press liked him, and you didn't have to worry that he'd embarrass you on the stump. Someone said that Eisenhower appealed to people's hearts and Stevenson to their intellect. Since more people have hearts than intellect, Eisenhower won. But that 1952 Democratic Convention was Adlai Stevenson's hour in the sun. He came out of nowhere to win the nomination on the third ballot. And Dick Russell went back to the Senate, which was probably just as well. Had he lost to Eisenhower, that would have been cited as additional evidence that the South was a liability to the Democratic party.

One day in May 1954, I was giving a speech in Lafayette, Georgia, about the many fine things our administration was doing to educate the children of the state—both black and white. I firmly believed that the principle of separate but equal meant exactly that. Those of us who were committed to maintaining segregation were morally obligated to see that the facilities provided for black citizens were as good as those that the whites enjoyed. This had not always been the case in Georgia, but the revenues from the sales tax helped us to upgrade our services to blacks. I had barely started that speech in Lafayette when a friend passed the word that the *Atlanta Journal* was trying to get in touch with me. I immediately knew what had happened. Within minutes, I had borrowed a DC-4, and in less than an hour I was back in Atlanta. Forty-five minutes later, I made a statement to the news media on the lawn of the executive mansion. The U.S. Supreme Court, I said, has "reduced our Constitution to a mere scrap of paper." That day the court had outlawed segregated schools in the case of Brown versus the Board of Education.

The decision implementing the ruling in Brown versus the Board didn't come down until 1955, which was after I was out of office. So, that was one battle I didn't have to fight. My one notable contribution to the debate over the Brown decision came in the form of a little book called *You and Segregation*. This book was published by the Vulcan Press in Birmingham, Alabama, in November 1955. Although I have since changed my views about the wisdom of segregated education, many of the points made in that book are as valid today as when it was written over thirty years ago. There were two primary legacies of the Brown decision. One was the integration of schools. The other was the transformation of the Supreme Court from a judicial to a quasi-legislative body. History has shown the first legacy to have been beneficial. The second has been an unmitigated disaster.

Throughout the fifties and sixties, the Warren Court went about reshaping American society with one precedent-shattering decision after another. The founding fathers of this country originally conceived of the federal government as serving a very few limited functions, with all other rights and responsibilities reserved to the states. Even at the federal level, government power was limited by being divided among three branches of government. What the courts have been doing over the past thirty years, beginning with the Brown decision, is to arrogate more and more power to themselves. By finding all sorts of hidden meanings in the Constitution, the federal courts have been telling Congress and the state governments what sorts of laws they can pass. That has effectively wiped out the sovereignty of state governments (which is supposedly guaranteed by the tenth amendment to the Constitution) and, on a federal level, has made the judiciary the supreme branch of government, not just one of three co-equal branches. Thus, what the founding fathers saw as a delicate system of checks and balances has been turned into a judicial tyranny.

To be more precise, the situation is not so much *judicial* tyranny as tyranny by the judiciary. It wasn't enough to set aside other branches and levels of government, the Supreme Court also began ignoring the decisions of earlier courts. What was important was not the separation of powers and the tradition of constitutional law, but the political and sociological opinions of the justices. I suppose we should have seen this coming years earlier. When Roosevelt was unable to work his will on the judiciary by expanding the Supreme Court from nine to fifteen justices, he began a policy of appointing judges because of their ideology, not their knowledge of the law or their judicial temperament. This policy has been continued by his successors. Of the nine justices who rendered the Brown decision, none had ever served as a judge on a court of general jurisdiction, either state or federal. None had ever served on a state appellate court and only two on a federal apellate court. Yet, these judicial neophytes reversed the decision of the Supreme Court rendered in 1895 in the case of Plessy versus Ferguson, a decision that for nearly sixty years had held that separate-but-equal schools were not in violation of the fourteenth amendment. And what great authority on the United States Constitution enabled them to see that the federal courts had been in error for six decades? It was a Swedish sociologist by the name of Gunnar Myrdal, who took it upon himself to tell black and white Americans how they ought to live together. Yankee carpetbaggers were bad enough, but at least they were fellow Americans. You would think that a Swedish sociologist would have enough to study in his own country, which has got to be the biggest cesspool of social pathologies this side of the Iron Curtain. But the Warren Court laid more store in what he had to say than in the political processes and legal scholarship of our own country.

The Supreme Court was so strong on the utopian ideal of integration that it forgot that you can't alter the customs and mores of a people overnight, and you can't change a man's heart at the point of a bayonet. I suspect that the Southern position on this great moral issue was best expressed in the following statement:

> Ideally there should be brotherhood among human beings; God is our Father; we are adjured to love each other and be each other's keepers. Yet, Arabs and Jews are fronting each other today in Palestine, dealing out death and destruction, spurning cooperation. India, having gained the boon of independence, has its streets littered with the dead of its irreconcilables. After a thousand years of smoldering effort Southern Ireland finally shook itself free from England; and even then the bad feeling did not die, for the same old bitterness prevailed during the recent war in the face of common danger.
>
> In the Southern states there are special conditions of comparative numbers of Negroes and whites and inbred psychological attitudes and customs that constitute as deep-seated a problem as the tangled situations in Ireland, Palestine, and India. Time and tact are necessary parts of the cure.

That eloquent statement was not made by Herman or Eugene Talmadge. It was not made by Orval Faubus or Strom Thurmond or any other white defender of segregation. It was made by the black educator Joseph Winthrop Holley. No man did more for the black people of Georgia during the first half of this century, and no man was more committed to the future progress of the black race. But Dr. Holley knew something that Gunnar Myrdal and Earl Warren and Hubert Humphrey never learned—"You Can't Build a Chimney From the Top." (That was Dr. Holley's motto and the title of his autobiography.) Unfortunately, the judges and bureaucrats and "social engineers" thought otherwise. As I left Georgia for the United States Senate in January 1957, court-ordered chimneys were under construction all over the South.

Part Two

The
Senate
Years

9

Work Horses and Show Horses

It rained all day in north Georgia. Three Boeing 707 jetliners approach-ed Dobbins Air Force Base in Marietta and attempted to land. Betty and I were in Air Force Two, along with Vice President and Mrs. Agnew, Congressman Phil Landrum and his wife, Treasury Secretary-Designate John Connally, and various senate leaders. We dropped to within 150 feet of the runway and then flew on. We tried again and returned to a holding pattern. We were diverted to Atlanta to wait for a break in the weather. Radio checks indicated that we wouldn't be able to land in Winder, Gainesville, or Athens, Georgia, or in Greenville, South Carolina. At the direction of Vice President Agnew, we headed for the nearest open military base—at Charleston, South Carolina. In all, the three planes that touched down in Charleston carried fifty-three United States Senators, seventeen members of the House, and fifty-seven staff members and friends of the man we had come to bury. After thirty-eight years in the Senate, Dick Russell was coming home.

I HAD KNOWN DICK FOR NEARLY fifty years, from the time he was speaker of the Georgia House and I was a teenage page. He was elected Governor of Georgia in the depths of the Depression and proceeded to make state government more frugal and more responsive to the people. (He cut his own salary by $4000,

161

trimmed the state budget by twenty percent, and reduced the number of bureaus, departments, and commissions from 102 to 17.) He first took the oath of office as a U.S. Senator on January 12, 1933, and served continuously until his death on January 21, 1971. He is the only man in American history to have spent more than half his life in the Senate. Because he never married, Dick was able to devote his full time and energies to his job. Until his final illness, he would put in twelve and fourteen hour days before returning to his modest bachelor apartment to read a book or watch a ball game on television. Next to the Senate, his two great passions in life were history and baseball.

When I was Governor of Georgia, I probably could have picked up the phone and sought Dick Russell's help on just about any matter affecting the state. But I knew that he was a busy man with heavy national responsibilities. So, whenever possible, I tried to go through his principal aide, Leeman Anderson. (Leeman had worked for Papa before going to Washington to join Russell's staff.) Still, I maintained close personal and professional ties with Dick and was active in his campaign for president in 1952. Although his failure to win the presidential nomination was a bitter disappointment, Dick continued to serve his state and nation until his dying day. During his years in office, six different men entered the White House. They lasted anywhere from three years (in the case of Kennedy) to twelve (in the case of Roosevelt), but Dick went on and on. As chairman first of the Armed Services and later of the Appropriations Committee, he had a good deal of official power. As president pro tem of the Senate, he was fourth in the line of presidential succession. However, Dick Russell's influence went beyond job titles and was based on a good deal more than longevity of service. His intellect and his dedication to the national interest earned him the respect of colleagues who disagreed with him on virtually every substantive issue. When Ted Kennedy was first elected to the Senate, he asked his brother Jack how he could learn to be a good senator. And Jack is supposed to have said, "Go to Dick Russell."

Fortunately, I didn't have to have anybody tell me to go to Dick Russell. I knew that Dick would be there waiting to help me in any way he could. Not only is that how he was personally, it is also

how the Senate used to be. Freshmen senators would show deference to their senior colleagues and, in turn, would learn the ways
of the Senate from them. Dick held a little reception for me when
I got to Washington and helped introduce me around. He saw that
I was appointed to the Agriculture Committee my first year in the
Senate and to the Finance Committee shortly thereafter. Without
Dick's assistance, I might have had to wait several years for those
assignments. Although we rarely discussed how we were going to
vote on an issue, he and I saw eye-to-eye nearly 100 percent of the
time. No doubt, Georgia benefited from our close working relationship. When two senators from the same state don't get along,
it's the folks back home who suffer. I remember Jack Javits and Ken
Keating of New York always used to be at each other's throats.
When an issue arose, they used to race to see who could be first
to make a statement on the senate floor or get his name in the *New
York Times.* I'm not sure what the people of Georgia would have
thought if Dick Russell and I had carried on like that.

For most of his life, Dick was a vigorous man who seemed in the
best of health. But every once in a while, he'd go into a coughing
fit that would last for two or three minutes. His face would turn
purple, and you'd think he was about to have a heart attack. Up
until 1957, Dick smoked three packs of cigarettes a day; however,
he quit overnight when his doctor told him he had emphysema.
His health deteriorated noticeably in the late sixties until he had to
use a cane to get around the Capitol. He had an oxygen tank in his
senate office and another one in his apartment. Before any of this
became apparent, though, Dick knew that time was running out
for him. I remember one day his turning to me on the senate floor
and saying, "Herman, I'm not going to be around much longer."
I said, "Don't talk that way, Dick. Your father lived to a ripe old
age, and your mother had a long, useful life. You'll be around for
years to come." But on this, as on so many other things, Dick was
right. He entered Walter Reed Army Hospital for the last time on
December 8, 1970. In his final hours he gave his proxy vote to Bob
Byrd, who was running for senate Democratic whip against Ted
Kennedy. At 11:40 A.M., on January 21, 1971, the opening session
of the Ninety-Second Congress formally adjourned. Two hours
later, Dick Russell was dead.

Much of the federal government had come to a halt to pay its final respects to a fallen giant. He was the one senator of our time who deserves to be ranked with Webster, Calhoun, and Clay. He was only one of seven men to lie in state in the Georgia Capitol. And yet, his funeral was a simple affair, as he was laid to rest over the hill from his old ancestral home. His coffin was carried out the front door of that home and brought to a green tent in the family burial plot, while the Marine Corps Band played "Nearer My God to Thee" in a driving rainstorm. Only two of his senate colleagues—Hubert Humphrey and Lawton Chiles—made it through to the gravesite. The rest of us, who had been turned back by the weather, delivered our prepared eulogies over a special television hookup from Charleston, South Carolina. Harry Truman once wrote that "if Russell had been from Indiana or Missouri or Kentucky, he may well have been President of the United States." What Dick wrote of himself was considerably more modest. The *Congressional Directory* contains glowing and wordy biographies of our national legislators. But under the name of the foremost legislator of this century were only these words, "Richard Brevard Russell, Democrat of Winder, Georgia."

Dick Russell was the supreme example of the sort of senator we don't see much anymore. During my twenty-four years in Washington, I saw a marked decline in the quality of our national leadership. For years, reformers criticized the seniority system and the "senate club," and I suppose some of the complaints were well taken. But it's only common sense that you don't do away with an arrangement that is working tolerably well unless you have something better to take its place. Over in the House of Representatives they've pretty much scrapped the seniority system, and look where it's gotten them. Instead of having a few responsible leaders and a passel of eager workers, you have several hundred would-be chiefs and damn few Indians. The Senate hasn't gone quite that far, but there's a good deal more parochialism there now than when I arrived in 1957. It used to be that folks thought of themselves as Americans and not primarily as labor or management or farmers or blacks or members of some other special interest group. Now, the parochial interest comes first and the national interest second. Naturally, that fragmentation has been reflected in the quality of men and women the voters have sent to Washington.

One of the wisest men I knew in the Senate arrived there long before the deterioration of recent years. Old Carl Hayden of Arizona served in the U.S. Congress longer than any other man in the history of the nation. He came to the House of Representatives when Arizona became a state in 1912 and then was elected to the Senate in 1926. He left when he declined to run for an eighth term in 1968. When he came to Washington (the year before I was born), William Howard Taft was president; when he left, Richard Nixon was preparing to take office. The first opportunity Carl had, he made a longwinded speech in Congress. After he was done, Frederick Talbott of Maryland took him aside and said: "Well, son, you just had to say it, didn't you? Remember, that speech will always be in the *Record*. Someday you may want to change it, but you can't. There are two ways to be a Congressman—to be a show horse or a work horse. One way will get your name in the paper. The other will win you votes and the respect of your colleagues." As far as I know, that was the only speech Carl Hayden ever gave in his fifty-six years in Congress.

Before he came to Washington, Carl had been sheriff of Maricopa County, Arizona. He could remember seeing Geronimo's hostile signal fires in the distance. One of his favorite stories was about the time some old churchwomen complained to him about an Indian chief outside of town who had three wives. As sheriff, it was Carl's job to do something about it. So, he rode out to see the chief and told him: "Under the white man's law, you can have only one wife. Now, you pick out the one you want to keep and tell the other two you don't want them." Well, that old chief took this all in in silence. Then, after a few minutes, he just grunted, "You tell 'em." Seeing he had met his match, Carl got on his horse and rode back to Phoenix. That was one of the few times anyone got the best of Carl Hayden.

Carl and I used to eat lunch in the senate dining room (sometimes we'd be the only ones in there), and he'd give me advice on how to be a good senator. Even though he stayed in Washington until he was ninety years old, his mind was as keen as the day he stepped off the train from Arizona. At the end, he was walking with little shuffling steps, but there was no greater work horse in the Senate. Had there been an upper age limit on senators, the nation would have been denied the benefit of Carl's wisdom and experience. Of course, I've seen some senators grow senile with age. Theodore Green of Rhode Island had sense enough to remove himself when he was no longer able to function; Jim Murray of Montana did not. Carter Glass of Virginia tried to run his senate office from a hospital bed. Still, it is best to deal with individual cases as they arise rather than establish a hard-and-fast rule concerning retirement. For the most part, the people can be trusted to decide who's doing an effective job and who isn't. Once an eighth-grade schoolgirl in Arizona was asked on a test to name the three branches of the American government. She wrote, "The President, the Supreme Court, and Mr. Carl Hayden." You can't produce respect like that with congressional reform.

If Carl Hayden was the Senate's most notable work horse, the biggest show horse I knew in my twenty-four years in Washington had to be Wayne Morse. Wayne was born and grew up in Wisconsin, where his childhood hero was Fighting Bob La Follette. He went west to Oregon as a young man and became dean of the University of Oregon Law School a mere two years after receiving his own law degree. He went to Washington as a special assistant to the attorney general in 1936, served as West Coast maritime arbitrator from 1938-41 and as head of the Railway Emergency Board from 1941-44. In 1944 Wayne returned to Oregon and was elected to the U.S. Senate. That body would never be the same again.

Like his hero Bob La Follette, Wayne started out as a Republican, and he remained one for the next eight years. In 1952, however, he bolted the party to back Adlai Stevenson for president against Dwight Eisenhower. For several years thereafter, he called himself an Independent. In the Senate, Wayne had a desk by himself, halfway between the Republicans and the Democrats. In an institution where seniority and committee assignments are determined by the two major parties, that put him in an untenable position. Bob Taft, who was party leader for the Republicans, had Wayne thrown off all the committees he was on. (When Wayne unsuccessfully appealed this action to the entire Senate, one of his staunchest defenders was Russell Long. No two men could have been farther apart ideologically, but as Huey Long's son, Russell had a soft place in his heart for longwinded mavericks.) Eventually, Wayne drifted over to the Democratic side of the aisle, but he was no more of a yes-man as a Democrat than he had been as a Republican. He and Alaska's Ernest Gruening were the only two senators to vote against the Gulf of Tonkin Resolution, which gave President Lyndon Johnson a blank check to widen the Vietnam conflict without a declaration of war.

Wayne was a feisty little fellow with a mustache that would bristle whenever he got worked up about something, which was most of the time. Wayne held the record for the longest senate filibuster (22 hours and 26 minutes in 1953) until it was broken by Strom Thurmond in 1957. Most politicians are enamored with the sound of their own voice, but Wayne outdid them all. I remember once when I was a freshman senator I had been given the typical freshman chore of presiding over the Senate on a Friday afternoon. No business was being conducted, and all the other senators were fixing to leave for the weekend. That is, all but Wayne Morse. Wayne got up at four o'clock in the afternoon and talked until seven or eight at night. There wasn't another soul in that chamber except for Wayne and me. But you would have thought that he was holding forth before 100,000 people in the Roman amphitheatre. In 1968 Wayne lost his seat to Bob Packwood, a thoroughly "respectable" moderate Republican who recently has done a right impressive job on the issue of tax reform. Wayne was all set to make a race to regain his old seat when he died in 1974. I'm not sure that he accomplished a hell of a lot in his four terms in office, but the Senate was a much duller place without Wayne Morse.

The most powerful senators do not always hold the most important official positions, and those with the most important positions do not always wield much power. Throughout the 1940's and early '50's, the post of majority leader was a case in point. In the late 1930's, the Senate had been run by majority leader Joe

Robinson of Arkansas. Between them, Joe Robinson and Franklin Roosevelt could get just about any bill they wanted passed. The one notorious exception was FDR's plan to expand the Supreme Court from nine to fifteen members. Quite a few observers think that Joe Robinson literally killed himself trying to work that infamous bill into law. For the next fifteen years or so, the majority leader was either a drudge who did the bidding of more powerful senators or a ceremonial leader who didn't do much of anything. Alben Barkley, who was majority leader during Truman's first two years in office, was a pretty good example of the latter. Barkley was such an entertaining speaker that he was always off lecturing someplace. When he became vice president in 1948, he was succeeded as majority leader by Scott Lucas of Illinois. Lucas lasted two years, until he was defeated for reelection by Everett Dirksen. The man who replaced Lucas, Ernest McFarland of Arizona, was also defeated after two years, losing to Barry Goldwater in 1952. Both Lucas and McFarland were conscientious fellows who spent too much time in Washington and not enough wooing the folks back home. When the Republicans took over the Senate in 1952, Bob Taft became majority leader. And the Democrats were in general disarray.

If no one was really eager to take the job of majority leader when Scott Lucas was defeated for reelection in 1950, there was even less enthusiasm about the post of majority whip, which carried no glamor and quite a few menial responsibilities. So, when Bob Kerr of Oklahoma pushed Lyndon Johnson for the job, the party caucus was more than willing to let Johnson have it, even though he had been in the Senate for only two years. When Ernest McFarland lost his bid for reelection in 1952, the office of party leader seemed jinxed. Moreover, with the Republicans in control of the Senate, the top Democrat was now only the minority leader. Once again, Lyndon was ready and willing to accept a job that nobody else seemed to want. Besides, he had made many friends and few enemies working under McFarland, who was essentially a figurehead, and parlayed that personal good will into the position of party leader. (The fact that as a fellow Texan he was a political protege of house speaker Sam Rayburn didn't hurt, either.) As Dick Russell said of Lyndon in 1953: "He doesn't have the best mind on the Democratic side of the Senate; he isn't the best orator; he isn't the best parliamentarian. But he's the best combination of all those qualities."

I met Lyndon Johnson when I came to the Senate in 1957 and got to see him in action as majority leader for the next three years. (He ascended to that position when the Democrats regained control of the Senate in 1955.) Like many of his colleagues, Lyndon didn't know quite what to expect from me. The man I was replacing—Walter George—was one of the most respected members of the U.S. Senate. He had been in that body since November 1922 and had risen to the rank of president pro tem. At the 1952 Democratic National Convention, Senator George had told me that he was unlikely to seek another term in office and urged me to run for his seat. In the meantime, however, George became chairman of the Foreign Relations Committee and was convinced by President Eisenhower and Secretary of State Dulles that he carried the weight of the world on his shoulders. Consequently, he was ready to change his mind and run again, even though he was 78 and in poor health. But by the time he had made that decision, I had raised too much money and was too far ahead in the polls. And this time, George didn't have FDR to build up a sympathy backlash for him by trying to purge him. In 1956 I did what Papa had failed to do eighteen years earlier—I forced Walter George from the U.S. Senate. In fact, seeing that he would lose badly, Senator George pulled out of the race.

I would not have been surprised to encounter some animosity when I got to Washington, a freshman senator replacing such a national monument as Walter George. Undoubtedly, some of my new colleagues were resentful of me. But not Lyndon Johnson. He was as courteous and thoughtful as he could be. Knowing Lyndon, however, he may simply have been trying to head off a potential troublemaker. You see, with the exception of Dick Russell, the folks in Washington knew me only as young "Hummon," son of the wild man from Sugar Creek. They had Papa pegged as a fire-eating maverick in the tradition of Huey Long and Theodore Bilbo. And I was supposed to be a kind of junior wild man. All they knew about my years as governor was my fight against integration, not the things I had done to bring economic and social progress to Georgia. So Lyndon, and quite a few others, treated me with kid gloves until they saw that I wasn't going to start foaming at the mouth. There was an almost audible sigh of relief when my first speech in the Senate was about the folly of foreign aid, not a call for a second attack on Fort Sumter.

In dealing with me and with every other member of the Democratic caucus, Lyndon Johnson proved himself to be a master of persuasion. He made it a point to know every senator intimately. He knew our hopes, our fears, and our aspirations. And he knew how to count votes. (On one of the few occasions when Lyndon miscounted and was a vote short on an important issue, he simply yelled across the senate chamber to J. Allen Frear of Delaware, who had voted his true beliefs, "Change your vote!" Frear did, and Lyndon won.) He knew the issues on which he could win and those on which he would lose. When victory was possible, Lyndon did whatever was required to win. He would praise, threaten, cajole, and bribe (not with money, but with political preferment, which to a senator was more important than money). When victory was not possible, he wouldn't fight. He was champion of many causes but a martyr for none. His own political advancement was Lyndon Johnson's most important cause. And for that reason, he was probably the most effective majority leader in the history of the United States Senate.

During my years in public life I've known quite a few political families (in addition to being part of a pretty important one myself). But the most famous and controversial of them all was the Kennedy family. Not since FDR has there been a politician in this country who has stirred up the powerful feelings evoked by the Kennedy brothers. That makes it mighty hard to evaluate those boys objectively. But once you get past all the love and hate and special pleading, you find that Jack, Robert, and Ted Kennedy were three men with different virtues but many of the same defects. Although I was not close to any of them, I did serve in the Senate with all three and was able to form definite opinions of them.

Jack had come to the Senate four years before I arrived and had impressed enough people that he almost got nominated for vice president in 1956. What I knew of Jack I liked. He was a pleasant and witty fellow with a lot of Irish charm. He had the best intellect of the three brothers and probably would have been quite happy as a history professor if his father hadn't pushed him into politics. I remember that wherever he would go to speak, he would always send pulses fluttering among the women in the audience, as if he were some rock and roll star. I knew that Sander Vanocur had been covering him for NBC News, so I asked Sander why women were so taken with Jack. "Well, Senator," Sander said, "he's been on TV a lot, so they recognize him. Also, he's one of the few politicians around who doesn't have a bald head and a pot belly. Never underestimate the power of plain old lechery."

Bobby was the middle of the three Kennedy brothers (the third of four if you count Joe, Jr., who was killed in the war). However, he came to the Senate last and served for the shortest period of time. Bobby must have had some attractive qualities, because large numbers of people (especially the young and the black) were drawn to him. But he didn't have the personality and charm that his brothers had. He always seemed a little too ambitious and a little too abrasive. Jack had built his early political career on being a senator. However, Bobby seemed to be in the Senate as an afterthought. He was uncomfortable staying in Lyndon Johnson's cabinet, and he wasn't foolhardy enough to challenge Johnson for the presidency in 1964. So, he had to have some political office from which to stay visible while waiting for his turn in the White House. When Bobby packed his carpetbag and moved from his home state of Massachusetts to New York to run for the Senate, it seemed too much a matter of political convenience. But Bob Kennedy was a harder worker than Jack and was generally better prepared on the issues. Because he was a serious and driven political animal, he didn't seem to enjoy life as much as his brothers did.

Ted Kennedy is the youngest and the only surviving brother. When people think of him, they usually think of the family legacy, of presidential politics, of a no longer fashionable political philosophy, or even of the Chappaquiddick tragedy. His role as a United States Senator seems almost incidental to Ted Kennedy's political identity. And yet, he has served in the Senate longer than either of his brothers. In fact, if he is reelected in 1988 and serves out his full term, Ted will join Dick Russell as only the second man in American history to spend more than half his life in the Senate. (He came to the Senate in November 1962 at the age of 30 and will turn 61 on February 22, 1993.) During his first few years in the Senate, Ted was a low profile work horse who refused to make a point of the fact that he was the president's brother. But after Jack and Bobby were killed, both the torch and the spotlight passed to Ted. Your typical senator will do just about anything to get people to take him seriously as a presidential candidate. In contrast, Ted has had to make announcements to keep from running in five separate presidential campaigns—1968, '72, '76, '84, and '88.

Every time that Ted has taken himself out of the running for the presidency he has concentrated on his senate duties. I don't doubt that there is a part of him that wants to carry on the presidential legacy of his brothers. But there is another part that would be content to make a permanent career of the Senate. It's no accident that he had such difficulty answering Roger Mudd when Mudd asked him in a television interview in 1980 why he wanted to be president. When he finally did run for the top office that year, his campaign was totally inept until he had lost any realistic chance of winning. The most memorable speech he gave in that campaign (and perhaps in his entire life) was at the Democratic National Convention in New York—after he had withdrawn from the race. Ted Kennedy would probably never make a good president, but he has the makings of a fine senator. He gets along well with his colleagues, even with those at the opposite end of the ideological spectrum. (For example, he had a very cordial relationship with Jim Eastland of Mississippi, who was an arch conservative and a staunch segregationist.) When my younger son Bobby drowned in Lake Lanier in 1975, Ted sent me a handwritten note of condolence. (Most other senators simply had their secretaries prepare a letter to which they affixed their signatures.) Such gestures never make the evening news, much less the history books. But that kind of personal concern is remembered after a vote or a speech on some transitory issue is long forgotten.

☆ ☆ ☆

It is impossible to think of American politics during the thirty years following World War II without thinking of one of my most controversial and best loved senate colleagues—Hubert Horatio Humphrey. With Hubert the controversy came long before the love. When I got to Washington in 1957, Hubert had been stirring things up for a full term in the Senate, but with very little effect. Southerners were mad at him for his role in getting a civil rights plank through the 1948 Democratic National Convention, and most of the experienced politicians on Capitol Hill saw him as a wild-eyed visionary with more solutions than there were problems. Moreover, with the possible exception of Wayne Morse, I never saw anyone who liked to talk as much as Hubert. When he had an eight-hour audience with Khrushchev in 1958, there were a lot of folks who felt sorry for Khrushchev. At the time he sought the Democratic presidential nomination in 1960, Hubert was probably the most left wing candidate ever to make a serious run for the White House. His friend Lyndon Johnson affectionately referred to Hubert as a bomb thrower.

I'm not sure when the nation started taking Hubert to heart. It surely wasn't in the sixties. As senate whip under Mike Mansfield, he steered the 1964 civil rights bill to passage. And as vice president under Lyndon Johnson, he defended America's presence in Vietnam. As everyone knows, civil rights and Vietnam tore this country apart in the sixties. In the process, Hubert made powerful enemies at both ends of the political spectrum. All those wounds were opened again when Hubert ran against George Wallace and George McGovern for the 1972 Democratic presidential nomination. It seemed unlikely that they would heal soon. But by 1976, folks who had never said a good word for Hubert were wishing that he would make one final run for the presidency. He seemed like the friendly, gregarious corner druggist. He was not a dashing young prince like Jack Kennedy; but folks sort of felt that if they took sick and were out of medicine in the middle of the night, Hubert was the type who would get out of bed, open up the pharmacy, and bring it to them. Unfortunately, Hubert's hour had already passed. Even then, he was dying of cancer.

In the Senate, we were a bit ahead of the rest of the country in warming up to Hubert. Except on agricultural matters, he and I disagreed on the vast majority of issues that came before the Senate. But it was impossible to be around Hubert for any length of time and not like him. He was always warm and thoughtful. And even when he was telling you that you were dead wrong in everything you believed, he had a twinkle in his eye. He was the sort who remembered birthdays and attended funerals. He also had the quickest coordination of mind and tongue of anyone I have ever known. I'll never forget an incident when we were working on the Rural Development Act back in the early seventies. I took Hubert to a meeting of county commissioners in Georgia. These were Wallace people. They saw Hubert as a know-it-all Yankee liberal who probably looked down his nose at the South and its mores. When he started to read a prepared speech, they just sat there skeptical as hell. Then, Hubert threw that speech away, looked them in the eye, and started talking man-to-man. Before he was done, Hubert had won over every one of those county officials. The words may have come off the top of his head, but the conviction was from the bottom of his heart.

In 1976, a cancer-ravaged Hubert Humphrey declined to make a fourth campaign for the presidency and settled for reelection to the Senate. In late 1977, he made his last trip to Washington. President Jimmy Carter stopped in Minnesota to give him a ride on Air Force One. Hubert told the Senate, "For at least twenty years I have been trying to get aboard Air Force One... just the thought of it, the vibrations, gave me new hope." It was like Hubert to express optimism to the very end. You looked at his white hair and his emaciated body, and you would hardly recognize the man. Then you'd look into his eyes and hear him start to talk, and you knew it was Hubert. When he was dying, he spoke before the Senate in what had to be the most emotional scene I would witness in my twenty-four years in Washington. Senators on both sides of the aisle stood up and cheered him for his life, and quite a few wept at the thought of his approaching death. As his days drew to a close, Hubert tried to sum up what the years in public life had meant to him. He said: "Barry Goldwater and I sit in the Senate sometimes late at night and talk about the big and small things we have done. The Senate is a place filled with goodwill and good intentions, and if the road to hell is paved with them, then it's a pretty good detour."

10

Reconstructed
But Unregenerate

On October 10, 1975, I was awarded an honorary Doctorate of Humane Letters from Morris Brown College in Atlanta. As senator I had helped get books for the school library and had assisted in making it a depository of public records. I had always gotten along well with the school's president, Dr. Robert Threatt, and knew that he appreciated my efforts on behalf of his college. But I was surprised when the school gave me that degree and declared me Georgia Man of the Year for 1975. In conferring the honor, Dr. Threatt said that I had been "a friend when friends were needed and when friends were hard to find." The award citation called me "a strong proponent of education, political sage, defender of constitutional law, champion of rural development, and friend to Morris Brown College." I've received more honors than I can remember during my years in public life, but this one was kind of special. You see, Morris Brown is a predominantly black college. It had been over twenty years since the NAACP had declared me an "enemy of the Negro people." We've all come a long way since then.

WHEN I TOOK MY SEAT IN THE SENATE in January 1957, the Eisenhower administration was preparing to implement the Brown decision, and Attorney General William Rogers was drafting civil rights legislation so sweeping that it practically made

177

Harry Truman look like a Ku Kluxer by comparison. Eisenhower himself was no ideologue, but his closest political allies were folks who thought that the only way the Republicans could become the majority party was to move away from the conservative principles of Robert A. Taft. Truman had gone for civil rights because he thought there was no way he could lose the South. The liberal Republicans were going the same route because they thought there was no way they could win the South. Both parties were bending over backwards to woo the urban liberals and black voters. A few non-Southern senators were sympathetic to the principle of states' rights, but political realities were such that this would be a predominantly Southern fight.

About a year before I came to the Senate, the Southerners in Congress drafted a "Declaration of Constitutional Principles" that came to be known as the "Southern Manifesto." It was basically a statement of support for those states and localities lawfully resisting forced integration. It also contained a prophetic warning to the rest of the nation, asking "the states and people who are not directly affected by these decisions to consider the constitutional principles involved against the time when they too, on issues vital to them, may be victims of judicial encroachment." The idea for the statement came from Strom Thurmond, and he originally drew up a fire-eating draft that had to be toned down a little so it would sound moderate and responsible. In all, this document went through six revisions until it was in a form that was generally acceptable to the Southern caucus. In addition to Strom, Dick Russell, John Stennis of Mississippi, Bill Fulbright of Arkansas, and Price Daniel of Texas worked on that final draft. It was signed by ninety-four of the 109 Southern congressmen and nineteen of the twenty-two Southern senators. Because Lyndon Johnson was senate minority leader, he was not asked to sign the manifesto. The only two Southern senators who refused to sign it were Estes Kefauver and Albert Gore of Tennessee.

The nineteen Southern senators who were waging the battle for states' rights and local self-government included some of the finest statesmen and most honorable human beings I have ever known. Heading the list was my senior colleague from Georgia, Dick Russell. If there were two things that Dick couldn't stand, they were hypocrisy and self righteousness. He felt that, along with political expediency, those were the two motivating forces behind the drive for civil rights. Back in the forties and fifties, most of the black population in America was still concentrated in the South. So "civil rights" laws were really sanctions aimed at the white Southerner. I suspect that about one per cent of the population of Minnesota was black, but the biggest champion of civil rights was Hubert Humphrey. It's easy to pontificate on race relations when your biggest ethnic minority is Swedes. Of course, the armchair quarterback always thinks he knows how to run the football team, and the bachelor uncle always thinks he knows how to raise the kids. But just try shoving that know-it-all sports fan out of his armchair and on to the field where he has to contend with 250-pound linebackers. Or let uncle sit with those kids for a whole weekend. You know they'd both be singing a different tune mighty quick.

Back in 1949, Dick figured that if integration was such a good thing, the Yankees ought not to be denied its blessings. So he introduced a bill in the Senate "to reduce and eliminate racial tensions and improve the economic status of the American people by equitably distributing throughout the several states those citizens belonging to the two largest racial groups included in the population of the United States who of their own volition desire to change their place of residence." You would think that all the great Northern advocates of civil rights would have been standing in line to co-sponsor this far-sighted piece of legislation. But for some reason they were right cool to the idea. There's more than a little truth to the adage that a neo-conservative is a liberal whose kids have just been bused.

Another fellow who was usually in the vanguard of the Southern resistance was my cousin Strom Thurmond. Since he had been elected to the Senate in 1954 (in a write-in campaign when the party bosses kept his name off the ballot), he didn't have Dick Russell's seniority. Still, he had won considerable fame for his 1948 race against Truman and was generally regarded as one of the most hardline segregationists in American politics. But Strom was not a racist. When he was Governor of South Carolina, he abolished the poll tax and built a number of parks and schools for blacks. He was also vigorous in his prosecution of white men accused of lynching a black. Strom was always fiercely independent. He stood up for what he thought was right and, as Ralph Yarborough found out, never let anyone push him around.

Strom was a warm and friendly fellow, and he made important contributions to the Southern cause. But he wasn't always a team player. I remember that when we Southerners were fighting the 1957 Civil Rights Bill we had managed to get it watered down to the point that we could live with it. So in order to avoid antagonizing our colleagues any further, we had agreed not to filibuster. That is, everyone agreed except for Strom. He decided that he would filibuster singlehandedly if he had to. After taking a Turkish bath to get rid of excess body fluids, he walked onto the senate floor at 8:54 P.M. on August 28 and proceeded to hold the floor for twenty-four hours and nineteen minutes. A couple of times Barry Goldwater broke in to talk about the military pay bill, while Strom took some much needed relief. He had some malt tablets and party snacks up at the podium with him and managed to wolf down some ground meat in the cloakroom those two times he yielded the floor to Barry. But the man's endurance was remarkable. Several of us rode him pretty hard for continuing that filibuster when we had agreed to stop. Still, you've got to hand it to Strom. Many more people know that he filibustered for over twenty-four hours than even remember what was in that '57 bill when it was finally passed. You might say he won for losing.

In addition to being a strong advocate of states' rights, Strom was an arch-conservative on just about every issue that came before the Senate. It got to the point that he could no longer stand to be in the Democratic Party, even as a Southern Democrat, so he went over to the Republicans during the Goldwater campaign of 1964. The rest of us in the Southern caucus remained Democrats and continued to vote with the party on organizational matters, but we voted our consciences, rather than the party line, on substantive issues. That usually put us considerably to the right of the leadership of both major parties. There were exceptions, however. Bill Fulbright voted with the Southern bloc on civil rights and with the ultra-liberals on just about everything else, particularly foreign policy. As chairman of the Foreign Relations Committee during the sixties, he was a vocal opponent of the Vietnam War and became something of radical pin-up boy.

Sam Ervin was another senator who didn't fit the stereotype of the boll weevil Southerner. On balance, his voting record was pretty conservative. But Sam had such a passionate commitment to the Bill of Rights that he would often vote with the left-wing civil libertarians. To his mind, strict adherence to the Constitution was the only true conservatism. He gained a good deal of fame in the late sixties and early seventies for his opposition to government surveillance of the New Left and became a national folk hero when he chaired the senate Watergate Committee in 1973-74. (Twenty years earlier he had been instrumental in the senate censure of Joe McCarthy and had long championed the political and civil liberties of American Indians.) Liberals who wanted to like Sam could never quite understand his vigorous opposition to all "civil rights" legislation. It would have been easy if they could have called him a racist, but racism was foreign to Sam Ervin's nature. As a lawyer, he often defended blacks free of charge and was invariably kind and courteous in his dealings with persons of all races and stations in life. If people wanted to know why Sam Ervin opposed the sham of "civil rights" legislation, all they had to do was listen to his well-reasoned constitutional arguments. But in politics it is always much easier to ride the bandwagon than it is to think. That's why statesmen like Sam Ervin are a rare and vanishing breed.

I'm sure that our Southern opposition to civil rights was largely shaped by the customs and mores of our region. We sincerely believed that we had devised the best means for organizing race relations, but we were not arrogant or foolhardy enough to insist that other areas of the country follow our example. If the Yankees would leave us alone, we were more than happy to leave them alone. The genius of our federal system of government lies in the cultural diversity it permits. What the social engineers wanted to do was to obliterate sectional distinctions and make the country fit some preconceived design. You can do that if you're running rats through a maze, but not when you're dealing with human beings.

We didn't think it was the better part of wisdom to try to regulate social relations across the length and breadth of this country from some bureaucracy in Washington, D.C.

It was a tragic mistake to have instituted slavery in this country in the first place. It was also a mistake not to have extended the full rights of citizenship to black people once they were freed. But that situation was largely corrected by the thirteenth and fourteenth amendments to the Constitution. Under our form of government, blacks had every right to demand equal treatment under the law. In those instances where segregation was used to keep blacks in an inferior position to whites, it violated constitutional law and elemental principles of human decency. But the so-called "civil rights" laws that were proposed in Congress from the late 1940's to the late 1960's had little to do with equality under the law. They were designed primarily to force a mixing of the races at every level of Southern society and to punish any Southerner who valued the right to associate with persons of his own choosing.

Sam Ervin always made an important distinction between civil liberties and "civil rights." Civil liberties are constitutional freedoms guaranteed to *all* citizens regardless of race, creed, color, or previous condition of servitude. They are enumerated in the Bill of Rights, and their application to racial minorities is made clear by the fourteenth amendment. Without exception, civil liberties protect an individual from governmental encroachment on his personal freedom. "Civil rights" laws, however, have the exact opposite effect. Although they are usually drafted in neutral language, they are intended to confer special privileges upon certain groups of people precisely because of their race or some other distinguishing characteristic. Rather than limiting the power of government over the private life of the individual, civil rights laws greatly expand the power of government to enforce the special privileges of some favored minority group.

Back in the 1950's and '60's folks supported civil rights legislation because it was seen as a blow against racial prejudice. That's a very noble sentiment, to be sure. So was the sentiment that got Prohibition passed right after World War I. The world would no doubt be a lot better place without booze or racial prejudice. But when you try to outlaw either one, you create more problems than you solve. We all know what a travesty Prohibition was. The damage done by the philosophy of civil rights is not so apparent, but it's been every bit as harmful to the social fabric of this country. Over the last twenty to thirty years, too many Americans have stopped thinking of themselves as individual citizens who stand equal before the bar of justice. They see themselves as members of special-interest groups, as "victims" of society who deserve preferential treatment. They look at those of us who don't fall into some government approved minority group and say: What are you going to do for me?

With the extension of "civil rights" to so many different groups in society, the property rights of individuals have become largely a thing of the past. Owning property used to mean being able to do what you wanted to with it so long as you didn't endanger public health or safety. That included the right to do things that other folks might regard as stupid or unfair. If I wanted to rent an apartment and the landlord said, "I'm sorry, I don't rent to people who smoke cigars and chew tobacco," that would be a malicious and bigoted action on his part. But since it's his apartment, he's got the right to be malicious and bigoted. Unless, of course, he's discriminating against a government approved minority group. There are some cities in this country where that landlord would be in violation of the law for turning down a prospective tenant who was homosexual. When you deny the property rights of all citizens in order to guarantee special privileges to a particular group, it is almost impossible to draw the line with that one group. If the government can use its coercive power to protect blacks from private acts of discrimination, every other group from illegal aliens to transsexuals will want to get in on the act. And there will always be ambitious politicians ready to oblige them.

Once a group of people has tasted special privilege, it's kind of hard to say, "That's enough; you can't have any more." Neo-conservatives argue that such things as forced busing and racial quotas are perversions of civil rights. That's nonsense. They are logical outgrowths of the sort of special-interest politics that lies behind all the civil rights initiatives of the post-war era. In the Brown decision, the Supreme Court said that separate-but-equal schools violated the constitution because Gunnar Myrdal thought they might have an adverse psychological effect on black children. If that's the case, then minimal desegregation is obviously not enough. You have to have racial balance to make the sociologists happy and keep the children well adjusted, even if it means destroying the concept of the neighborhood school. If integration in the workplace is desirable, racial quotas are the next logical step, even if they mean trampling on the rights of white workers with better qualifications and more seniority. I have no doubt that we are better off living in an integrated society than in a segregated one, but I'm also convinced that we would have eventually gotten there without federal intervention. Civil rights have created new racial tensions and a special-interest mentality that is tearing this country apart. But, ironically, that is more true in the North than in the South. Blacks and whites in the South have had to learn to live together in a new way. Up north, they're getting acquainted for the first time.

Someone once asked George Washington what the purpose of the Senate was. He just poured a little bit of his coffee into a saucer and said, "To cool things down." I doubt that Hubert Humphrey or Paul Douglas or any of the other liberal torchbearers I met in the Senate when I got there in 1957 would have agreed with the father of our country. But the Senate was originally meant to be the world's greatest deliberative body. Senators have always been elected for staggered six-year terms, and, until early in this century, they were chosen by state legislatures rather than by direct vote of the people. One of the greatest traditions of the Senate, which has made it such an impressive deliberative body, is the custom of unlimited debate. This has allowed a dedicated minority the chance to enlighten, or at least restrain, a headstrong majority. One of the most memorable uses of this custom occurred during the Truman administration. At the time, President Truman was so incensed at some striking railroadmen that he had legislation introduced that would have allowed him to draft them into the Army. It passed the House overwhelmingly and appeared headed for certain passage in the Senate. Now, Robert A. Taft, who was ordinarily no great champion of organized labor, thought that

that was unfair. So he delayed the bill until reason prevailed. Unlimited debate was the only tactic we Southern senators had to slow the juggernaut of civil rights.

In years past filibusters were conceived primarily as delaying actions, and there was no requirement that the speaker stick to the topic being debated. Back when Huey Long was filibustering in the 1930's, he would give recipes for pot likker and oysters with Roquefort dressing and tell stories about his uncle. (His longest filibuster—fifteen hours and thirty-five minutes—ended when his colleagues wouldn't allow him a recess to leave the floor, and he had to give up to go to the bathroom.) Under Dick Russell's leadership that was to change. He insisted that we all confine our remarks to the merits of the legislation being discussed. If we were to lose, it would be with dignity, not looking like a bunch of obstructionist clowns. And, because of an innovation I suggested, the debate would not end because any of us had to make a beeline to the men's room.

For as long as anyone can remember, filibusters had been a test of physical endurance. And since the Southern senators were getting older, the opposition figured it could win simply by wearing us down. But my experience standing watch in the Navy told me that we could easily outfox that strategy. I said, "Look Dick, this is as simple as ABC. We've got nineteen senators on our side. That's one general and eighteen troops. You divide those eighteen troops into three platoons of six men each. A platoon will go on duty for one twenty-four hour period. You divide each of those platoons into squads of two men each. Those two men will be responsible for filibustering for eight hours. They can take turns talking and resting. Then, when the eight hour watch is over, another squad will replace them. That means that each of us will be on duty for eight hours and then have two days off."

When Lyndon Johnson was majority leader of the Senate and was trying to pass Eisenhower's 1960 Civil Rights Bill, he thought he could wear us down by holding round-the-clock sessions. Well, while we were getting plenty of rest with our platoon system, the opposition was wearing itself down by having to keep a majority of senators close to the floor. You see, the Senate had a rule that each member could make only two speeches during a "legislative day." Now, the legislative day began when the Senate convened and ended when it adjourned. That could be a period of time ranging from several minutes to several months. The only way the opposition could hope to thwart us (short of cutting off debate, which required a two-thirds vote) was to keep the legislative day going until we all had given our two speeches. That meant preventing adjournment. But you have to have a quorum (i.e. a majority of senators present) to do that. So the anti-filibuster senators would have to take catnaps on cots out in the corridors so they could come in and answer the roll call whenever we'd ask for a quorum count. We'd come in well rested and clean-shaven, with a hearty breakfast under our belts, smiling from ear-to-ear. "Good morning," we'd say. "It's a lovely day, isn't it?" And those haggard Yankees, who hadn't seen the daylight in weeks, would shoot us some mighty nasty looks.

Debate on that 1960 civil rights bill began on February 15 and lasted until April 8. The opposition tried to invoke cloture (shut off debate) on March 10, but lost 42-53. At that point, Lyndon Johnson and Attorney General Bill Rogers got together and removed some of the more offensive provisions of the bill. We knew that the old order of race relations would have to go. A full century had passed since the War Between the States, and blacks who had fought valiantly in the recent world war were beginning to demand their rights as free and equal citizens. We weren't naive enough to want to return to the old days of Jim Crow. We were simply asking to be allowed to settle our own problems in our own way and in our own time. In the early 1960's, Dick Russell expressed our position right well. He said:

> I believe the Negro *has* been imposed upon. He *has* been subjected to indignities. But we shouldn't upset the whole scheme of constitutional government and expect people to swallow laws governing their most intimate social relations. The tempo of change is the crux of the whole matter. Any realist knows that the "separate but equal" doctrine is finished....
>
> Every Negro citizen possesses every legal right possessed by any white citizen, but there is nothing in

either the Constitution or Judeo-Christian principles or
common sense and reason which would compel one
citizen to share his rights with one of another race at the
same place and at the same time.

One of the main reasons why we filibustered against that 1960 bill
is that we had been burned badly in 1957. We had been talked out
of blocking that earlier bill by assurances that federal troops would
not be used to enforce court orders. We were pretty naive to have
believed that. Eisenhower, after all, was a general. He knew that
you cannot maintain civilized society without obedience of the
law. A professional politician might have backed down when
Arkansas governor Orval Faubus defied the court order to
desegregate Central High School in Little Rock in the fall of 1957.
But not Ike. When he called in federal troops to integrate that
school, we knew he meant business. At the time I said that "the
spectacle of the President of the United States using tanks and
troops in the streets of Little Rock to destroy the sovereignty of the
state of Arkansas" reminded me of "the destruction of the
sovereignty of Hungary by Russian tanks and troops in the streets
of Budapest." That might have been overstating the case a bit, but
the South had gotten the message loud and clear. As Earl Long
told Leander Perez, "The feds have got the atom bomb."

While I was doing my part for the Southern cause up in Washington, the real battles were being fought back in the states, where
court orders and federal laws were being enforced—if not always
at bayonet point, as in Little Rock, at least with the massive power
of the federal bureaucracy. The only really tangible challenge we
had to face when I was governor involved the efforts of a young
black man named Horace Ward to enroll in the University of
Georgia Law School. In an attempt to maintain both segregation
and equal opportunity, the state had offered to pay the tuition of
any qualified black student who wanted to attend a black or
integrated law school. But Horace Ward refused to take us up on
this offer and insisted on being admitted to the University. I
instructed our state attorney general, Eugene Cook, and our

special counsel, Buck Murphy, to be prepared to fight the case in the courts if necessary. As it happened, Mr. Ward was drafted into the Army, and the case became moot. When he had completed serving his country, he did enter law school (though not at the University of Georgia) and became an outstanding attorney. Years later I had the privilege of nominating him for a federal judgeship.

Horace Ward's draft board and Senator George's well-deserved retirement spared me any further conflict with the feds, but Marvin Griffin was not so lucky. He had waited dutifully, if not patiently, for six years to become governor, only to take office in the middle of a second period of Reconstruction. It was almost as if Sherman, when he got to the sea, had waited a few generations—until we were sure that he was gone—and then turned around and marched back. And poor Marvin was standing right in his way. Marvin and Roy Harris went around the South helping to organize chapters of the White Citizens' Council and conferring with other public officials about the common threat to our way of life. The legal doctrine most frequently advocated at that time was something called "interposition." The idea was that the governments of the sovereign states would interpose themselves between their citizens and dictatorial actions of the federal government. John C. Calhoun and other Southern statesmen had been pretty enthusiastic about this doctrine, but that was back before the feds got the A-bomb. Marvin didn't think that interposition was quite strong enough, so he came out for state "nullification" of federal laws. Since neither doctrine had much chance of succeeding, it made good political sense to go down taking the harder line. Besides, "nullification" was easier to pronounce than "interposition."

By the late 1950's it had become clear to me that all of this talk about interposition and nullification might play well politically but would do absolutely nothing to return control of public education to the states and communities of the South. So on Tuesday, January 27, 1959, I took to the floor of the Senate and proposed the following constitutional amendment:

> Administrative control of any public school, public
> educational institution, or public educational system

operated by any state or by any political or other subdivision thereof, shall be vested exclusively in such state and subdivision and nothing contained in this Constitution shall be construed to deny to the residents thereof the right to determine for themselves the manner in which any such school, institution or system is administered by such state and subdivision.

Since the speech I gave introducing this amendment stirred quite a bit of comment back home in Georgia, let me quote a little bit of it here:

> With the exception of seeking the salvation of his immortal soul, man has no greater responsibility than seeking that his young are educated to the fullest extent of their abilities and are equipped spiritually and intellectually to achieve mankind's highest destiny....
>
> [I]t is essential to the future welfare of the nation that all citizens face up to the two incontrovertible facts of the situation. They are these:
>
> 1. Regardless of whether one accepts it or not, the Supreme Court's school decision is an accomplished fact which will remain so until it either is reversed by the court itself or is nullified or modified by Congress or the people; and
>
> 2. Regardless of whether one likes it or not, the overwhelming majority of the people of the South will neither accept nor submit to the forced implementation of that decision and there is no prospect of any change in that position within the foreseeable future.

> I am convinced that the historians of the future will record as one of the gravest and most costly mistakes of our nation the decision of the Supreme Court to make judicial questions out of matters of human relations which the sum total of the experience of mankind dictates should be left to the orderly process of evolution.
>
> But now that the court has arrogated unto itself the

189

authority to release the unknown contents of this Pandora's Box, I submit, Mr. President, that it is now incumbent upon Congress to act to provide for the resolution of the resulting problems and tensions in a way compatible with American constitutional concepts.

That way, Mr. President, lies in the recognition of the fundamental fact that public schools in the United States are local institutions which have been established and are operated and financed by local people on the local level.

Unfortunately, less than a quarter of the Senate was on hand to hear my speech. Fourteen Democrats and seven Republicans were either sitting at their desks or drifting in and out of the senate chamber, and few of those seemed to be listening to what I had to say. So, I was rather surprised to see that speech get front page coverage throughout the state of Georgia. Since I was proposing a way of circumventing the Brown decision, you would have thought that I would have been praised by the segregationists and denounced by the liberals. What actually happened was closer to being the other way around. Since both sides knew what I thought about the Brown decision, they pretty much ignored the fact that I was rawhiding the Supreme Court again. Instead, they focused on my calling the court's decision an accomplished fact that we would have to learn to live with. Roy Harris gave me hell in his paper, the *Augusta Courier,* for having sold out to the integrationists. On the other hand, Ralph McGill couldn't have been more lavish in the praise he gave me in the *Atlanta Constitution.* That such a statement "should come from Sen. Herman Talmadge," Ralph said, "will surprise many, chiefly those outside his native state. But it will not so affect those who know him well. He is a politician of consummate skill. But he also has courage and character. He has affection for his state... [H]e has the necessary integrity to tell his people the truth." The truth was that Ralph McGill was looking to the future and Roy Harris to the past. As for me, I had my hands full with the dilemmas of the present.

☆ ☆ ☆

After eight years of Eisenhower, the Democrats were returned to power in the election of 1960. John F. Kennedy won the presidency that year in one of the closest and most controversial races in American history. Civil rights was not really an issue in that election. The Republican candidate, Richard Nixon, pretty much endorsed the Eisenhower-Rogers approach, which was to proclaim the Republicans the party of Lincoln and then settle for whatever the Southern Democrats in the Senate were willing to accept in the way of civil rights. Since blacks and white Southerners both remained pretty strong for the Democratic Party, the Republicans figured they had reached the point of diminishing returns in their push for civil rights. Kennedy's problem was to keep both the blacks and the white Southerners reasonably happy and in the Democratic fold. That meant a lot of bold rhetoric and little aggressive action. So for the South, the 1960 election was essentially six of one and half-a-dozen of the other. Or so it seemed.

As I mentioned earlier, I knew Jack Kennedy in the Senate and found him great fun to be around. Like Estes Kefauver, Jack was something of a publicity hound, but he had a lot more common sense than Kefauver. When Adlai Stevenson refused to express a preference for a running mate after winning the Democratic presidential nomination in 1956, both Kefauver and Kennedy went all out for the vice presidency. Kefauver won the nomination narrowly, but most of the Southern delegates backed Kennedy. Over the next four years, Jack was absent from the Senate a good deal because he was running for president. In particular, he always seemed to be absent when civil rights issues were being debated. As president, he tried for awhile to keep civil rights on the back burner, but there was too much public pressure in the other direction. When a small minority of white Southerners started using violence against civil rights workers, there was a great sympathy backlash in the North. So Kennedy was more or less forced to come up with a sweeping civil rights program. Then after he was murdered, that program ceased to be merely a controversial piece of legislation and became the legacy of our martyred president.

It's one of the great ironies of recent history that Jack Kennedy, who in life was a moderately conservative Democrat and a thorough pragmatist, should have been transformed by death into a great liberal idealist. It's maybe even more ironic that his brother Bobby, who was probably more conservative and more pragmatic than Jack, should find himself carrying the torch of that liberal idealism. When Bobby got up to speak at the 1964 Democratic Convention in Atlantic City, you would have thought that it was the Feast of Pentecost all over again. Saint Jack had been called to his heavenly home, but he had left brother Bobby behind to comfort the bereaved multitudes. Those delegates went absolutely berserk. They cheered and danced and wept and did everything but speak in tongues. As attorney general, Bobby had wiretapped Martin Luther King, but now he was the white champion of black power. It's almost as if he felt he had to overcompensate for all the moderation that he and Jack had ever shown on the race issue. If he could redeem every unkept promise of the New Frontier, then maybe folks would think that's what his brother would have done had he lived. Every time a black revolutionary put up a picture of one of the Kennedy brothers, it was as if Jack had never ducked a civil rights vote or courted a Southern governor. Jack Kennedy only wanted to be president. Bobby wanted to be a Prophet of the Lord.

If Jack and Bobby Kennedy were show horses on the issue of civil rights, Lyndon Johnson was the work horse. Having known Lyndon as majority leader of the Senate, I knew that if he ever became president, he would be pretty effective in getting legislation passed. But it came as quite a surprise to me that he would become a crusader for civil rights. When he was a congressman, and during his early years as a senator, Lyndon had consistently voted against the civil rights programs of the Truman administration. But when he became majority leader of the Senate during the Eisenhower years, all of that began to change. He shifted his loyalties from the Southern bloc to the national party. And since 1948, the national party had been strong for civil rights. Still, Lyndon seemed more of a follower than a leader on this issue. At the 1960 Democratic Convention the Southern delegates supported him for president, and when he didn't get the nomination, he was chosen as Kennedy's running mate primarily to bring Southern support to the ticket. We thought that in his heart Lyndon was still one of us.

Like Harry Truman, Lyndon inherited the presidency under very difficult circumstances. In several respects, it was even worse for Lyndon than it had been for Truman. Although people grieved for Roosevelt, they knew he was a sick man who didn't have long to live. Kennedy was a young man whose death came as such a shock that just about everyone remembers where he was when he heard the news. As mediocre as people thought Truman was, he had at least been a political ally of Roosevelt's. Johnson was a ticket balancer who had been scorned by Kennedy's inner circle. So Lyndon came into office with a lot to prove. If Bobby was carrying the Kennedy torch in a very personal sense, Lyndon was now carrying it in a public way. Lyndon may have figured that the only way he could make those New Frontiersmen respect him, and carve himself a niche in history in the process, was to out-Kennedy Kennedy. If Jack had a few social welfare initiatives in the tradition of the New Deal, Lyndon would launch him a War on Poverty and go all out to turn America into a Great Society. If Jack had a little police action going on over in Vietnam, Lyndon would commit half a million troops to stopping Communism dead in its tracks. If Jack was content to march along with the civil rights movement, Lyndon was intent on leading the parade.

Lyndon Johnson will probably go down as one of the most successful and least effective presidents in American history. His success was due in large part to his great political skills. Many men have a passion for food or drink or sex or making money. For Lyndon it was politics. It was his natural element, what literally kept him alive. He had had a bad heart attack back in the 1950's. Most men in that situation would have looked around for a less stressful life than being majority leader of the United States Senate, let alone a candidate for President of the United States. But not Lyndon. His heart didn't give him a bit of trouble while he was wheeling and dealing in the White House and making life-and-death decisions as leader of the free world. But when he left office he was lost, and in less than four years he was dead.

Lyndon Johnson was the consummate politician, but his success ultimately undid him. Whereas a lesser man would have had to deal with compromise and defeat, Lyndon managed to get most of what he asked for from Congress. But what he asked for was unwise. By insisting on having both guns *and* butter, he put burdens on the economy that we are still paying for today. The Vietnam War tore this country apart as nothing had since the War Between the States. And Lyndon's civil rights program helped drive the races farther apart. White people felt that their rights were being sacrificed to make up for past injustices to blacks. And the blacks themselves got caught in the tide of rising expectations. After the ink had dried on all of the civil rights bills, far too many blacks were no better off than they had been before. When "civil rights" failed to take them to the promised land, they felt that they had been tricked. And in a sense they had.

In the spring of 1964 the United States House of Representatives passed the most sweeping civil rights bill in the history of this country and sent it on the Senate. It had ten separate sections, or "titles," which collectively gave the federal government unprecedented power to control the affairs of state and local governments and to regulate the activities of private individuals who might be engaged in "interstate commerce." Those of us opposed to the bill knew that if it passed, the tenth amendment to the Constitution and property rights as old as the tradition of common law itself would be nothing but distant memories. However, in the wake of the Kennedy assassination and against the backdrop of massive demonstrations, any bill with the words "civil rights" on it—no matter how poorly drafted or how oppressive its provisions—was treated as Holy Writ by a large percentage of the American people. And politicians survive by going along with what is popular. Again, it was up to us Southern senators to reason with our colleagues, even if we had to do it around the clock for weeks on end.

So Dick Russell rounded up his troops, and the liberals put out their cots in the corridors of the Capitol as the world's greatest deliberative body prepared to debate a bill that would profoundly alter the American way of life. Although we Southerners were a small minority, our ranks included some of the most powerful and influential men in the Senate. You see, when a Southern state found a senator it liked, it had a tendency to send him back for term after term. Since power and influence in the Senate were determined largely by seniority, that meant that the South had long exerted a force beyond its numbers. That was evident in a whole variety of ways, both large and small. Our members chaired important committees, they had close personal ties with other senators, and they knew parliamentary procedure and the rules of the Senate inside out. They also had perks, such as hideaway offices where they could relax during filibusters while their opponents were sacked out on army cots in the halls.

One of the most opulent of those hideaway offices belonged to Allen Ellender of Louisiana. He had been Huey Long's leader in the Louisiana legislature back in the 1930's. When Huey was shot, his widow filled out his unexpired term. Then Ellender ran for the seat at the next election and held it thereafter. Ellender had a crystal chandelier, a marble fireplace, a bar, and a private kitchen in his hideaway. And, like so many natives of Louisiana, he was a superb cook (he could whip up the most delicious and exotic omelettes you would ever want to eat). We have no hereditary House of Lords in this country the way they do in Great Britain. But for years the grand old men of the Senate formed a kind of aristocracy of experience. Things are a lot more democratic now, but we have lost a certain civility in the process. And the government doesn't work nearly as well. Too many young fellows are trying to get on television rather than learning how to get things done. Now that television is coming to them, right in the senate chamber itself, it's a wonder that any work gets done at all.

We knew that there was no way in hell we could muster the necessary votes to defeat that civil rights bill, but we thought we could filibuster long enough to get the other side to agree to amendments that would make it less offensive. We had several tactical advantages that tended to offset the numerical advantage the liberals enjoyed. For one thing, we could keep fifty-one of them hopping with frequent quorum calls. Hubert Humphrey, who was managing the bill for the Democrats, and his Republican counterpart Tom Kuchel clocked their troops to see how fast they could get in the chamber for a quorum call. On one afternoon in April, it took them twenty-two minutes to get everyone together for the first roll call and over an hour for the next one. That weekend we caught them napping, with over half their men out of town, and managed to force an adjournment. From that point on, Hubert and Kuchel ran a much tighter ship. A senator would just be sitting down to dinner at a restaurant or just getting to D.C. Stadium for a ball game, and the message would come over the loudspeaker—all senators please return to the Capitol for a quorum call.

The other big tactical advantage we had was the fact that we needed only thirty-four votes to prevent cloture. That meant getting fifteen senators to go along with the nineteen in our bloc. They didn't necessarily have to be opponents of civil rights, either. The tradition of unlimited debate was something that many senators valued very highly, so it was quite rare for the Senate to invoke cloture, regardless of the issue. Hubert knew that initially he didn't have nearly enough votes in his caucus to stop the debate. So his strategy was to let the filibuster drag on until enough senators were so irritated with us that they would be willing to deal with him. On the one hand, he had to placate absolutists in his own camp who saw any compromise as surrender. On the other, he had to woo senators who wanted to vote for some kind of civil rights bill but who had reservations about certain provisions of the bill under consideration. If he could manage to put together a coalition of sixty-seven votes from those two groups, he could stop the debate and pass the bill without having to deal with us at all. The man who held the key to that strategy was the senate minority leader, Everett McKinley Dirksen.

Hubert and Dirksen got along pretty well because they were cut from the same cloth. Both were highly partisan men who worked hard for the interests of their respective parties. They were also orators who loved to hear themselves talk. Philosophically, Dirksen was most comfortable as a Midwestern conservative. He idolized Bob Taft, and he did everything he could to keep the Senate from censuring Joe McCarthy. But Dirksen was first and foremost a Republican pragmatist. He knew that the majority of Americans were eager to see a civil rights bill become law, and he wasn't about to let the Republicans be on the wrong side of history.

Everett Dirksen had an instinctive sense of drama. He was the greatest actor I had ever seen in or out of the theater. Ronald Reagan is right impressive on the TV or movie screen, but Dirksen belonged on the stage. He was a throwback to the days when they didn't have microphones or loudspeakers, and an actor had to rely on the resonance of his own voice to be heard. He was one of the few senators who could draw a crowd of other senators just to hear him speak. And it didn't matter what the subject was. He could send chills up and down your spine talking about his favorite flower, the marigold. Whenever an important issue was being debated, we'd wonder where Dirksen would wind up. Dick Russell said it would be wherever the cameras were.

On June 12, 1964, after seventy-five days of debate and a sixty-seven-day filibuster, the Senate imposed cloture by a vote of seventy-one to twenty-nine. This was the first time in history that cloture had been voted on a civil rights bill. Hubert and Dirksen had cut enough deals to isolate the Southern opposition. In some respects, the bill we finally voted on was even more vindictive toward the South than the version that had originally been proposed. In that original bill, the federal government would have had the power to initiate action against discrimination in employment anywhere in the country. In the final senate version, that power was restricted to where there "existed a pattern or practice of massive resistance in any geographical area." That meant that you would have federal bureaucrats roaming around in Georgia, Mississippi, and South Carolina, but not in Dirksen's Illinois. (This business of singling the South out for special punishment would be repeated in an even more highhanded way in the Voting Rights Act of 1965.) When the cloture vote finally came, we were joined by only a handful of non-Southern allies—including Barry Goldwater of Arizona. Senator Clair Engle of California, who had been paralyzed by a brain tumor, was brought in in a wheelchair. Unable to speak, he voted for cloture by pointing to his eye.

The vote on the Civil Rights Bill of 1964 finally came on June 19. In the week between cloture and the final vote, senators rose, one-by-one, to show their true colors. Although he knew that he would take a beating in the press and lose the presidential election in November, Barry Goldwater said that he would vote against the bill because it was unconstitutional and would create a police state mentality. Old show horse Dirksen wasn't about to let that one pass. So he got up and lit into Barry in his best Shakespearean voice. "There is an inexorable moral force that moves us forward," he said. "No matter what the resistance of people who do not fully understand, it will not be denied. Utter all the extreme opinion that you will," he continued, pointing his arm directly at Barry, "it will not be denied." Dick Russell was in the middle of his final speech when Ted Kennedy, who was presiding over the debate, rapped his gavel and said, "The time of the gentleman from Georgia has expired." And so it had. The bill passed by a vote of seventy-three to twenty-seven. Dick summed matters up pretty well when he said "I have no apologies to anyone for the fight that I made. I only regret that I did not prevail. But these statutes are now on the books, and it becomes our duty as good citizens to live with them."

11

A Time to Build

When I was an officer in the United States Navy, I served aboard ship with another white Southern officer, Mack Perry, and quite a few black enlisted men. These blacks were from the North, and they were mostly stewards, cooks, bakers, orderlies, and the like. Although their immediate superiors in the chain of command were Northern whites, they would never go to these officers with their problems. Instead, whenever they were in trouble or needed help, they would seek out Mack Perry or myself. They knew that we lived in a segregated society, and they probably had been taught that in the South blacks were "second-class citizens." But they somehow sensed that Southern whites would have a concern and understanding for them that they couldn't find in their Yankee officers. In talking to white Southerners who served in other branches of the military, I have learned that this was a common phenomenon. That may suggest why, twenty years after the civil rights upheavals of the sixties, race relations are generally better in the South than in the North.

ONE OF THE REASONS WHY Northerners find it so difficult to understand race relations in the South is that Yankees tend to see the race before they do the individual. In fact, someone once said that the tendency in the North is to love the race and hate the individual, whereas in the South it's just the opposite. In Margaret

Mitchell's great Southern novel *Gone With the Wind*, there's one memorable scene where some officious women from Maine become absolutely aghast when Scarlett O'Hara suggests that they hire a black woman to look after their children. Not only do they not want to get that close to a black person, but they also act right condescending to one of Aunt Pittipat's faithful old black servants. This gets Scarlett so indignant that she thinks: "What damnably queer people Yankees are!... They didn't understand negroes or the relations between negroes and their former masters. Yet they fought a war to free them. And having freed them, they didn't want to have anything to do with them, except to use them to terrorize Southerners. They didn't like them, didn't trust them, and yet their constant cry was that Southerners didn't know how to get along with them." Those lines were written in the 1930's to describe the situation during Reconstruction, but they remain largely true even today.

When I was growing up in the South, it probably would have come as a shock to ninety-five percent of the white people and a substantial majority of the blacks to learn that some folks thought it downright immoral for persons to prefer associating with others of their own race. To us in the South, that seemed about as natural as chittlin's, okra, and country music. It was simply a matter of taste, custom, and individual preference. As long as segregation was not used as an excuse for inequality, it really had no moral significance whatsoever. Of course, any honest person would have to admit that from the time of Reconstruction on, segregation had often been used as a means to assure the inequality of blacks. Nevertheless, as a principle, the notion of a "separate-but-equal" society was sound. I think most Southern blacks would have preferred that kind of society to dealing with the animosities created by outside forces trying to impose integration on the South. Back in 1948, Joseph Winthrop Holley expressed a view on the matter that I'm sure reflected the thinking of most responsible Southern blacks. Speaking of outside agitators, he wrote: "How much would it profit us Southern Negroes (or the South, or the North, or the Nation) if these out-of-state individuals should gain for themselves by law their barren point, but lose for us the good-will of our white neighbors with whom all of us must live? The

Northern Negro could, of course, go back North with his pride fattened, but we Southern Negroes, to whom the victory meant nothing, would be left to endure the blazing antagonism that this shotgun union would arouse."

Inequality, not segregation, was the major problem that plagued blacks from the time of Emancipation until the gains of the recent past. In the period immediately following World War II, that inequality was starting to break down even as segregation remained firmly in place. Blacks had previously been held back by a lack of political and economic power. However, in the late forties and early fifties they began voting in record numbers, and the economy of the South began to expand. So white politicians began courting the black vote by using some of the funds generated by this economic boom to upgrade the facilities serving black citizens. In other words, we began moving toward an equal, as well as separate, society. Whether white officeholders were helping blacks out of the goodness of their hearts or simply to gain political advantage is beside the point. What is important is that significant progress was being made without federal intervention and without forced integration. I campaigned among blacks from the time I was governor in the early fifties until I left politics after the 1980 election. I remember, in particular, speaking before the annual ham-and-egg festival down at Fort Valley College, where Julian Bond's father had been president for so many years. About a decade later, in the early sixties, I became the first white politician to speak before an influential black organization called the Hungry Club. The person who introduced me said, "Well, Senator, this is the first time you've ever been here." And I said, "This is the first time you've ever asked me."

As governor I did more for the black people of Georgia than any of my predecessors, and probably more than all of them put together. I've already mentioned how we equalized the pay of black and white school teachers and provided school buses for black students. (By the time I went out as governor, the school buses in Georgia daily traveled a distance equal to thirteen trips around the world.) About half the money appropriated by the School Building Authority went to black schools, even though only a third of the state's population was black. We spent over

$3.7 million for classroom buildings and dormitories at black colleges and universities. We constructed an Academy for the Negro Blind at a cost of almost half a million dollars and spent nearly as much for new buildings at the State School for the Negro Deaf. But my proudest accomplishment was building a modern, fireproof, one thousand-bed psychiatric hospital for black patients. This facility was praised by mental health authorities as being one of the best in the nation. The old hospital it replaced was a run-down firetrap that was unfit for human habitation. I couldn't help but notice that none of the Yankee do-gooders who were always protesting the immorality of segregation ever had a damn thing to say about the condition of that old building. Nor was there a word from the NAACP. They were too busy denouncing me as an "enemy of the Negro people."

When I was getting ready to run for the Senate back in 1956, I did so with the urging of quite a few white politicians. Despite the things I had done for blacks as governor and my active solicitation of black support, I figured that M.E. Thompson would get the majority of the black vote. After all, in the late forties I had favored the Democratic White Primary and he had opposed it. Although I hoped to receive some black votes in the privacy of the polling place, I was enough of a realist not to expect the public endorsement of any prominent blacks. Well, I was wrong. Robert Parks, a black undertaker and political leader from over in Cedartown, came to see me. He said that up to that point he had opposed me in my various races for public office. But he had seen what I had done as governor and was convinced that I ought to be representing Georgia in the U.S. Senate. He didn't make his support contingent on my backing integration or taking a liberal stand on civil rights. He realized that it would be a waste of time for him to do so. He knew my views and my record, and he felt that, on balance, the black people of the state would be well served by my presence in the Senate. That meeting with Robert Parks began a political alliance that would last for the rest of my career in public office and a personal friendship that continues to this very day.

It was an act of political courage for Robert Parks to support me, just as it had been for Dr. Holley to support my father. There is considerable political pressure on black people to follow the liberal line. That began with the welfare policies of Franklin Roosevelt and remains all too true today. Most black political leaders have risen to power through the patronage of left wing political machines or, worse yet, by playing lap dog to rich liberals who like feeling morally superior to ordinary folks (giving cocktail parties for Black Panthers and the like). That may start to break down in the years to come, however, as more and more blacks see that welfare is a trap to keep them enslaved to political masters just as surely as they were enslaved to economic ones back before the War Between the States. Julian Bond tells about how blacks from the South arriving by Greyhound bus in Chicago will be greeted at the terminal by some party hack from the local Democratic organization. According to Julian, the hack will say, "You've got three kids, your husband's not here, you're on welfare. Just remember to pull the Democratic lever at election time." A lot of blacks are beginning to wise up and see how self-serving and hypocritical liberal "compassion" really is. All the polls show that ordinary black folks are much more conservative than their "leaders" seem to realize. Those leaders may turn around some day and find that they've got no followers. But until that time, the liberals will keep taking black votes for granted.

As the people continued to return me to the Senate, my support among black Georgians increased. I'm sure that most of them disagreed with my stand on civil rights, but they could see what Robert Parks had seen back in 1956—that good government is color blind. I figured that I could serve my black constituents better if I had a black on my staff. He would have a more personal understanding of their needs and problems and could serve as an inspiration and role model. So I asked Robert if he could recommend a good young black person to come and work with me. At that time, there weren't many black staff members in the Senate and none working for senators from the deep South. Robert gave me the name of a young fellow who was teaching in the public school system in Haralson County. Curtis Atkinson had an advanced degree from Columbia University, a quick, retentive mind, and a personality that made him popular with blacks and whites alike. In fact, many white citizens who needed help would ask for Curtis by name. He served as a liaison in my Atlanta office up until the time I left the Senate in 1981. He is currently assistant secretary of state in Georgia, which is the highest state house office held by a black.

I suppose it was a sign of the times that in 1968 I had a black opponent in the Democratic senatorial primary. He was an unknown Atlanta lawyer by the name of Maynard Jackson. When you are a prominent incumbent, as I was, the best way to deal with an obscure challenger is to keep him obscure by ignoring him, which is what I did. Maynard filed late for that primary and seemed to be running as something of an afterthought. He knew he had no chance of winning, but that campaign gained him some recognition and helped launch his political career. The next year he was elected Vice-Mayor of Atlanta and, in 1974, became the city's first black mayor. Maynard and I worked closely on issues affecting the city and enjoyed a cordial relationship. He's a bright fellow and did an effective job of representing the views of Atlanta's black majority. He was never really accepted by the whites, however, and some of his statements and actions created tension between the races. But there are few rougher jobs in or out of politics than being mayor of a big city. Maynard had quite a few crises to deal with, including a garbage strike and that horrible string of child murders. Unfortunately, a sensational TV movie has left a lot of people up north thinking that Maynard was more concerned with public relations than with stopping those murders. Of course, it's not the first time a Southern politician has been defamed by the Yankee media. They just never had a Southern black to do it to before. I guess that's what you call racial progress.

I suspect that one of the major differences between the way blacks live in the South and the way they live in the North is the more pervasive influence of the church down here. Not only is the black church a strong moral influence in the South, it is also a cohesive social force that helps to hold the black community together. One of the problems with totalitarian societies is that the state replaces the church, the family, the neighborhood, and all other institutions that are supposed to sustain us in our journey from the cradle to the grave. The best way to keep the government from trying to run people's lives is not to ask it to do what those other institutions ought to be doing. In the South we've always known that instinctively. And that goes for blacks as well as whites.

There's no question that black people living in the urban ghettos face some problems that are not of their own making. Too often they have to contend with sub-standard housing, unemployment, and a lack of marketable skills. Government giveaway programs haven't solved these problems, and some studies suggest they've only made them worse. But what's absolutely clear is that there are some problems in the ghetto that all the welfare in the world can't cure. Drug addiction, prostitution, illegitimacy, and violent crime are so rampant in those communities that a stable social structure and economic development are damn near impossible. These problems are moral, not political, in nature, and the church is better equipped to deal with them than the government could ever hope to be. You can't write this off as simply the viewpoint of a white politician with a segregationist past, either, because respected black leaders are beginning to say the same things themselves. When basketball player Len Bias died from an overdose of cocaine, Jesse Jackson got up at his funeral and said that more black people had died from drugs than from a Klansman's noose.

In a way, it's entirely fitting that the most dynamic black leader of our time (and probably of all American history) was a Baptist preacher from Atlanta. I never had the privilege of knowing Dr. Martin Luther King, Jr., but I could certainly see his impact on the way we live in this country. He set a standard for oratory that will not soon be equaled, and in a relatively brief life he inspired strong emotions in virtually everyone who knew his name. Some saw him as a great moral leader, others as a divisive force who encouraged disrespect for the law. No doubt, he was a bit of both. But it is difficult to imagine his becoming such a towering figure if he were anything other than a minister of the Gospel. It's not easy to win a debate with someone who can convince people he has God on his side. (Everybody *thinks* he has God on his side, but

Martin Luther King, Jr., was one of the few who could convince others that he did.) Today, when conservatives such as Jerry Falwell and Pat Robertson invoke God and morality in a political debate, liberals get in a race to see who can be the first to scream about the "establishment of religion." When Dr. King was preaching God and integration, all they could say was, "Amen, brother!"

At the time that Jimmy Carter was running for president back in 1976, a lot of folks couldn't figure out why he had the support of so many Southern blacks. He was not the most liberal candidate in the race (in fact, with the exception of George Wallace, he appeared to be the most conservative). And the conventional wisdom held that blacks were distrustful of Southern whites. What the conventional wisdom failed to note was the appeal of Carter's religious convictions. For the most part, your limousine liberals are either agnostics or folks who look upon the church as a cross between the country club and the United Way. When those people hear someone talk about being washed in the blood of the Lamb, they start to snicker and head for the door. But down south, we've heard that kind of talk all our lives. Most of us have been born again at least once, and some notorious backsliders have done it as many as a dozen times. What's more, the blacks tend to be even more fervently religious than the whites. Carter made a shrewd political move when he hung a picture of the Reverend Martin Luther King, Jr., in the Atlanta Capitol. He made an even shrewder move when he won the endorsement of the Reverend Martin Luther King, Sr., in his race for president.

The Reverend King, Sr., had been a right formidable presence among the blacks in Atlanta long before anyone had ever heard of his son. As pastor of the city's most important black church, he was the leader of his flock, and they followed him. But more important, after his son's assassination, Daddy King was left to carry on the name that had become synonymous with civil rights in this country. It was a kind of reverse inheritance. And when he and Dr. King's widow Coretta told the blacks that Jimmy Carter was a good Christian man who had their best interests at heart, Mo Udall and Birch Bayh and Fred Harris and Scoop Jackson and all the lesser liberals who had worked so hard for civil rights at the federal level didn't have a chance of cornering the black vote.

The fact that Carter managed to pass himself off as something of a conservative on social and moral issues, such as abortion, didn't hurt him either. Unlike some of your ultra-liberal whites, religious blacks don't endorse moral degeneracy. They've seen what it's done to their own community.

I got to know Daddy King fairly well during the last ten or twelve years of his life. I can't recall his ever trying to influence my views on any political issue (Coretta would come by the office from time to time to lobby for the Humphrey-Hawkins Bill and other legislation before the Senate), and I don't even know if he ever voted for me. But we had a warm personal relationship that transcended politics. He was originally a country boy from Henry County, an area where I have lived for the past forty years. By the strength of his character, he rose from obscure origins to a position of international prominence. But he paid a terrible price in personal suffering. Within a few years, his son Martin was tragically murdered, his other son A.D. drowned, and his wife was gunned down while she was playing the organ in church one Sunday morning. Daddy King accepted everything that life handed him, good or bad, like a Christian gentleman. He could be right hard-nosed at times, but he always forgave those who despitefully used him. In later years, he gave the invocation at several of my birthday parties. Whenever he'd see me, he'd say, "How's my senator?" I'm proud to have known the Reverend King and feel poorer for his passing.

Of all the black leaders who have appeared on the scene since the death of Martin Luther King, Jr., none has tried harder to pattern himself after Dr. King than Jesse Jackson. Like Dr. King, Jesse is an evangelical minister and a stemwinding orator. If you close your eyes and listen to him, it almost sounds as if Dr. King is alive again. But Jesse has got himself a different historical situation to deal with. After Congress passed the Voting Rights Act in 1965 and the Open Housing Act in 1968, there was hardly an area of public life where racial discrimination was still legal. If the government had gone to extraordinary lengths to strike down social barriers to racial equality and equality still had not been achieved, it was pretty clear that discrimination wasn't the only problem blacks had to contend with. Dick Russell had made that point back when we were debating the 1964 Civil Rights Bill. He said, "The greatest problem confronting the Negro is economic. Jackie Robinson and Ralph Bunche have no problem pursuing careers. The same goes for the Negro millionaires in Atlanta. You must bring up the low income groups... We've got to provide more jobs for Negroes. Just how, I can't say. I admit it's a difficult problem." It remains the single most difficult problem facing Jesse Jackson and other black leaders of the post-Martin Luther King era.

If you judge Jesse by his ability to inspire black folks, you've got to give him pretty high marks. But if you look at what he's actually done to improve economic conditions for his people, he doesn't come off nearly so well. In any movement there's a need for show horses as well as work horses. But for the blacks, showtime was when they were sitting in and marching and going to jail. Back then, Jesse was a young fellow who had to take a back seat to Dr. King. Now that it's worktime, Jesse is still trying to put on a show. His self-help group Operation PUSH seemed like a good idea, but it was so poorly run that it's been audited by the federal government to see what it did with all the money it got from the Carter administration. Jesse's sermons against drug abuse and in favor of homework get children started in the right direction, but there hasn't been enough followthrough. Jesse doesn't have the administrative ability or the temperament to be a political executive at any level, much less President of the United States. But as a candidate, he's a hell of a lot more interesting than the likes of Fritz Mondale or George Bush.

On most economic and foreign policy issues, Jesse is probably closer to Fidel Castro than to Ronald Reagan. That sort of puts him out of the mainstream of American politics. But it's inaccurate to say that he has pulled the Democratic Party way over to the left. The national Democrats started turning to the left under Roosevelt, and they really went off on the lunatic fringe when George McGovern rewrote the party rules in between the 1968 and 1972 presidential elections. Jimmy Carter kind of slipped into the Democratic nomination and the presidency itself by seeming to be all things to all people. But when he got into office, he pretty much became a captive of the leftwingers rather than the strong leader necessary to move the party in another direction.

So by the time Jesse Jackson ran for president in 1984, he wasn't saying much that the party activists didn't already believe on their own (the one exception being his hostility to Israel and the whole Zionist movement). If anything, Jesse's desire to win support within the national party probably pushed *him* to the left on social issues. At one time, he was a strong opponent of abortion and promiscuity, and he supported prayer in the schools. As a presidential candidate, he either abandoned or minimized his stands in all these areas. Jesse can probably do more for his people, and for white America as well, by preaching the basic moral values of the Christian church than by smooching Yasir Arafat or running to the left of George McGovern. The black leaders who are most likely to shape the future of this country know that it is time to stop marching and start building. Jesse Jackson has yet to get that message.

Civil rights have taken a mighty interesting turn in this country over the past fifteen to twenty years. There was a broad national consensus for anti-discrimination laws when they applied almost exclusively to the South. When the Brown decision outlawed segregated schools, the Yankees thought: "Well, that's all right; we don't have segregation up here. It's just those crackers down south who will be affected." Then when Everett Dirksen got that 1964 Civil Rights Bill amended so that the federal government could institute anti-discrimination suits *only* in the South, folks elsewhere breathed a sigh of relief. "Those rednecks never could govern themselves," they said. "But, of course, *we* can." Now, if there was ever any doubt that "civil rights" was primarily an exercise in baiting the South, it was laid to rest with the 1965 Voting Rights Act. For years prior to that act, barriers against black voting had been coming down all over the South, and blacks were registering and voting in record numbers. Moreover, this trend seemed destined to continue and even accelerate in the coming years. You would think that the civil rights activists in Washington would have been delighted to to see this voluntary progress on our part. But that's not the way the liberal mind operates.

Bert Lance, who's a great philosopher from down in our neck

of the woods, always likes to say, "If it ain't broke, don't fix it." However, liberals are never happier than when they're puttering around trying to fix unbroken things. And, of course when you do that, nine times out of ten you wind up breaking them in other ways. What the 1965 Voting Rights Act did was to put local election laws in the South under federal control. That way, when the expected increase in black voting took place, the Yankee liberals in Congress and the Department of Justice could claim credit for it.

In his autobiography, Sam Ervin describes the absurdity and vindictiveness of that Voting Rights Act mighty well. According to Sam:

> The Voting Rights Act of 1965 condemned the entire states of Alabama, Georgia, Louisiana, Mississippi, South Carolina, and Virginia, and forty counties in North Carolina, by a bill of attainder declaring, in substance, that they and their election officials had violated the voting rights of blacks..., and on that basis suspended the constitutional power of these states and counties under Article I, section 2, Article II, section 1, and the Tenth and Seventeenth Amendments to employ literacy tests as qualifications for voting. Even if any of these states or counties had registered without discrimination every person of voting age residing in them, it would nevertheless have been covered by this strange bill if 50 percent of its registered voters had voluntarily failed to vote in the presidential election of 1964, [even] if all the registered voters so failing to vote had been members of the white race.

That legislation seemed a trifle harsh. But we would have been much more inclined to accept it if its benefits had applied to the nation as a whole. We didn't want to be selfish and hog the assistance of those helpful federal bureaucrats. So we said to the proponents of the bill, "Y'all ought to be doing this over in your own states, too." For some strange reason, they didn't quite see things that way. All attempts to apply the provisions of that act nationwide have been soundly defeated.

Now, a person inclined to cynicism might jump to the conclusion that equal rights were meant to be unequally enforced. But that wasn't the case. The recent trend in civil rights that I mentioned awhile ago extended the blessings of federal coercion across the length and breadth of this fair republic. We first saw this happening when federal judges started looking at the Brown decision and saying, "This Swedish fellow doesn't think that our black children will have a very positive self image unless we get them going to school with whites. Now, up there in the North, you folks have got what we call *de facto* segregation. Whites tend to live in certain areas and blacks in others. That means that your neighborhood schools are predominantly white or predominantly black. We can't have that. If you want quality education, forget about buying more books or raising teachers' salaries. You take that money and you get you a fleet of buses. Put a bunch of your black children on some of them and a bunch of your white children on others, and bus 'em to each other's schools. Before you know it, your classrooms will all look about like the General Assembly of the United Nations. And make sure you do it with all deliberate speed."

Busing may not be the divisive issue it was a decade ago, but it's not easy to find a parent—black or white—who actually wants to see his children bused. Many rich folks get out of it by sending their kids to private schools where *de facto* segregation (or at least racial imbalance) exists because of income rather than geography. Working class whites (whom liberals always feel free to malign) don't like busing because it undermines the social integrity of their neighborhoods. Blacks (who are supposed to benefit from it) often see it as a form of benign racism. What the social engineers are telling them is something that even the most fire-eating segregationists of years past were never bigoted enough to say. That is that blacks have no right to control their own schools and their own neighborhoods, that they are too backward to learn unless they are sitting in a suburban classroom with a bunch of culturally superior white children, and that racial balance will be achieved for their own good whether they like it or not. About the only good that forced busing has done is expose a lot of self-righteous Yankees for the hypocrites they really are.

211

Over the past few years busing has had to take a back seat to racial quotas as the most flagrant abuse of civil rights in this country. Call it affirmative action, goals and timetables, or compensatory hiring, it amounts to pretty much the same thing—reverse discrimination. It all goes back to the habit of stressing the group and ignoring the individual. Here again, racial balance is seen as the overriding goal. Unlike busing, however, this is a game where there are winners as well as losers. For that reason, every group that can claim to have been disadvantaged at some point in the past is demanding special treatment. This includes various racial minorities, women, the handicapped, and sexual deviants. I have no doubt that members of all these groups have suffered from discrimination, but so have Jews, Irishmen, Orientals, and Southerners. If a man or a woman has been directly victimized, compensation should be made, preferably at the expense of those who have done him wrong. A generous society will collectively lend a helping hand to folks who have had it rough. But by trying to compensate a *group* for past injustices, affirmative action rewards people who have suffered no *individual* harm and does so at the expense of those who have done no *individual* wrong.

Most of the white males who support affirmative action are so well established in their professions that they will never have to suffer its consequences (just like the wealthy advocate of busing who sends his kids to an expensive, predominantly white private school). But what of the fireman or the construction worker who is passed over for a promotion to which he would otherwise be entitled? And what of the young person who can't gain admittance to the graduate or professional school of his choice or get a good job simply because of his race and sex? Is it justice or even compassion to rob one group of people in order to bestow undeserved benefits on another? Not in my book it isn't.

A lot of folks who sincerely believed in the ideal of a color-blind society feel betrayed by what has happened to the promise of civil rights in this country. My friend Morris Abrams is one of them. Morris helped get Dr. King out of jail early in his career, brought the law suit that eventually did away with the county unit system, and recently served on the U. S. Civil Rights Commission. Never did he dream that "civil rights" would one day result in racial quotas. What he and other well-intentioned liberals should have seen a long time ago is that social engineering, even of the most idealistic variety, is not the same as simple justice. Lord Acton once said, "Power tends to corrupt, and absolute power corrupts absolutely." He might have added that this is never more true than when that power is exercised on behalf of a worthy cause.

Obviously, I have serious reservations about some of the laws and court rulings that have been promulgated on behalf of "civil rights." But that doesn't mean I want to see blacks held back. Far from it. I just happen to think that genuine racial progress will come about only when people succeed or fail on the basis of their individual merit, not the color of their skin. Specifically, we need a society in which blacks can compete in the job market without the stigma of affirmative action and rise to positions of political prominence without setting one race against another. To the surprise of many, we've made much more progress toward those goals in the South than in the North. In Atlanta, in particular, we have a strong black middle and upper class and an abundance of black political talent. This became particularly evident on September 2, 1986, when the Democratic voters of Georgia's fifth congressional district went to the polls to choose between John Lewis and Julian Bond.

Most Americans got their first look at Julian Bond in 1968 when he led a delegation of dissident liberals who unseated the regular Georgia delegation of Lester Maddox at the Democratic National Convention in Chicago. He made a seconding speech for Eugene McCarthy at that convention and saw his own name placed in nomination for vice president. (He had to withdraw, because at age twenty-eight, he was seven years under the minimum constitutional age for vice president.) Julian had created something of a stir two years earlier when he went to court to force the Georgia legislature to grant him the seat to which he had been duly elected. You see, the legislature figured that his involvement in the anti-war movement made him unfit for public service. Julian won that court case and for the next twenty years served in the state legislature, first in the House and later in the State Senate.

Around the country people know these things about Julian. What many don't know is that he comes from an old Georgia family. Julian's father—Horace Mann Bond—was president of Fort Valley State College until 1945, when the family moved north to Philadelphia (Julian was five at the time). As governor, Papa always got on well with the black college presidents, and that included Dr. Bond. He'd go down to their annual ham-and-egg festival to socialize and see what he could do for the college. Julian claims that his daddy would always write Papa around appropriation time and send pictures of him breaking bread with the blacks. "Governor," Dr. Bond would say, "would you like me to send these pictures to the Atlanta papers?" I don't know whether that's true or not, but those pictures never got in the papers, and the school always got its appropriation. During the fourteen years that our public careers overlapped, Julian would call me from time to time, and we would cooperate on matters that concerned his constituents.

Back in the late sixties and early seventies, Julian earned himself something of a reputation as an advocate of black power. He'd command pretty good fees going around giving rabble-rousing speeches on college campuses. That was back when students felt that the way to show their great concern for humanity was to kidnap deans and burn down buildings. And Julian told them what they wanted to hear. (I don't know if he was just playing to the audience back then or if he has mellowed over the years, but Julian doesn't seem so wild-eyed anymore.) If black power means violent disturbances and antagonism toward white folks, then I want no part of it. But if it means greater political and economic responsibility for blacks, it makes a whole lot more sense than getting all worked up over something as trivial as racial balance in our social institutions. Julian understands that. In a joint interview that he and Roy Harris did with *Atlanta Magazine* back in April 1969, Julian said that the way to solve the racial problem in America was not by working for a fusion of the black and white races, but "by having an equitable division of power in this country."

That particular interview, by the way, is revealing for a lot of different reasons. I imagine that some folks were surprised that two men as different as Julian and Roy Harris would even agree to talk to each other. What's more surprising is how agreeable they were. Perhaps because of his background and his daddy's background, Julian seems more comfortable dealing with honest segregationists than with duplicitous liberals. In that interview, Julian claimed that Lester Maddox falls into the first category and Carl Sanders into the second. This is how he put it:

> Before I got to the legislature, I went with all the Negro legislators to see Governor Sanders. We mentioned a lot of problems to him. One thing was that there were no Negroes on any draft boards in the state of Georgia except in Atlanta. He said, "I'll have to study it." A year later I finally got to the legislature and I went to see Lester Maddox, and you know what Governor Maddox said? "Y'all fight in the Army, don't you?" He said, "You ought to be on the draft boards." He said it just like that. He didn't have to study it or anything.

> One thing that strikes me about Lester Maddox is that he comes from a very poor family. He knows what it means to be poor and he has a lot of sympathy, I think, for poor people. He doesn't care if the poor people are black or white, but if he thinks he can do something for poor people I think he'll try to do it. There are some things he's just more decent about than *any* other politician I've seen.

In 1986 Julian was ready to make his long-awaited move into national politics. The polls showed that he had heavy black support in a heavily black congressional district. He was smooth, intellectual, and articulate, and he had the backing of the city's black political establishment. What he did not count on was the popular appeal of his major opponent, John Lewis. Conventional wisdom held that Lewis would be the overwhelming favorite of the district's white minority but that Bond would beat him by piling up a sizable lead among the black majority. Unfortunately for Julian, the conventional wisdom proved only half right.

John Lewis didn't have nearly the national visibility of Julian Bond, but both men had been active in the civil rights movement for twenty-five years. Back in the early sixties, they had worked together in the Student Non-Violent Coordinating Committee, a kind of junior version of Dr. King's Southern Christian Leadership Conference. Julian would be giving eloquent speeches and dealing with the press back in Atlanta, while John was out organizing demonstrations and voter registration drives in some of the roughest parts of the South. When Dr. King marched on Selma, John Lewis was the first person to cross the Edmund Pettus Bridge. (He got his skull fractured and his picture on the cover of several national magazines.) When Julian Bond was denied his seat in the Georgia legislature, it was for endorsing a statement against the Vietnam War that John Lewis had drafted.

The fact that Julian and John ran against each other for Congress in 1986 rather than join forces against the white power structure proves that black voters were finally coming into their own politically. The results of that election may be further evidence that is the case. For years Julian had contended that white political bosses (particularly liberal ones) were taking the black voter for granted. What we found out in this election was that in Atlanta it was the *black* bosses who were taking the black voter for granted. Those bosses were backing Julian because they thought his way with words would make him a more effective congressman than John. (Also, as an Atlanta city councilman, John had challenged the bosses on a number of issues.) So they picked their man, only to see the voters go ahead and make up their own minds.

As expected, eighty percent of the whites in the fifth district went for John, because they saw him as the less dangerous of the two candidates. But John also picked up forty percent of the black vote, which was enough to put him over the top. Perhaps those blacks were simply voting against the machine or rewarding John Lewis for all the time he spent on picket lines and in jail. But it could be that when they went to the polls, the voters knew more than all the "experts" who thought that flashy Julian would be a more potent force in Congress. No doubt, Julian would have done better in press conferences and on the nightly news, but that's not what government is all about. It's about making laws,

not headlines. If that's what the voters of the fifth district were saying when they sent John Lewis to Congress, then black political
power really has come of age.

Of all the black political figures in America today, the most
impressive is the Mayor of Atlanta, Andrew Young. Like John
Lewis, Andy has done something that Jesse Jackson is apparently
unable or unwilling to do—he has made the transition from civil
rights activist to establishment politician. Jesse thinks he's still
back in the sixties, whereas Andy has kept pace with the times.
Although both are ordained ministers, Jesse is more the pulpit
orator, while Andy is most comfortable working behind the
scenes to bring people together. Back in the days when he was
with Dr. King, Andy kept a low profile. When a demonstration
was being planned or some issue needed to be resolved, Dr. King
would send a wild man like Hosea Williams in to scare the white
folks half to death. Then reasonable Andy would come in and
work out a compromise agreeable to all. (At least, that's the way
Hosea tells it.) Andy has followed a similar pattern during his
years in public office.

Andy first became well known nationally when he was elected
to represent the fifth district in Congress. As the first black congressman from the deep South since Reconstruction, he was obviously someone to watch. His politics were predictably liberal, but
he was more interested in building bridges than in shouting slogans. When busing became such a polarizing issue, Andy tried
unsuccessfully to work out a compromise solution. When Spiro
Agnew resigned as vice president and Richard Nixon appointed
Gerald Ford to take his place, Andy was the only member of the
Black Caucus to vote for Ford's confirmation. He knew that Ford
was a decent and honorable man and was realistic enough to
figure that there was no way in hell that Nixon would name someone ideologically acceptable to the Black Caucus. So, better to
make a gesture of good will than to take a pointless stand on principle. I personally knew Andy to be an effective and hardworking
member of the Georgia congressional delegation and a gifted
extemporaneous speaker.

Back around 1975, when Jimmy Carter was starting to run for president, Andy was far better known nationally than Carter was. So Andy's support, along with that of Daddy King, proved essential in establishing Carter's credibility among blacks. Andy and Carter sort of became symbolic of interracial politics in the New South. Thus, it was no surprise to anyone that Carter gave Andy an important post in his administration, but a few eyebrows were raised when that post turned out to be Ambassador to the United Nations. After all, Andy's background and reputation were in domestic politics, not foreign affairs. Of course, that may be what made the job attractive to Andy—it would help him develop a new area of expertise, which always looks good on a politician's *résumé*. It made sense from Carter's standpoint, too. He was showing that in his administration blacks would not be restricted to shaping urban and welfare policy. Besides a skilled, non-white negotiator seemed just what we needed at the U.N. But like a lot of the best laid plans, this one didn't work out so well.

Roy Harris always used to say that the press did him its worst disservice not when they misquoted him, but when they quoted him *too accurately*. That was surely the case with Andy at the U.N. He started sticking his foot in his mouth so often that even when he said something that wasn't all that outrageous, folks would interpret it as though it were. Poor Carter was in a bind. Here was his U.N. ambassador calling the Ayatollah a saint and saying that the Cubans had brought a stabilizing presence to Angola. (Unfortunately, he's still saying the latter.) To keep Andy on would invite continued ridicule from the press and criticism from the Republicans in Congress. To fire him would hurt Carter's image at the U.N. (which was no big deal) and in the black community (which *was* a big deal, because it was just about the only base of support that Carter had left). When Andy held a secret unauthorized meeting with the PLO and then tried to deny it, that was the last straw. He was forced to resign as pretty much of a failure—one of the most embarrassing figures in a generally inept administration.

Now, I've always believed that one of the truest measures of a man's character is the way he comes back from adversity. Anyone can look good when things are going his way, but it takes a special kind of human being to pick up the pieces of a shattered career and put them back together again. Papa did that after the Dean Cocking affair, and Andy Young did it after falling on his face at the United Nations. The Republicans came to power in 1980, and Andy's old boss was sent back to Plains, Georgia. The congressional seat that Andy had given up was now held by Wyche Fowler, a white man who was popular with his black constituents. The only important office that would be coming open was Mayor of Atlanta. In a city with a sixty-seven percent black population, the job was Andy's for the asking. The only question was whether he would continue Maynard Jackson's policy of antagonizing white folks or try to bring the races together. After his tenure at the U.N., people weren't too optimistic. One of the few establishment whites to believe in Andy at that time was Charlie Loudermilk, a rich conservative Republican who owned the largest furniture rental business in America. He backed Andy in every way he could.

In a sense Andy's performance as mayor was like history repeating itself, but it was not the history of his debacle at the U.N. You remember my saying that in the civil rights movement Andy would come in and make peace with the whites after a wild man like Hosea Williams would have them counting the family silver. (Hosea always said that Andy could do more things with white folks than a monkey could with a peanut.) Well, this time the wild man was Maynard Jackson. (Hosea's still around as a member of the Atlanta City Council, but he's regarded as something of a crank with no real power.) After Maynard got the white folks all stirred up during his eight years in office, Andy came in and got everyone working together for the good of the city. As he told a reporter for *Esquire*, "My job is to see that whites get some of the power and blacks get some of the money." In 1984 alone, the city of Atlanta saw seven billion dollars in new construction that brought with it 100,000 new jobs. That may not have been Andy's doing, but at least he knew enough not to stand in the way of economic development. The best way to fight a war on poverty is to maintain a healthy and growing economy. Andy put it right well when he said, "Politics doesn't control the world. Money does... You're not going to get nine million folks in Ethiopia eating unless you get money into their economy. If you want to bring about what we preachers preach about—feeding the hungry, clothing the naked, healing the sick—it's going to be done in the free-market system. You need capital. You need technology. You need marketing." It's unfortunate that Andy will never get as much publicity for sensible statements like those as he did for making himself into a horse's rear end over at the United Nations.

I have no idea what Andy Young's political future might be, but what he has done in Atlanta is an example of how blacks can gain their rightful place in American politics. When we have more black political leaders doing an outstanding job for people of both races, then color is going to start being less of a political issue. Blacks are not going to advance under the care of paternalistic white politicians or under a racial spoils system that tries to put whitey in his place. It is only when white people see that the interests of both races can be advanced by electing competent blacks like Andy Young that blacks will cease to be a political underclass in this country. If white Virginians can elect a black lieutenant governor, there's no reason why white Georgians cannot elect a black governor or U.S. Senator. Or, for that matter, why white Americans cannot elect a black president. Those barriers may eventually be broken down by persons who are not even on the political scene today. But when that happens, it will be because blacks have chosen to be more like Andy Young than Jesse Jackson. By that time we will have a society in which forced busing and racial quotas will seem as out of date as segregation does today. I'm optimistic enough to think that that might happen in my lifetime.

12

Our Daily Bread

Sometimes the calls start before sunup. The voice on the other end of the line may be sober and worried. But often these days it is slurred and not always coherent. Either way, the message is the same: "Things are bad for the farmer... Prices are low and debts are coming due... I'll lose everything... It hasn't been this bad since the Depression." (What the voices don't say, but only imply, is that alcoholism, divorce, and suicide are up in rural America—once a bastion of traditional moral values and religious faith.) Being an old farmboy myself, I'm already up when the phone begins to ring. That doesn't bother me. But what do I say to these hardworking, Godfearing people, who are seeing their lives fall apart in front of their eyes? I tell them I understand, that I'm for the farmer living well, that I couldn't do as much as I wanted to when I was in the Senate, that I can do even less now. My wife, Lynda, is up and cooking breakfast. She gives me a sympathetic look and says, "They're starting early today."

THE STATISTICS ALONE ARE ENOUGH to convince any fair-minded person that there is a crisis in American agriculture. But the statistics are not enough to persuade the ninety-eight percent of the population who do not live on a farm that they ought to care about the two percent who do. When David Stockman said that farmers are adults who ought to take their lumps in the free market, a lot of non-farm folks probably agreed with him. But what those people don't seem to realize is that some of the same economic forces that are shoving farmers off their land are also costing jobs in the steel and textile and auto industries. As we proceed to lose markets overseas and to import more and more of our essential goods and commodities, we are moving toward an economy based on fast food hamburgers and computer chips. The farm problem is not a problem just for farmers any more than national defense is a problem just for generals. Everyone who eats should be concerned about the source of our food. It doesn't just spring up on the grocery shelf on its own. And, as Merle Haggard said in a recent song, we don't want to have to buy our bread from the Toyota man.

How we deal with the farm problem will depend a lot on the sort of country we decide we want to have. And that is a debate that is at least two hundred years old. Every time a bank forecloses on a farm, the ghosts of Alexander Hamilton and Thomas Jefferson continue their struggle for the soul of America. Hamilton, you will remember, thought that we ought to be one society with a strong central government and central banking system. He believed in a high degree of industrialism and commerce. He had his eye on the future, and his vision has served us well. In my own lifetime, we have moved from the horse and buggy era to the space age. Air travel and interstate highways have brought us closer together. The simple invention of the elevator has made it possible for the country to grow vertically, as well as horizontally. The telephone has made instantaneous communication commonplace. And regional differences have begun to disappear. A shopping mall in Atlanta looks pretty much like one in Kansas City or Phoenix. Local TV newsmen are the same everywhere—the same blazer, the same blow-dried hair, the same bland Midwestern voice. The changes in this country may be a little hard to adjust to, but not very many folks would really want to turn the clock back. Especially not if it meant sacrificing the great advances we have made in medical science. As far as our standard of living is concerned, there never was such a thing as the good old days.

Compared to Hamilton, Thomas Jefferson was no visionary. He didn't see nearly as far. But what he did see, he saw well. He knew that it was necessary to make a life as well as a living. He knew that it is possible to look so far into the future that you forget where you are and where you came from. When Jefferson looked around him, he saw that the best citizens were the yeoman farmers. They had never heard of Adam Smith and the division of labor, and they couldn't have imagined a society in which folks made their living screwing in a single bolt on an assembly line, over and over again, for eight hours a day. For the most part, they didn't divide their labor—they did it all themselves. It might have been inefficient, but it made for social stability. Great societies have always been built by people who had their origins in the soil. (The Roman Army was drawn from the farm boys of Italy.) And when you have a mass movement of people off the farms, the society becomes transient and rootless and divorced from nature. That's something that Hamiltonian bean counters like David Stockman will never understand. When you get past all the undeniably crucial economic issues, the fundamental question facing us is whether it is possible for Jefferson's kind of people to live in Hamilton's kind of world.

Just recently a lot of college professors and newspaper columnists have started talking about "two Georgias." To hear them carry on, you would think that this was a real novel insight. But it's not. All my life I've known that there were "two Georgias"—one where the streetcars ran and one where they didn't. They used to call those two Georgias the Talmadge and the anti-Talmadge counties. (As you recall, the former consisted of poor dirt farmers who thought that their only friends on this earth were God Almighty, Sears Roebuck, and Gene Talmadge.) As both governor and senator I did what I could to bring those two Georgias together, and for thirty years I succeeded. In my last campaign the voters of metropolitan Atlanta finally turned away from me (for reasons I'll be a-comin' to in a later chapter), but the "other Georgia" remained faithful to me to the end. During my years in public office, the farmer knew he had a friend in Herman Talmadge. I guess it was just part of my heritage.

I remember when I was in high school, Mama and I would fill

up the car every morning with collards and turnip greens and eggs and butter and all the other things she produced on the farm. We would take them to a little store called the Telfair Cooperative Company and get credit for them. We would also buy our farm supplies there and get a bill at the end of the month for the difference. Then when we all moved to Atlanta after the farmhouse burned in 1930, Mama would go back to McRae every weekend to keep an eye on the farm and provide for the tenants who had stayed behind to work the land. (We saw that those folks always had enough to eat, when a lot of city people were going hungry during the Depression.) My mother was a shrewd business-woman who knew how to make a farm turn a profit. In 1933, she bought a pecan farm for $2,500. She grew enough pecans the first year to pay for the farm. Just before she died she gave that farm to me. I kept it for five or six years and then sold it for $100,000.

Many of the things I did as governor were designed to help all of the people—urban and rural. But the benefits were most keenly felt in those areas that had been farthest removed from vital public services. Increasing the number of hospitals helped all the people, but none so much as those who had previously lived one hundred miles away from the nearest hospital. Everyone appreciated better roads, but they were absolutely essential to those who depended on them to get their crops to market. Among the things we did specifically for the farmer, I am proudest of the statewide farmers' markets. The farmers would bring their produce directly to these markets and sell it to truckers who were shipping food to stores up north. By eliminating some of the middlemen, the farmer made a better profit on what he sold, and the consumer paid a lower price. While I was in office we tripled the number of markets from eleven to thirty-three. In 1945-46, the total sales in our farmers' markets stood at approximately $33.2 million. By 1953-54, they had risen to nearly $83.85 million.

If anything, my interest in agriculture increased when I went to Washington. In the Senate, most business is transacted in committees, and my first important committee assignment was Agriculture. Back in 1957, the farm population in this country was significant enough that senators were standing in line to get on the Agriculture Committee. By the time I left the Senate in 1980, you had to go out and beg people to serve. Being on that committee for twenty-four years, and chairing it for nine, was an interesting, sometimes frustrating, experience. You see, there is no such thing as a single agricultural interest. The same policy is not going to work to the advantage of all areas of the country or of all farm products. Consequently, there were different parochial interests within the senate Agriculture Committee. After those interests had been accommodated, we had to bring the resulting legislation to the senate floor and then, more often than not, reconcile it with whatever the House of Representatives had done with its version of the same bill.

Those reconciliation sessions could turn into real donnybrooks. I remember when Allen Ellender of Louisiana was chairman of the senate Agriculture Committee and his house counterpart was Bob Pogue of Texas. Both men were fine fellows and dedicated public servants, but neither one had what you would call a diplomatic temperament. Ellender was a hot-blooded Cajun who wasn't about to let anyone get the better of him in an argument. Pogue also had a short fuse. He was the sort who could be convinced of something by the sound of his own voice. The more he asserted his position, the more determined he became that he was right. There were several times I was certain that Pogue and Ellender would come to blows. From watching those two I learned how *not* to run a conference committee. When I got to be chairman of Agriculture and was running the reconciliation sessions, I would start out by having the conferees fine-tune those points on which they were in substantial agreement. Then, with everyone feeling in harmony with each other, we'd tackle the few points on which we disagreed. As a result, we managed to keep both our legislation and our blood pressure on an even keel.

It may be difficult at times to identify the common *positive* interests of agriculture, but farmers usually can agree on what, or whom, they're against. When I came to the Senate, they were pretty well agreed that one person they were against was Secretary of Agriculture Ezra Taft Benson. It wasn't that they had anything against Benson personally. (He was an attractive and pleasant fellow who became head of the Mormon Church in

1985.) Nor did they disagree with his free market philosophy as an ideal for which to strive. The problem was that Benson's emphasis on a totally free market in agriculture ignored the reality of the world in which we live. Our economy is riddled with special provisions for labor and industry and other economic interest groups. If everyone else would agree to compete in a free and open market, the farmer would be more than willing to forego some of the programs designed for his benefit. As it is, labor has the minimum wage law, unemployment insurance, and occupational health and safety regulations, along with whatever else the unions can win at the bargaining table. Every industry in this country has some kind of special tax loophole or write-off. All the farmer asks for is a chance to make a living in a profession where the odds are stacked against him. Farming is the greatest gamble on the face of this earth, because farmers are fighting the weather, insects, disease, labor, market prices, and, in recent years, shifts in foreign policy. They have to win every one of those battles to be successful. It's a little much to ask that, in addition to all his other struggles, the farmer also become a martyr for the principle of free enterprise.

Despite the general unpopularity of Ezra Taft Benson, the farm states stayed in the Republican column in the presidential election of 1960. But then, the Democratic Congress had stymied much of Benson's program and the Republican candidate Dick Nixon was doing his best to run away from it. Midwestern farmers probably figured that Bensonism was out regardless of who won the presidential election and that Nixon would be stronger than his opponent, Jack Kennedy, on other issues. As it turned out, Jack won and appointed former Minnesota governor Orville Freeman to be Secretary of Agriculture. As a city boy from Boston, Massachusetts, Kennedy didn't know beans about agriculture, and Freeman wasn't much better. But unlike Eisenhower and Benson, they deferred to the agricultural experts in Congress. When Lyndon Johnson, who *was* a farmboy, became president, he did pretty much the same thing. Lyndon concentrated on such issues as civil rights, Vietnam, and the Great Society and left the House and Senate to formulate farm policy. In fact, he didn't even replace Orville Freeman with one of his own men. For all I know, Lyndon may have forgotten that Freeman was even there.

A senator's position on agricultural matters may follow geographical lines, but it is seldom defined by political philosophy or party affiliation. On farm policy, I was almost always in agreement with liberals such as George McGovern and Hubert Humphrey. And some of my most congenial colleagues on the senate Agriculture Committee were Republicans. A case in point was George Aiken of Vermont. Although he hadn't been in the Senate as long as Dick Russell or Carl Hayden, Aiken was the old man among senate Republicans. He had been Governor of Vermont when Papa was Governor of Georgia, and back in Vermont they still referred to him as "Governor" rather than "Senator." Aiken was first elected to the Senate in 1940 and stayed there for thirty-five years. George Aiken spoke in an accent rarely heard in Georgia, and he came from a region where "Yankee" was not a term of derision. But he was a farmboy who got up before dawn, worked hard, and won the respect of everyone who knew him. Under senate rules, subcommittee chairmen are appointed from the majority party. But from 1958 to 1969, George was chairman of the Foreign Relations Subcommittee on Canada, and not a single Democrat was heard to object. (The fact that George was a good friend of majority leader Mike Mansfield didn't hurt.) You could always tell George Aiken by his red ties and his common sense. Like Papa, George was a fiscal conservative. He allowed that, "Some say you shouldn't prune except at the right time of the year. I generally do it when the saw is sharp."

Another enormously capable and level-headed Republican who served with me on the Agriculture Committee was Bob Dole of Kansas. Bob has gotten a pretty good press in recent years, but that wasn't always the case. Back in the early to mid seventies, he caught a lot of hell for being a partisan Republican. Of course his critics felt that the only proper place for a Republican was at the end of a yard-arm. Bob became party chairman right as Watergate was heating up and, in 1976, was picked to be Jerry Ford's running mate because Jerry wanted a quick-witted hatchet man who would let him continue playing the nice guy. As a rule, the sages in the press don't like for politicians to be smarter than they are. If, in addition to being smart, the politician also has a caustic wit and a conservative philosophy, he's asking for trouble. But Bob Dole's skills as a legislator eventually became so obvious that even folks who didn't like what he stood for (which included most of the press) had to admire his ability to get things done. When the Republicans took over the Senate in 1980, Bob became chairman of the Finance Committee. Then when Howard Baker retired in 1984, Bob replaced him as majority leader and, by all accounts, has been the most effective one since Lyndon Johnson. Bob Dole takes his job seriously but is still able to laugh at himself. In a profession where there are far too many inept and self-important people, he's like a breath of fresh air.

The man who probably did the most for agriculture during my twenty-four years in Washington was not a fellow senator at all, but Secretary of Agriculture Earl Butz. Earl entered Richard Nixon's cabinet shortly after I became chairman of the senate Agriculture Committee. (I replaced Allen Ellender, who moved over to chair the Appropriations Committee when Dick Russell died.) During the five years he was in office, Earl was an out-spoken fellow who made plenty of enemies. Like Bob Dole, Earl had a quick wit, but he wasn't always discreet or diplomatic in the way he used it. Because of the intense press coverage of every-thing they say and do, politicians have to be on guard at all times to keep from embarrassing themselves. Fine public servants as diverse as Barry Goldwater and Andy Young have damaged their careers by making off-the-cuff statements that were later blown out of proportion by the media. Earl Butz had the same problem. He finally lost his job when an ethnic joke he told off-the-record was made into a big campaign issue during the 1976 presidential election. Unfortunately, more people probably remember him for that one joke than for all the good he did as Secretary of Agriculture.

Regardless of what the press and the professional politicians might have said about him, the farmers loved Earl Butz. Like Ezra Taft Benson (under whom he had served as Assistant Secretary of Agriculture during the fifties), Earl believed in the free market. But unlike Benson, he was not a fanatic or an ideologue about it, and he used his influence and position in Washington to expand overseas sales of American farm products. That kept farm profits up and helped reduce our foreign trade deficit at a time when oil imports were playing hell with our balance of payments. As a result, we also had high food prices that got the consumer up in arms. I'm glad to say that Earl stood his ground and let folks know that it wasn't the farmer who was taking advantage of them. When someone at a banquet in Chicago asked him about high food prices, Earl said, "You had beef here today. I don't know what it cost. But just putting an empty plate in front of you probably would have cost $9, with all those built-in services." When he was Secretary of Agriculture, Earl would come by my office two or three times a week, and I got to know him well. He did a fine job in one of the most thankless positions in government. No Secretary of Agriculture can please all the *farmers*, much less the general public. In fact, most secretaries are so unpopular when they leave office that you'd have a hard time rounding up enough pallbearers to carry them to the cemetery.

To some extent American farmers are victims of their own success. When they are able to produce enough food to saturate the foreign and domestic markets, prices must go down. There are few attractive alternatives to the sort of overproduction that would deny farmers their livelihood. During the Depression, when millions of Americans went to bed hungry at night, farmers were killing little pigs and plowing their crops under to keep the bottom from dropping out from under farm prices. That seemed like such a waste that the government started buying up and storing surplus production. But the cost of preserving these surpluses got to be prohibitive. And the policy still did nothing to feed the hungry. The problem was solved temporarily by the food shortage during World War II. Then during the fifties, Ezra Taft Benson tried unsuccessfully to move the federal government entirely out of agriculture. It wasn't until the sixties that Congress tried in any systematic way to feed the hungry with farm surpluses. The result was a well-intentioned program that has gotten out of hand in recent years.

229

In 1961 the U.S. government started a pilot food stamp program in eight "distressed areas" of the country. This was expanded to include the entire nation in 1964. The program issued recipients coupons that could be redeemed at just about any grocery store for domestically produced food. Since the stamps were sold to beneficiaries at less than their monetary value, they were designed to supplement a family's food budget. When George Aiken and I drafted the original food stamp legislation, our intention was to provide for widows and other destitute persons who had no other means of feeding themselves. Well, before you know it, hunger had become a political fad, and liberal politicians were running around the country turning up starving and malnourished folks everywhere. Eligibility requirements were relaxed to the point where striking workers and college students from middle-class homes were getting food stamps. Then in the Carter administration, the government started giving the stamps away to people enrolled in the program. In many cities today, food stamps have become just another form of currency that can be used to purchase everything from cocaine to a woman for the night. Too often greed has been a more important factor than need in determining who benefits from food stamps.

A much more effective piece of legislation I was instrumental in passing when I was chairman of the senate Agriculture Committee was the Rural Development Act. This was a classic case of a program that helped the entire nation by specifically aiding rural areas. Basically, we were trying to attack two different but related problems—the exodus of people from the countryside and the decay of our nation's cities. The first of these problems began to appear in the late 1940's and had reached crisis proportions by the early 70's. In the twenty-five years immediately following World War II, thirty million people left our farms and villages for larger cities. As farming became more productive, it became profitable for fewer and fewer individuals. Consequently, communities that had depended on agricultural employment for their economic health began to decline. Rural folks either couldn't find jobs or were woefully underemployed. Youngsters who went off to college had no career opportunities to lure them back.

At the time we were drafting the Rural Development Act, about

125 young people were graduating from high school each year in Telfair County. Most left and never came back. Educating each of those kids through the twelfth grade and providing them with other government services cost the county about $5,000. So for every one hundred who left, the county lost an investment of $500,000. Telfair County and similar rural areas were exporting the capital they had invested in these young people along with some of their best educated and potentially most productive citizens. At the same time, they were also exporting some of their worst educated and least productive citizens, those who formerly would have been laborers on farms and in rural villages. They couldn't find jobs at home either.

So where did all these people go? To the cities, of course. Some of the better educated found careers in business or the professions. But quite a few of the others wound up on welfare, adding to the great urban plague of crime, pollution, narcotics, and overcrowding. Through a total lack of planning, we ended up with a situation in which seventy percent of the people were living on two percent of the land. Throughout the 1960's the only solution that had been offered to this problem was to pump billions of dollars into the cities ($160 billion, to be exact) to try to make them more livable. It was a noble effort, but the problems were always multiplying faster than the solutions. By the early seventies, the cities were worse off than they had been before we spent the first dollar. It was obvious to me that what we were trying to do was equivalent to damming up the Mississippi down around New Orleans with a structure that was sure to break apart, when it might have been easier and wiser to build a number of smaller dams upstream. Building those smaller dams was the focus of the Rural Development Act of 1972.

As chairman of the senate Agriculture Committee, I was one of the authors of the Rural Development Act, but a good deal of the credit for that bill must also go to Hubert Humphrey, who chaired a subcommittee on rural development. (I knew that Hubert would sometimes slough "unimportant" work off on his staff, so before I appointed him to chair this subcommittee, I asked him, "Hubert, will you work at this?" He said, "Herman, I will"; and he did.) The legislation that Hubert and I finally came up with began by defining "rural areas" as those with populations of no more than ten thousand, all of which were eligible for the full range of programs authorized by the act. Communities with populations between ten thousand and fifty thousand were eligible only for loans and grants for actual commercial and industrial development. At the time that the bill was passed, there were 13,200 communities of ten thousand or less in this country and more than 720 of ten to fifty thousand. All told, these communities contained nearly eighty million people.

The bill provided rural areas with grants and loans to help them develop industrial parks and related facilities. An even larger chunk of money went into the planning and building of water and sewage systems. We also started a program to test the feasibility of nationally coordinated fire protection in rural areas. As you can see, many of these initiatives were national-level versions of things I had done as Governor of Georgia. In our federal system of government the states are the laboratories where we test out new ideas to see if they work before instituting them nationwide. The success of the Rural Development Program lay in the fact that it was not wild social experimentation but only a means to help local communities put tested and proven policies to work. This couldn't have been done without assistance from the federal government. That is because our rural areas simply do not have enough equity and lending money for housing construction and business expansion. Nor do our towns and villages have the tax base to finance the civic improvements they so desperately need. What they do have are yeoman farmers and other solid country folk. All they needed was a chance to survive. And that's what the Rural Development Act gave them.

If I had an easy or simple solution to the farm problem in this country, I'd know what to tell the frightened people who call me early in the morning. I know that the more efficient farms will continue to flourish. That includes what is commonly called agribusiness, but also many smaller, family farms that are doing right well producing on a modest scale. In fact, quite a few farmers in America are making a profit. But those who are not are often in very dire straits. We can't save them all, nor should we try. What we can do is help some of the marginal farmers make the transition to other occupations where they can make a living. This is an area where rural development can continue to play a very constructive role. If a man is forced off the farm, he ought to be able to find employment in the community where he lives rather than have to pull up roots and face the squalor and anonymity of the big city. That may not be possible in each and every case, but it is the ideal we should be working toward.

The government must continue to help the farmer, but the best way to do that is to look at our agricultural policy and make damn sure that well-intentioned programs are not simply making matters worse. Assistance should be targeted to those most in need, not to wealthy weekend farmers or passive investors who are simply looking for a lucrative tax write-off. But even a thorough overhaul of farm programs is not going to solve the problem facing American agriculture. At best, those programs treat only the symptoms and not the cause of the problem. Nothing hurts the farmer more than an inadequate market for his products, and nothing would help him more than a larger market. Ironically, his productivity makes it virtually impossible to find that larger market in the United States. Only by feeding the hungry of the world can the American farmer continue to feed himself.

In our modern economy it is downright impossible to separate agriculture from foreign policy. Back in the early to mid-1970's, when the United States was a reliable exporter of food and a weak dollar made our products internationally competitive, the farmer lived well. Now, in addition to bad weather and mounting debt, he has to contend with shrinking overseas markets and an overvalued dollar. One of the best things Richard Nixon ever did was to sell American wheat to the Soviets. One of the worst things Jimmy Carter ever did was to declare a grain embargo. (Once you refuse to sell a product, for whatever reasons, your buyers start to look around for a more reliable supplier.) Also, for nationalistic purposes, there are far too many countries in the world that bar or restrict American agricultural imports. As long as we ignore economic reality and permit unilateral free trade, our balance of payments will suffer. We will continue to export industrial jobs overseas, and our farmers will continue to face bankruptcy and despair at home. But that needn't be the case. Fair trade is one issue on which the self interest of various sectors of the economy coincides with the national interest. We no longer need to be separated as labor and industry, farmers and city dwellers, Hamiltonians and Jeffersonians. We can come together as *Americans*—ready to be great again.

13

Permanent Interests

As the clerk of the Senate calls the roll, the vote is so close no one can be certain of the outcome. Radios are on all across the nation, as folks keep count to see if the magic number of sixty-seven can be reached. It hasn't been by the time the clerk gets to the T's. "Mr. Talmadge?" he says. Knowing it will probably be the most difficult vote I will cast in my career in the Senate, I say "Aye." I did it twice. Once on March 16, 1978, and again on April 18 of that year. I did it despite the fact that the vast majority of the American people and an even larger majority of Georgians wanted me to do otherwise. I did it despite a huge volume of mail urging me not to. Doing it went against my political instincts and personal predilections. But that didn't matter. There comes a time in every politician's career when he has to choose between the dictates of his constituents and the dictates of his conscience. When the issue involves national security, he better be sure that his conscience wins. Mine did when I voted for ratification of the Panama Canal Treaties.

DURING MY TWENTY-FOUR YEARS in the U.S. Senate, I had no direct role in formulating American foreign policy. I never served on the Foreign Relations or Armed Services Committees, and my advice on international affairs was rarely sought, except when the issue pertained to agriculture. But several times a year, matters of national security would be debated on the senate floor and a vote would be taken. So it behooved all of us senators to learn as much as we could about foreign policy, even if it wasn't our area of special interest. I knew this before I ever set foot in Washington. It's true that my political background had been as Governor of Georgia and that Georgia had no foreign policy. But I was a student of history, and I had seen international relations first-hand in the South Pacific during World War II. When I challenged Senator George, who was chairman of the Foreign Relations Committee, one of my major campaign issues was the wastefulness of our foreign aid program. And that was the topic of my first official speech in the Senate.

There's an old saying that war is too important to be left to the generals. Well, foreign policy is too important to be left to the foreign policy "experts." You have an entrenched bureaucracy in the State Department and the Foreign Service that remains substantially unchanged regardless of which party is in control of the White House and the Congress. These officials are sometimes referred to as the "permanent government," and elected politicians are often intimidated by them. These fellows are supposed to know so much more than we do that when they say the taxpayers ought to cough up tens of billions of dollars in foreign aid, it is easier to agree than to challenge them with mere common sense. But when the experts have their way on issue after issue, we begin to lose any semblance of representative government. And when I look at some of the messes those experts have gotten us into over the years, I'm convinced that we'd be better off turning our foreign policy over to a level-headed Georgia dirt farmer.

When I think of foreign policy, I remember a little aphorism that Charles De Gaulle always liked to quote: "France has no permanent friends. France has no permanent enemies. France has only permanent interests." That's the sort of philosophy that ought to guide American foreign policy, and it's the one I've always used in deciding how I would vote in matters of national security and international relations. Whether you're talking about arms control, terrorism, human rights, or anti-Communist insurgencies in Central America, the only question that needs to be asked is whether or not a given course of action furthers the permanent interests of the United States. We get off the track only when we lose sight of that principle or when we are so misguided by illusion or ideology that we forget what our permanent interests are.

I served in the Senate during the administrations of six American presidents—three Democrats and three Republicans. On the whole, I would say that the three Republicans steered a steadier course in foreign affairs. But this had more to do with the intellect and temperament of the men involved than with party affiliation. The first of these men, Dwight Eisenhower, was supposed to have been a great soldier who was out of his element in politics. What the folks who bought that stereotype didn't seem to realize was that any man who was Supreme Commander of the Allied Forces in World War II had to be one hell of an international politician. (David Eisenhower's recent book on his grandfather makes that point pretty convincingly.) Eisenhower ended the Korean War and projected an image of strength without involving American troops in any other conflict. He had the courage to act when necessary and, perhaps more important, the wisdom to know when not to. He was also the last American president to combine diplomatic respect abroad with a bi-partisan foreign policy at home.

Richard Nixon was Eisenhower's vice president and got a good deal of on-the-job training in foreign policy after Ike's nearly fatal heart attack forced him to delegate many of his presidential responsibilities. That experience served Nixon well when he finally won the presidency himself in 1968. Most American politicians are primarily interested in domestic issues. But not Richard Nixon. He thought the country could pretty much run itself domestically but needed a president for foreign policy. Nixon and his chief national security adviser Henry Kissinger were a couple of realists who had a pretty good grasp of where our permanent interests lay and did whatever was necessary to advance them. By cutting our losses in Vietnam and opening the door to Red China, Nixon helped box the Soviets in. When he was in the Navy in World War II, Nixon could sit at a poker table for so long that he got the nickname "Iron Butt." That same tenacity paid off time and again in his dealings with other heads of state.

When Jerry Ford replaced Nixon after the Watergate scandal, folks were mighty relieved that that whole sordid fracas was behind us. But the nation's foreign policy suffered. Watergate weakened the presidency and consumed so much of Nixon's time and attention that he wasn't able to enforce the terms of the Vietnam peace treaty. So instead of maintaining the sort of stalemate we had won in Korea, we had to sit in front of our televisions in April of 1975 and watch helicopters lifting off the roof of the American embassy in Saigon. Try as he would, poor Jerry Ford was powerless to do anything about it. In the post-Vietnam era Congress and the people were so sick of foreign entanglements that we just about withdrew from the world arena. The CIA was kicked around in public for being a clandestine organization (which is what it's supposed to be); countries all around the world were falling to Communism; and the same liberal politicians who had gotten us into Vietnam fifteen years earlier were warning us never to make the same mistake again. Of course, they hadn't the foggiest idea what the mistake really was and seemed to forget that they were the ones who had made it.

About the only thing Jerry Ford did to restore America's standing in the world was to send in the Marines to retake the Mayaguez when it was seized by Cambodia. (That was a real tonic after those helicopters in Saigon.) Of course, he did start the annual economic summits and helped expose the Soviets for the hypocrites they are by getting them to sign the Helsinki accords. But when folks think of Jerry's foreign policy, they're likely to remember his saying in a campaign debate with Carter that the Poles, who have been under Soviet domination since shortly after World War II, are a free and independent people. Jerry Ford was a decent man who did his best in a bad time. But for both good and ill, he was not another Nixon.

It is interesting to speculate on how the world might have been different had Nixon been elected president in 1960 instead of '68. But history is a record of what did happen, not what might have happened. It was John F. Kennedy, not Nixon, who took the oath of office on January 20, 1961. And we are still feeling the effects of what he did during the next one thousand days. But for the tragedy in Dallas, Jack Kennedy could have been a great president—or a total failure. As it is, he said and did some good things but also made some mighty blunders. If you read his inaugural address and other statements he made about Communism, he sounds more like Ronald Reagan than he does the liberals of today (and that includes his own brother Ted Kennedy). Like Reagan, Jack Kennedy knew that the Soviets are indeed an evil empire, that dealing with them is not like dealing with a political opponent at home. (In the 1960 election he took a harder line than Nixon, running against the so-called "missile gap" and advocating the armed overthrow of Castro in Cuba.) But like Reagan, Jack found that the tough talk and grand commitments had to give way to reality. Kennedy stood up to the Communists in such places as Cuba, Berlin, and Vietnam. And yet, when the dust had settled, the world was a little less free than before. I suspect that Nixon would have promised less and delivered more.

One fellow who made a habit of promising more than he could deliver was Kennedy's successor as president—Lyndon Johnson. Now, politically Lyndon could always deliver the goods, whether it be votes on a bill or funding for a program. But because he was such a consummate politician, he thought there was a political solution to every problem. That's where he got into trouble both at home and abroad. If there were poverty and racism in this country, he figured he could eliminate the one with federal programs and the other with federal laws. If the Communists were making inroads in Southeast Asia, he figured that a show of American force would bring them to heel. Lyndon had little patience with problems that might take a long time to solve and simply refused to admit that politics might not be the answer to every human dilemma. His one notable success in foreign policy was the invasion of the Dominican Republic. Like Reagan's little foray into Grenada, it was quick, decisive, and not too costly in either blood or treasure. In other words, it was pretty much the opposite of Vietnam.

The last man to serve as president during my years in Washington, and the first to serve a full term in the post-Vietnam era, was Jimmy Carter. When Carter took office, two of the lessons we were supposed to have learned from Vietnam were that it was pointless to try to use military force to contain Communism and that it was immoral to back right-wing dictatorships simply because they were pro-American. As a result, the Soviets and their various surrogates ran roughshod over a passel of Latin American and third world countries, and free-lance thugs like Somoza and the Shah of Iran were replaced by even more dangerous fanatics like Daniel Ortega and the Ayatollah Khomeini. A foreign policy dedicated to world peace and human rights produced less of both because our leaders acted as if they believed an "inordinate fear of Communism" was worse than Communism itself. On matters that required attention to detail, such as the Panama Canal Treaties and the Camp David accords, Carter scored impressive triumphs. His mistakes came on broad policy issues. Some might say that he couldn't see the forest for the trees. It would be more accurate to say that he saw a forest that really wasn't there.

One region where the permanent interests of this country have been in jeopardy for the past thirty years is Latin America. Back in the early part of the last century, President James Monroe warned any European power that might be thinking about it that we wouldn't take too kindly to any colonization in this hemisphere. When Spain tried to call our bluff in Cuba at the turn of the century, Teddy Roosevelt and the Rough Riders showed the world that America keeps its solemn commitments. Unfortunately, when Castro came to power in Cuba half a century later, we were lulled into thinking that he was a democratic leader, not the agent of a foreign power. Anyone who looked at the man's background could have seen his ties to Soviet Communism. But American liberals figured that since Castro had overthrown a dictator, he must be another George Washington. By the time folks realized he was infinitely worse than what he had replaced, Castro had established a Soviet beachhead ninety miles south of Key West. Eisenhower could see that the only way that menace would be removed was through armed force. It's just too bad that Ike didn't stay in office long enough to see us through a D-Day in Cuba.

Whatever virtues he may have possessed, Jack Kennedy was

not in the same league with Eisenhower as a military strategist. He bought a flawed invasion plan from the CIA and then botched even that by calling off air support at the last minute. Many brave men were betrayed to death or prison, and Cuba remained unliberated. But the worst geopolitical consequence of the Bay of Pigs fiasco was that Castro and his Russian sugar daddies figured that the Monroe Doctrine didn't apply to them. Within a year and a half they had offensive missiles installed in Cuba and pointing at us. They must have assumed that if Kennedy had lost his nerve over conventional air support in the spring of '61, he was unlikely to go to the brink of nuclear war in the fall of '62. Thank God, they were wrong.

I was down in Brazil attending a NATO conference during the Cuban Missile Crisis, so I must have been one of the few Americans who didn't think that the end of the world was around the corner. At the conference, we got reports of what was happening, but without the hysterical interpretations of the U.S. news media. Looking back on that crucial week some twenty-five years later, I have to give Jack Kennedy high marks for staying cool under enormous pressure and, in the process, atoning for his behavior at the Bay of Pigs. (It was sort of like a grade-B war movie, where the nervous kid turns tail and runs in the first reel, only to find his courage and save his platoon by the end of the film.) But the deal he had to strike with Khrushchev got the missiles out while leaving Castro in. And the combined forces of the CIA and the American underworld were never sufficient to restore Cuba to a pro-American despotism. We couldn't even manage to slip Castro an exploding cigar or something to make his beard fall out.

We continue to suffer from the legacy of that Bay of Pigs debacle. Castro is firmly entrenched in Cuba, spreading subversion from there all over the hemisphere and sending mercenaries as far away as Africa. As a result, the Monroe Doctrine has become more a historic curiosity than a living document. Had we removed Castro in 1961, the missiles never would have come into Cuba in 1962. And we wouldn't have had to promise to leave Castro alone in order to get them out. The current debate over aiding the anti-Communist freedom fighters in Nicaragua is a result of the failure of our policy in Cuba. Also, the Soviets have drawn the reasonable conclusion that if we can't stop them from colonizing less than one hundred miles from our shores, we can't stop them anywhere. Cuba was the first Communist country not geographically connected to another Communist country. But it has not been the last. And if the Sandinistas stay in power, it won't even be the last in this hemisphere.

Advancing our permanent interests does not mean fighting everywhere. We are a great and powerful country, but we are not omnipotent. And as our liberal friends never tire of reminding us, we can't afford to be the world's policeman. (Bill Fulbright put it best when he said that the United States government has no proper quarrel with any country's domestic policies, no matter how obnoxious, just so long as it doesn't try to export them.) Sometimes the pragmatic, diplomatic, and *self-serving* thing to do is to be conciliatory toward a potential adversary. That's the course of action that Jimmy Carter and his three immediate predecessors took toward the Republic of Panama. And it resulted in a treaty arrangement that is serving our national interests.

Americans are justifiably proud of the Panama Canal. For its time, it was such a marvel of engineering that some folks took to calling it the eighth wonder of the world. We had built it and paid for it and had every moral and legal right to keep it. But our national interest lay in maintaining access to the canal, not in asserting sovereignty over it. I had been through the Panama Canal during World War II, and I knew that it was located in jungle territory where a few guerillas could hide and completely sabotage its operations. There's no telling how many Marines it would take to keep that canal open if the Republic of Panama didn't feel like cooperating with us. And the nationalistic feeling was running so high down there that turning the canal over to the Panamanians was the price we would have to pay for their cooperation.

As I've already mentioned, the people of Georgia were dead set against our relinquishing a square inch of American soil—especially if it meant giving in to blackmail. (Old Rudyard Kipling put the matter well when he said, "If once you have paid him the Danegeld/You are never rid of the Dane.") Perhaps the issue would have stirred less controversy had it come up thirty years earlier, when the United States was strong and proud. But after losing Cuba and being humiliated in Vietnam, we had lost something of our strength and pride. To many, "giving away" the Panama Canal seemed like the last straw. And in letter after letter, my constituents told me just that. When President Carter first asked me how I would vote on the treaties, I told him that I might hold my nose and vote "yes," but I wasn't ready to make up my mind yet. I suspect that quite a few of my colleagues felt the same way.

Although I had no role in drafting the Panama Canal Treaties, which were passed on March 16 and April 18, 1978, and took no relish in voting for them, they might not have become law had I yielded to political expediency and opposed them. First of all, it took sixty-seven votes in the Senate to ratify the treaties. When the roll was called, sixty-eight senators voted "aye." Had I gone the other way, several other Southern Democrats might have followed suit. (For example, my Georgia colleague Sam Nunn was very much interested in how I would vote.) On the merits of the case, the treaties should have won substantial, if not enthusiastic, support. But politicians who are not contemplating early retirement usually find survival more attractive than martyrdom. These days it's hard to find anyone who has much good to say about Jimmy Carter's presidency, but his handling of the Panama Canal Treaties was a diplomatic and political marvel only slightly less impressive than the canal itself.

Although I disagreed with Jimmy on a good number of issues, I can't help but think that he got too much blame for his failures and too little credit for his successes. This is particularly true of his foreign policy. It is probably the greatest irony of Carter's career that he was turned out of office because of something that happened in the Middle East. When folks went to the polls in 1980, they were hopping mad that our hostages had been in Iran for over a year. Had the rescue mission succeeded back in April of that year (even with loss of life), Carter would have been hailed as a strong president and probably reelected. After all, he began rebuilding our defenses, played the "China card" adroitly, and negotiated an arms control agreement that it took Ronald Reagan six years to repudiate. But all of that was much less vivid in people's minds than the images of blindfolded hostages and desecrated American flags we saw on the nightly news. It didn't even seem to matter that two years earlier Carter had helped to construct a framework for peace in the Middle East with the miracle of Camp David.

If you look at the way the public responded to Carter's policy in the Middle East and the way it's responding to Reagan's, you'd have to conclude that dead Americans are a far more valuable political commodity than live ones. Not only did all of the hostages in Iran come back alive, but fewer Americans died at the hands of hostile powers under Carter than at any time since the administration of Herbert Hoover. Hundreds have been murdered by Middle Eastern terrorists since Reagan took office. By some perverse logic, that makes Reagan a strong leader and Carter a wimp. I bring this out not to deify Carter or to condemn Reagan, but to suggest that the record future historians will look at may be different from what know-it-all political pundits have to say on TV talk shows. When history has scraped the Teflon off of Ronald Reagan and hosed the tar-and-feathers off of Jimmy Carter, we may see that both were very human men who did their best in the most dangerous and lonely job a person could ever hold.

One of the major problems with American foreign policy during this century is that we have swung back and forth too often between a couple of radically different philosophies about how to deal with other nations. One philosophy, which is commonly called internationalism, would have the United States trying to run the world either through military or diplomatic means. Theodore Roosevelt and Woodrow Wilson popularized that approach and accomplished a great deal with it. But internationalism almost always promises more than it can deliver. (World War I, after all, did *not* make the world safe for democracy.) It is one thing to say that we want to see freedom prosper everywhere in the world. It is quite another to say, as Jack Kennedy did in his

244

inaugural address, that, "We shall pay any price, bear any burden, meet any hardship, support any friend, oppose any foe to assure the survival and success of liberty." It's stirring words like those that sent Cuban freedom fighters to their death at the Bay of Pigs, that got the citizens of Free Berlin to thinking we'd tear down that hideous wall, and that gives oppressed people everywhere the false hope that America will risk nuclear war to save them from Communist aggression.

Whenever internationalism gets us into too much trouble, we are usually in for a spell of its opposite—isolationism. After Theodore Roosevelt planted the American flag all over the world, William Howard Taft quietly dismantled much of that empire. After Woodrow Wilson negotiated the Treaty of Versailles, the Republicans in the U.S. Senate refused to ratify it. What followed Wilson was a period of isolation that didn't really end until the Japanese bombed Pearl Harbor. Then for about twenty years after World War II (including my first decade in the Senate), Americans agreed on a bi-partisan return to Wilsonian internationalism. It gave us the United Nations (which is just an updated version of the League of Nations), the CIA, and the Korean War. It also caused Dwight Eisenhower to send Air Force technicians to Indo-China to service American planes being used by the French. At the time, Dick Russell warned that that action might lead to "piecemeal United States involvement in the war there." That was in 1954. Ten years later, the Gulf of Tonkin Resolution gave us just such an involvement, followed by a new wave of isolationism that has made bi-partisan foreign policy a thing of the past.

Like Dick Russell, I had grave reservations about U.S. involvement in a ground war in Asia. Granted, we had to challenge Communist expansion somewhere, but Cuba seemed of more strategic importance than Vietnam. If the Vietnamese could outlast the French, who had colonial ties there, they could certainly outlast the Americans, who had only an ideological commitment. And Dick Russell and I were not the only ones who thought that way. Two of our most heroic generals from World War II, James Gavin and Matthew Ridgeway, warned against a military involvement in Vietnam. So did newspaper reporters and diplomats who were close enough to the scene to know what was going on.

And surprisingly, so did senate majority leader Lyndon Johnson. I have no way of knowing what Eisenhower would have done had he remained in office during the sixties, but our subsequent policy in Vietnam was, in one sense, an escalation of commitments he made in the fifties. And once those commitments had been made, it was the duty of every patriotic American to close ranks behind our commander-in-chief. As Dick Russell put it, "Where the American flag is committed, I am committed."

If escalation in Vietnam was not initially the idea of military men or conservative politicians, you might wonder how we got so heavily involved there by the mid-sixties. There is no simple answer to that question, but part of the answer lies in the difficulty of pursuing liberal internationalism in a nuclear age. We were to make the world safe for democracy, but not at the risk of nuclear war. To fight in Cuba or Berlin or Hungary or Czechoslovakia would have been to invite a confrontation with the Soviets. That didn't seem to be the case in Vietnam. We needed only to keep the Chinese at bay, as we had in Korea, and pretend that the Vietnamese peasants were Jeffersonian agrarians. Douglas MacArthur once said that in war there is no substitute for victory. The major flaw in our Vietnam policy (other than being there in the first place) was that we were always looking for a substitute for victory. And we eventually found one—defeat.

At the same time that Vietnam was splitting the country at large, it was also dividing the Democratic caucus in the U.S. Senate. When the Gulf of Tonkin Resolution was passed authorizing President Lyndon Johnson to widen the war, only Wayne Morse and Ernest Gruening voted against it. But over the next two years, the anti-war bloc in the Senate grew, as more and more of Lyndon's former allies and proteges turned against him. Among Southern Democrats, the most notable defection was Bill Fulbright of Arkansas. Bill was a Rhodes Scholar and a former president of the University of Arkansas. He had come to the Senate in 1944 (four years before Lyndon) and had accumulated enough seniority to become chairman of the Foreign Relations Committee. Although he voted with the Southern bloc on civil rights, Bill was pretty liberal on most other issues. For that reason, Lyndon considered him a friend and felt betrayed when Bill had his committee conducting a televised inquiry into Vietnam from the Caucus Room of the Old Senate Office Building. Harry Truman had once called Fulbright an "over-educated son of a bitch." God knows what Lyndon must have called him.

At the beginning of our involvement, Lyndon had been far more skeptical about Vietnam than Jack Kennedy had. It's anyone's guess as to whether he would have gone in there the way that Kennedy did had he been elected in his own right in 1960. But having inherited a war, Lyndon wasn't about to admit that he couldn't finish what Kennedy had started. Also, Vietnam revealed an aspect of Lyndon's character that would have taken most Americans by surprise—his deep sense of intellectual inferiority. Here he was, the graduate of a little known teachers college in Texas, associating with scholars and eggheads from America's top universities. If fellows like McGeorge Bundy, Walt Rostow, Dean Rusk, and Bob McNamara told him that a limited war could bring freedom to South Vietnam and stability to a region that would otherwise go Communist, Lyndon nodded in agreement and sent more troops. Had he gone with his gut instinct rather than listening to the "experts" on Vietnam, Lyndon might have served another four years in office. As it was, he left the White House branded an appeaser by the Right and a war criminal by the Left.

One measure of the effect of Vietnam on American politics is the fact that Richard Nixon, who had lost the presidency to Jack Kennedy by a narrow margin in 1960 and the governorship of California to Pat Brown by a wide one in 1962, made it to the White House in 1968. Six years after he had held what he called his "last press conference," Nixon was leader of the free world. At that point, he began to wind down the war that Johnson had escalated, while making other—more astute—initiatives in foreign policy. Unlike his 1968 presidential opponent, Hubert Humphrey, Nixon was not publicly identified with Johnson on the war. And his reputation as a hardliner on national security made it unnecessary for him to prove his toughness the way Kennedy felt he had to. As for intellect, Nixon had his own resident egghead in Henry Kissinger. On the eve of the 1972 election, Nixon was able to announce that peace was at hand, and he carried all but one of the fifty states. The sixties had given us Kennedy's assassination and Johnson's withdrawal from politics. But when Richard Nixon was sworn in to his second term in office, it looked as if the American presidency was at last in firm and capable hands.

14

A Third-Rate Burglary

One day during the early part of 1973, I was sitting in my senate office when I got a call from the majority leader, Mike Mansfield. The first thing he said when I picked up the phone was, "Herman, will you serve on the Watergate Committee?" That sort of took me aback. I knew that such a committee was being formed, but I certainly didn't see myself as a prospective member. So I said: "Mike, as you know, I'm already carrying a pretty heavy load. I'm chairman of the senate Agriculture Committee, vice chairman of the Finance Committee, chairman of the sub-committee on health of the Finance Committee, and a member of the Joint Committee on Internal Revenue and Taxation and the Democratic Policy Committee." Well, Mike just came back as if I hadn't even opened my mouth and asked again, "Herman, will you serve on the Watergate Committee?" I said, "Mike, since you put it that way, how can I refuse?"

AS YOU CAN TELL, I wasn't exactly eager to accept that assignment Mike was offering me. In fact, I was put in mind of a story Abraham Lincoln used to tell about a fellow who was tarred and feathered and ridden out of town on a rail. "If it wasn't for the honor of the thing," he said, "I'd just as soon walk." Everyone in Washington knew that on June 17, 1972, five burglars had been caught in the office of Democratic Party chairman Larry O'Brien in the Watergate complex. It was later discovered that they were working under the direction of E. Howard Hunt and G. Gordon Liddy, a couple of low-level officials in President Richard Nixon's reelection committee. In the fall campaign, Nixon's Democratic opponent, George McGovern, had tried to make an issue out of this incident. But nobody paid much attention to him. Political espionage is as old as politics itself. It was inconceivable that anyone higher than Hunt and Liddy could have been involved in that stupid and pointless break-in. Anyone who knew anything about politics agreed with Nixon's press secretary Ron Zeigler when he called the whole escapade a "third-rate burglary."

Although I had endorsed Scoop Jackson for president, I wasn't very heavily involved in the 1972 campaign. Still, I had known Richard Nixon and George McGovern for most of my years in Washington and had definite impressions of those two men. In different ways, I liked them both. Nixon was vice president when I entered the Senate in January, 1957, and he had administered my oath of office. He was too busy running around the world for Eisenhower to spend much time presiding over the Senate, but my relationship with him was always pleasant. He actively courted the South in 1968 and made several overtures in our direction during his first administration. With the exception of his Family Assistance Plan, I thought that his policies as president were sound, and he seemed a good bet for reelection in 1972.

Nixon had had his share of political setbacks, but he always struck me as a shrewd and canny politician. I couldn't believe that he would do anything as stupid as to try to steal an election he had already won. Domestically, folks were worried about inflation, but they didn't have much confidence that the Democrats could bring it under control. And on the foreign policy front, Nixon's record was right impressive. His credentials as an anti-Communist made it possible for him to withdraw from Vietnam and make an opening to China. Also, Georgians appreciated the fact that he had twice tried to appoint a Southerner to the U.S. Supreme Court. And we loved those liberal-bashing speeches of his vice president, Spiro Agnew. Nixon would always be a

Yankee, but he was *trying* awful hard to act like a Southerner. The only way he could lose the South in '72 would be if the Democrats nominated George Wallace.

Philosophically, I was much closer to Richard Nixon than I was to George McGovern, but I knew George a lot better personally. It would be hard to find a more affable, sweet tempered man. He distinguished himself as administrator of Kennedy's Food for Peace program in 1961-62 and then came to the Senate from South Dakota in 1963. For the next seventeen years, George and I served on the Agriculture Committee together, until both of us were defeated for reelection in the Reagan landslide of 1980. George was a hard worker, and he and I were in almost complete agreement on agricultural issues. Based on his war record, I would also judge him to be a patriotic American. He flew a number of bombing missions during World War II, while Nixon was learning how to play poker aboard ship and Kennedy was getting his PT boat rammed by a Japanese destroyer. But this was not the George McGovern people saw in 1972.

I don't know whether it was his experiences in the war or his being a preacher's son that did it, but George was so devoted to the ideal of peace that he blinded himself to the reality of World Communism. He supported Henry Wallace in 1948 and acted as if the only obstacle to peace on earth was the American military. I'm sure that he disapproved of the way the Soviets treated their own people, but he seemed to feel that they would behave much better internationally if we'd just be a little nicer to them. It's the old theory of feeding the tiger in the hope that he'll eat you last. The majority of the American people rejected the Henry Wallace-George McGovern approach to foreign policy in 1948 and have continued to reject it ever since. But when Vietnam became a burning issue in the late sixties and early seventies, a vocal *minority* did start to take that extreme pacifist line. When they began looking around for a leader, there was George ready to head the parade.

To this day folks are still puzzled how a non-charismatic fringe candidate from a sparsely populated state like South Dakota could have become the standardbearer of the nation's majority party. The fact that he wrote the rules by which the party selected its candidate didn't hurt. After all the dissension at the 1968 convention in Chicago, the Democrats figured they needed to assure certain interest groups that they would be more fully represented at future conventions. So George was appointed to head up a committee to rewrite the rules for delegate selection. Not surprisingly, the new rules were heavily tilted toward George's kind of people. For example, Charles Kirbo, who was state party chairman in Georgia and a prominent Atlanta attorney, was defeated in his race for delegate by an eighteen-year-old unwed mother.

The other presidential candidates in 1972 were all playing by the old rules. Take Ed Muskie. He went around getting endorsements from as many prominent politicians as he could find. (He would have been better off working the unwed mothers.) The bosses and elected officials were backing Ed because they liked the fact that his philosophy was close to Hubert Humphrey's, while he lacked some of Hubert's liabilities. You know, the anti-Vietnam crowd never forgave Hubert for publicly backing Johnson's war policies. Muskie backed those same policies, but as a senator from Maine, not as vice president. (Obscurity sometimes has its advantages.) Whereas Hubert seemed a little too bubbly and emotional, Ed was earnest, maybe a little plodding. Hubert reminded folks of a boy scout, Ed of a scout master. Ed's appeal lay in his image as a dispassionate, thoughtful fellow. Unfortunately, that image was shattered when he lost control and began sobbing during a speech in the New Hampshire primary. (The editor of the *Manchester Union-Leader* had printed some unkind gossip about Ed's wife.) When your appeal depends on image, you have nothing to fall back on when the image is gone. The Muskie bandwagon pulled out of New Hampshire with nobody left aboard.

After New Hampshire, Muskie took a beating in the Florida primary and effectively pulled out of the race. Many of the people who had been supporting him switched over to Hubert, whose campaign was beginning to pick up steam. There were all sorts of minor candidates who had been in the race for part of that year (Shirley Chisholm, Wilbur Mills, Scoop Jackson, Fred Harris, Sam Yorty, Vance Hartke, Gene McCarthy, and Milton Shapp) and others who had considered running and then thought better of it (principally Birch Bayh and Harold Hughes). So as the campaign wore on, it began to shape up as a three-man race, with George McGovern on the left, George Wallace on the right, and Hubert Humphrey in the middle (the fact that Hubert could be regarded as a middle-of-the-roader said a lot about how far the Democrats had moved to the left). When Wallace was shot and paralyzed while campaigning at a Maryland shopping center, that pretty much narrowed the race down to Hubert and McGovern.

From 1948 on, the Democratic Party has moved to the left politically and to the north geographically. (In 1964, the Goldwater campaign started pulling conservative Southern Democrats into the Republican Party, and that trend continued with the "Southern strategy" Nixon pursued in 1968.) Of course, in politics whenever one group takes power, its members eventually start to squabbling among themselves. That's what happened to the liberal Democrats in the late sixties and early seventies. One faction backed Lyndon Johnson on the Vietnam War, and the other opposed the war. When Lyndon dropped out of the 1968 race, that pretty much left Hubert leading the first faction and Bobby Kennedy the second. The anti-war folks did look to Gene McCarthy to carry their banner when Bobby was still trying to make up his mind about running for president, but Gene never had enough fire in his belly to lead a political movement for very long. With him out of the picture and Bobby dead from an assassin's bullet, the anti-war left needed someone to rally behind in 1972. The logical choice would have been Bobby's younger brother, Ted Kennedy.

Teddy may have been the runt of the litter, but there was a huge political advantage to being the heir of *two* martyred brothers. The fact that one of those brothers had made the initial commitment of troops to Vietnam and the other had supported the war until shortly before he started running for president didn't affect the Kennedy myth any more than Jack's spotty senate record on civil rights had. (In 1960 the Kennedys had been to the right of Hubert Humphrey, but now they were to his left, even though Hubert had finally come to oppose the war.) The leadership of the anti-war Democrats and perhaps the nomination itself seemed Ted Kennedy's for the asking. But among his senate colleagues, there were serious questions about Ted's personal habits—specifically his drinking, driving, and womanizing. Now, there had always been a tacit understanding within the Washington press and among fellow politicians that a man's personal life was his own business as long as it didn't affect his ability to perform in office. Washington was filled with men who liked to drink and run around. Everyone knew that Jack Kennedy had an eye for the ladies, and Estes Kefauver had hung his coonskin cap on a few bedroom walls. But Teddy didn't even bother to be discreet about his shenanigans. It was almost as if he were playing Russian Roulette with a loaded gun, hoping it would go off. On July 18, 1969, it did.

That Chappaquiddick tragedy occurred on what should have been a weekend of triumph for the Kennedys. One of the few initiatives of Jack's administration that had not gone sour was the space program. That program achieved its historic goal when Neil Armstrong stepped onto the surface of the moon the night after Ted Kennedy drove off the bridge at Chappaquiddick. So instead of clamoring for a return to Camelot, folks started comparing Teddy's panic with the calm of the astronauts or even with Jack's resourcefulness back in the days of PT-109. Teddy's 1972 campaign, and perhaps his prospects for ever becoming president, died with Mary Jo Kopechne. Almost by default, George McGovern inherited the support that would have gone to Teddy. With Muskie, Wallace, and the also-rans out of the race, it came down to a confrontation between Hubert and McGovern in the California primary. When McGovern won that primary, he locked up the nomination and assured Richard Nixon's reelection.

While Nixon was busy putting together new coalitions for the Republicans, McGovern was just as busy tearing old ones apart for the Democrats. It was not enough that he had completed the job of turning the South from solidly Democratic to solidly Republican; he also alienated organized labor, Jews, urban political organizations in the North, and rank-and-file party members. What he had left was the solid support of hippies, homosexuals, draft card burners, bird watchers, and radical feminists. They put on such a show at the convention in Miami Beach that George didn't even get around to giving his acceptance speech until three in the morning. At that time, the only people who were up were insomniacs and early risers. From what I hear, George's speech was enough to cure the insomniacs and send the early risers back to bed.

His campaign had hardly gotten under way before it was revealed that his running mate, Thomas Eagleton, had been treated for psychological problems. (The fact that he agreed to run with George caused some people to wonder if he had been fully cured.) The first month of George's general election campaign was spent getting rid of Eagleton and trying to find someone willing to take his place. By the time Sargent Shriver agreed to do so, the only question remaining was how badly George would lose. As it turned out, he carried only Washington, D.C., and Massachusetts. So when George claimed that the election had been stolen from him at Watergate, it was about like a last place baseball team claiming it had lost the pennant because of some bum call an umpire had made in the early innings of a mid-season game.

With Nixon's landslide reelection, the end of American involvement in Vietnam, and the return of our POW's, Watergate wasn't exactly at the top of the national agenda as we headed into 1973. But Mike Mansfield was eager to see that scandal fully investigated and got the Senate to pass a resolution setting up a select committee to do so. Mike had several good reasons for going this route rather than entrusting the matter to one of the standing committees. For one thing, the whole range of presidential campaign activities, which is actually what the resolution charged us with investigating, cut across the jurisdiction of several of the standing committees. For another, Mike wanted this investigation to appear as fair and non-partisan as possible. All of the relevant standing committees had members who might be open to the charge of partisanship just because of who they were. Now, the Republican leader Hugh Scott could use any criteria he wanted to pick the three minority members of the select committee, but Mike Mansfield set himself pretty rigid guidelines in appointing the four Democrats. Principally, he was bound and determined to find the four least likely to be running for president.

I accepted my appointment to the committee because I couldn't very well turn down a personal request from my majority leader, and I figured that the whole thing would be over in a few weeks. The first hint we got that that might not be the case came on Friday, March 23, 1973. That was the day that Judge John Sirica was scheduled to sentence Hunt and Liddy and the five Watergate burglars. On Tuesday of that week, James McCord, a former CIA agent and one of the five burglars, had written a letter to Judge Sirica. Without coming right out and saying it, McCord implied that Hunt and Liddy were not the highest officials connected with the burglary, and he stated categorically that political pressure had been exerted to keep the defendants silent and to cover up important facts in the case. Since McCord was being encouraged by Judge Sirica and his probation officer to come clean, there was a good chance of his testifying before our committee. I thought that might make an otherwise boring assignment a little more interesting.

Burglary was a daily, even an hourly, occurrence in Washington, D.C. But Jim McCord was not your typical second-story man. From all appearances he was a patriotic American. He had served his country faithfully for thirty years—first in the Army Air Corps during World War II, later as an FBI agent, and finally for nineteen years as a security officer with the CIA. He now worked with Nixon's reelection committee, but more out of conviction than political ambition. Common sense said that a man like McCord wouldn't be mixed up in this sleazy burglary unless he thought he was serving some higher national purpose. But what was that purpose? What exactly were those five men looking for in Larry O'Brien's office? Only a full-scale investigation could reveal the answer.

That investigation was being run by the man who had been hired as the committee's chief counsel, Sam Dash. At first glance, Sam was not a physically intimidating man. He was a mousy little college professor with a balding head and glasses. But when he started in to questioning a witness, he was a real tiger. He took a right serious attitude toward his job and conducted a thorough investigation. At times, it seemed almost too thorough, dragging out longer than any of us had anticipated. But then, as the case unravelled, it got to be bigger than even Sam could have predicted. My concern was that we get the facts of the case without making a damn circus out of the investigation. The Kefauver hearings had been bad enough, but the image of the Senate had been permanently damaged by the McCarthy witch hunts back in the mid-fifties. The last thing we needed was a partisan vendetta that could be written off as McCarthyism of the left. I knew that Sam Dash would be fair. The only question was whether he could control the young Turks he had hired to conduct the investigation.

Sam divided the investigation into three phases. The first was to deal with the Watergate break-in and coverup, the second with dirty tricks in the campaign, and the third with political financing. Sam appointed Jim Hamilton to head up the first phase, Dave Dorsen the second, and Terry Lenzer the third. I had confidence in the first two men, particularly in Jim Hamilton, who was a mature and level-headed fellow and a fine lawyer. However, Terry Lenzer was another matter. Since he had been fired from the Nixon Justice Department, there was an apparent conflict of interest in his being on the committee's investigating staff at all. He had a long history of involvement with left-wing causes and had been one of the attorneys representing the Berrigan brothers. From day one, Lenzer was out to hang somebody, and it didn't matter who it was so long as it was a Nixon loyalist, if not the president himself.

Sam Dash's Republican counterpart was a young fellow from Nashville by the name of Fred Thompson. Physically, he and Sam were about as different as any two men could possibly be. Fred was a big, hulking fellow who put you in mind of Hoss Cartwright on the "Bonanza" television program. He handled himself well for being only thirty years old. Like so many Southerners of his generation, Fred had grown up in a Democratic home but had switched to the Republicans in the sixties. He had campaigned for Richard Nixon and believed in the president's innocence. He figured that the best interests of the Republicans would be served if he could keep the investigation from turning into a lynching without looking as if he wanted to make it into a whitewash. He could show flashes of temper from time to time, but he didn't have the prosecutorial intensity of Sam Dash. Fred would sit back, puffing on his pipe, taking everything in. Then he'd ask some pertinent question in a pleasant Southern drawl. Republican though he was, I felt a lot closer to Fred than to the likes of Terry Lenzer.

That select committee was an interesting cross-section of the Senate. We had an Hispanic (Joe Montoya of New Mexico), a Japanese American (Danny Inouye of Hawaii), four Southerners (Chairman Sam Ervin of North Carolina, Vice Chairman Howard Baker of Tennessee, Florida senator Ed Gurney, and myself), and a New England Brahmin (Lowell Weicker of Connecticut). Two of these men were injured veterans of World War II—Gurney walked with a limp because of artillery wounds in his legs, and Inouye had lost his right arm on the Italian front. On the Republican side, there were two future presidential candidates in Baker and Weicker. Mike Mansfield, however, had succeeded in his effort to find the four Democrats least likely to aspire to higher office.

I'm not exactly sure why Joe Montoya was appointed to that committee. He was as nice and friendly a man as you would ever want to meet, but he was hardly a skilled interrogator. Joe had spent his entire adult life in politics. He had been elected to the New Mexico state legislature in 1936, when he was twenty-one years old and a senior at the Georgetown University law school. He spent the next twelve years serving in both houses of the legislature and the eight years after that as Lieutenant Governor of New Mexico. He came to Congress in 1957 and to the Senate in 1964. While he was pursuing a political career and maintaining a law practice, he became the sole owner of Western Van Lines. Joe spoke Spanish fluently and was something of an expert on Latin America. Someone has suggested that Sam Ervin and Mike Mansfield put him on the committee because most of the Watergate burglars were Cubans. I don't know if that's true, but he did correct our pronunciation of Spanish terms on a number of occasions.

Because Joe was such a warm and decent fellow, it was downright embarrassing to watch him during those hearings. We all had staff assistance in preparing for the questioning of witnesses, but we were also able to improvise when a question we had intended to ask had already been answered or a new line of inquiry developed. With Joe it was almost as if he hadn't heard any of the previous testimony. He'd just read the questions his staff had typed for him on three-by-five cards, ignoring what had gone before and not following up on what the witness was saying to him. Those of us who cared for Joe felt like you do when a dear friend is giving a serious speech with his fly open, and there's no way you can get his attention. They say that whenever Joe's turn came to question a witness, the water level in the country would drop because folks watching on TV would take the opportunity to go to the bathroom.

Fortunately, the other three Democrats on the committee were a lot more effective than Joe. Danny Inouye, for example, had been a deputy public prosecutor in Honolulu and knew how to make a witness squirm. Although he was a liberal Democrat, anyone launching a partisan attack on Daniel K. Inouye usually ended up looking like a bigot and a know-nothing. Two months after his seventeenth birthday, Danny and his family were getting ready to attend an early morning church service when they heard that the Japanese had bombed Pearl Harbor. Less than a year later Danny was in the 100th Infantry Batallion in Europe, and his family was in a government internment camp. In the Po Valley in Italy, Danny helped lead an assault on a hill that was heavily defended by the German infantry. He personally eliminated two machine gun crews with grenades before the krauts put him out of action. Danny lost his right arm because of injuries he suffered that day. He received the Distinguished Service Cross for his role in the Po Valley attack and three purple hearts for wounds he incurred in other battles. When he retired from active duty he had risen to the rank of captain. So you can understand why folks didn't take too kindly to John Ehrlichman's lawyer referring to Danny as "that little Jap."

In a way, though, you have to sympathize with any lawyer whose client is being grilled by Danny Inouye. Danny was so cool and self confident that he put his adversaries ill at ease. He was a physically striking man who was named in one poll as the sexiest member of our committee. (For what it's worth, I was voted the most intelligent.) And he had a perfect voice for the airwaves. You would have thought it belonged to a disc jockey on an easy-listening radio station. Except that what he had to say was anything but laid-back. He could pursue a line of questioning without relying on his notes, getting off the track, or playing to the crowd. He did such a professional job that the syndicated columnists and political experts thought he was the second most effective man on the committee. Modesty constrains me from saying who they thought was the first.

Over on the Republican side of the table, you had the two most partisan members of the committee, only they were partisans of different causes. Lowell Weicker was doing his best to attack the Nixon administration, and Ed Gurney was trying just as hard to defend it. In fact, Gurney was so obviously carrying water for the president that he quickly destroyed his credibility and effectiveness. Many people watching those hearings probably believed that Ed was part of the cover-up. That was unfortunate. Like tens of millions of Americans, Ed Gurney believed in Richard Nixon's innocence and thought that the Watergate investigation was simply an attempt by the president's enemies to blame him for the misconduct of some of his low-level subordinates. Gurney was a native of New England who had moved to Florida and become the first Republican senator elected from that state since Reconstruction. If nothing else, his spirited defense of the White House helped keep our investigation honest.

If Joe Montoya was the least effective member of our committee, Lowell Weicker was the most obnoxious. At 6'6" and 250 pounds, Lowell is the biggest man in the Senate. But he doesn't look rugged like Fred Thompson. He's got too much baby fat on him. As heir to the Squibb pharmaceutical fortune, Lowell was born with a silver spoon in his mouth. His parents were living in Paris when Lowell was born in 1931 but soon moved back to New England. He had an aristocratic upbringing, going to prep school and then graduating from Yale in the class of '53. After finishing up at the University of Virginia Law School, where he was a classmate of Ted Kennedy's and John Tunney's, he was elected to the Connecticut legislature. He later served as Mayor of Greenwich, Connecticut, where a lot of rich New York commuters live, and went to Congress in 1968. He came to the Senate in 1970 and has been raising hell there ever since.

At first, you'd think that Lowell was a Republican more by inheritance than conviction. But, in fact, he's a throwback to the sort of country club Eastern Seaboard Republican that controlled the party in the forties and fifties. Since Goldwater whipped the pants off Nelson Rockefeller and Bill Scranton back in 1964, Lowell's sort of Republican has been a dying breed. He's one of the few surviving descendants of senators like Jacob Javits, Clifford Case, and Mac Matthias. I guess Lowell figures he's carrying the torch of liberal Republicanism all by himself now. While still a freshman senator, he actually campaigned for a spot on the Watergate Committee and threatened to take the matter before the entire Senate if he didn't get his way. Lowell was sure that Sam Dash and his staff weren't capable of conducting a thorough investigation, so he hired his own personal staff to do a little free-lance snooping. Many of the damaging leaks from the committee could be traced directly to his office. (It got to the point where we could read the day's testimony ahead of time in that morning's *Washington Post*.) Everyone who watched the hearings knows what a show horse Lowell was in public, but you figure that a little bit of that is in the nature of the political beast. Let me tell you, though, he was that way in private, too. I remember Dick Russell always used to say to beware of any man who will demagogue behind closed doors.

If the Watergate investigation dealt a politically fatal blow to the White House, it did quite a bit to enhance the image of a number of Southern politicians. On the Ervin Committee alone, four of the seven senators were from Southern states. On our committee staff, Fred Thompson, Jim Hamilton, Rufus Edminsten, and quite a few lower ranking individuals were native Southerners. Over on the house Judiciary Committee, which voted the articles of impeachment against the president, you had Barbara Jordan and Jack Brooks of Texas, Walter Flowers of Alabama, Trent Lott of Mississippi, and Caldwell Butler of Virginia. Leon Jaworski, who took over for Archibald Cox as special prosecutor after Cox was fired, was from Texas. And Jim Neal, who prosecuted

Haldeman, Ehrlichman, Mitchell, and others, hangs out his shingle in Nashville, Tennessee. A typical reaction to all of this came from a fellow who lived in Shaker Heights, Ohio, which is not a part of the deep South. After he heard Sam Ervin and me give our opening statements at the committee hearings, this fellow said, "God, I wish that Huey Long were still alive!"

In many ways Sam Ervin was the ideal chairman for that committee. At age seventy-six, he obviously didn't have higher political ambitions, and his solidly conservative voting record laid to rest any notion that he had ideological reasons for wanting to "get" the president. Sam was an experienced trial lawyer and a veteran of eight years on lower state courts and six years on the state supreme court in North Carolina. During his eighteen years in the Senate, Sam had earned a reputation as a right formidable constitutional scholar and a man of unquestioned personal integrity. What took us all by surprise, however, was the way the nation made a folk hero out of him.

For years Southern politicians had been used to being the objects of derision and ridicule. And few men were more "Old South" in their manner and lifestyle than Sam Ervin. His way of talking was a typically Southern blend of old fashioned rhetoric and homespun humor. He quoted the Bible, Shakespeare, and the U.S. Constitution. He had lived all his life in a town with fewer than fourteen thousand residents, and he and his wife had lived for fifty years in the same house. He was a decorated veteran of World War I, a devout Presbyterian, and a past Grand Orator of the Masonic Lodge. Physically, he looked like a big butterball turkey. If they had wanted to, the cartoonists could have had a field day with his quivering jowls and his jumping eyebrows. But instead of making fun of Sam, the urban sophisticates took this old country lawyer to heart. In fact, they came damn near to making "Uncle Sam" Ervin synonymous with the United States itself.

Now, Sam's folksiness was completely authentic, but there was an element of calculation in the way he let it show. This business about being an "old country lawyer" was a perfect example. In Washington, it was well known that Sam was an honors graduate of the Harvard Law School and had a brilliant legal mind. Down south, however, we've always believed that if a man had intellectual abilities, they would show through on their own without his having to brag about them. The trick was to make it in the big city without losing your country roots. The more modest, unassuming, and down-home a Southerner is, the more likely he is to have achieved distinction in the North. It's only the social climbers who try to lose their Southern "taint."

Uncle Sam's Republican counterpart was Howard Baker, the senior senator from Tennessee and vice chairman of the committee. Howard did an absolutely brilliant job of balancing himself between Lowell Weicker's crude attacks on the administration and Ed Gurney's inept attempts to defend it. As an attractive Southern Republican, Howard was already a rising political star. He had established himself with the conservative wing of his party by twice challenging Hugh Scott for the position of senate minority leader (he eventually won that post when Scott retired in 1976). Of course, Howard may have figured that the job should have been his by inheritance, since he was Everett Dirksen's son-in-law. Howard's father had also been a member of Congress, and his sister was married to a Republican congressman from Virginia. No question about it, Howard Baker was a political animal. He was also about as smooth and savvy as they come. Although he maintained enough folksy charm not to seem uppity, there was a lot of "New South" in him as well.

Without a doubt, the Watergate investigation made Howard Baker into a major figure on the national political scene. But the final outcome of that sordid affair also set the limits of how far he could go in the 1970's. First of all, daily television exposure brought Howard into millions of American homes, just as it had done more than twenty years earlier for Estes Kefauver, the man whose seat Howard now occupied. Howard's evenhanded, non-partisan manner impressed moderates in his own party, independents, and quite a few Democrats. Add that to his hardcore Southern and conservative support, and you have a valuable political property on your hands. Moreover, he came across as witty, articulate, and oh-so-very reasonable. If Nixon and Agnew had served out their terms in public office in great public disfavor, there would have been a vacuum of leadership within the Republican Party. Being one of the few Republicans actually helped by Watergate, Howard would have been in an ideal position to rush in and fill that vacuum. Instead, the resignation of Spiro Agnew catapulted Jerry Ford into the vice presidency, and Nixon's own resignation elevated him to the White House. Since Howard had no ideological grounds on which to challenge a sitting president of his own party, it would have seemed overly ambitious of him to have tried. So he had to sit out the 1976 campaign.

The years since '76 have been better for Howard Baker as a statesman than as a politician. He was elected minority leader of the Senate in 1977 and became majority leader when the Republicans took control of the Senate in 1981. He proved to be an outstanding legislator and parliamentarian during his eight years as party leader. If the Senate could have elected a prime minister for this country, Howard would have won hands down. But that's not the way our chief executive is chosen in the United States. In 1980, Howard was too busy running the Senate to make a full-time race for the presidency and sort of got lost in the crowd. Since he left the Senate in 1985, he's had plenty of time to run for office but not much national exposure. (Perhaps his role as Reagan's chief of staff will put him back in the limelight.) Besides, Watergate ceased to be a potent political issue after the 1976 election. By now, it's safely tucked away in the history books.

But then, things might have been different had Jerry Ford picked Howard to run as vice president in '76. For one thing, Jerry might have won the election. Two of the main advantages Jimmy Carter had going for him against Ford (beyond the normal assets of a Democratic candidate) were his Southern background and public revulsion with Watergate. Although Bob Dole, the man Ford did choose that year, is a superb political leader (who is eminently qualified to be vice president or even president), he wasn't able to help the ticket in either of those areas. Howard would have helped in both. I realize the vice presidency isn't much of an office (Dole called it inside work with no heavy lifting), but for that very reason it would have left Howard plenty of free time to run for the top spot in 1980. Had that happened, Ronald Reagan might be remembered today as a former actor who was once Governor of California.

Of course, Sam Ervin and Howard Baker weren't the only native

Southerners to gain favorable exposure as a result of Watergate. I had been in the Senate for sixteen years when Mike Mansfield appointed me to that committee, and I believe that my labors had been beneficial to the country at large. But where I was known outside Georgia, it was probably still as Gene Talmadge's son. In fact, there were quite a few people who thought that I was my daddy, despite the fact that he would have been eighty-nine years old in 1973. Well, with Watergate, I not only became a nationally known politician but a star of daytime television as well. The commercial networks carried those hearings from gavel to gavel, and PBS ran them on video tape at night. People would come up to me in airports and ask for my autograph in places like Chicago, Los Angeles, and Denver. Yankees who were running for everything from dog catcher to Congress back in their local communities would stop by the office to get their picture taken with me. (Let me tell you, *that* was quite a novel experience for a Southern segregationist.) At one point, my mail was up to 3,500 letters a day. I appreciated the attention, but I managed to ignore the occasional suggestion that I run for president. If my years in public life had taught me anything, it was that in the mid-1970's it would be next to impossible for a politician from Georgia to be elected President of the United States.

With Harry Truman at Ft. Benning, Georgia, 1950

Governor Talmadge with President Dwight Eisenhower

Senators Talmadge and Russell with President John Kennedy

Georgia visit: (L-R) Talmadge, Russell, Henry Cabot Lodge, Lyndon Johnson, William F. Knowland

To Herman Talmadge
from his friend
Lyndon B Johnson

(L-R): Phil Landrum, Talmadge, President Richard Nixon, Fletcher Thompson, Russell

Orientation flight in a McDonnell F-101 "Voodoo"

Talmadge welcomes fellow Georgian, President Jimmy Carter

(L-R): Robert Byrd, Henry Kissinger, Stuart Symington, Talmadge, Strom Thurmond, Daniel Inouye

Agricultural Committee members (L-R) Hubert Humphrey, Carl Curtis, James Allen, Talmadge

Friend and senate colleague Russell Long

Talmadge, Senator Sam Nunn greet Anwar Sadat

Conferring with Senator John Stennis of Mississippi . . .

. . . and Senator Robert Dole of Kansas

The seventy-seven $100 bills presented as evidence

Talmadge loyalists never waivered in their support

Lynda Cowart
Pierce, now Mrs.
Herman Talmadge

Celebrating a birthday with "Miss Mitt" Talmadge

15

A Lesson in Civics

Who can ever forget the image? The President of the United States walks up the steps of the helicopter in the back yard of the White House, waves goodbye to the nation that had reelected him overwhelmingly less than two years earlier, and disappears into history. They say he left the office in disgrace, and I suppose he did. There's no question that had he tried to hold on, the House would have impeached him. Nor is there much doubt that he would have been convicted by the Senate. But you had to pity the man when he sat in the Oval Office for the last time the night before and announced that he was resigning the presidency. Or that morning when he broke down while bidding farewell to his staff. When that helicopter lifted off the White House grounds, it marked the end of the biggest series of political blunders in our nation's history.

OUR HEARINGS BEGAN ON THE MORNING of May 17, 1973. Sam Ervin called the committee to order with a hand-carved gavel given him by the Cherokee Indians of North Carolina. The game shows and soap operas had been indefinitely preempted as the cameras of CBS, NBC, and ABC were trained on our proceedings. However, the first day of hearings wasn't anything to take people's minds off "The Newlywed Game" or "The Edge of Night." We heard a couple of well-groomed young men talk about the organization of the White House staff and the Committee to Reelect the President (popularly known as CREEP). We also heard the arresting officers talk about what they had found at the Watergate building on the early morning of June 17, 1972. This was all old hat to folks who had been following the case for several months, but Sam Dash was trying to lay a foundation for the testimony of the more important witnesses who were to come. The first of these was Jim McCord, who took the stand on the following day.

As you recall, it was McCord's letter to Judge Sirica that got folks to wondering just how high in the government this Watergate mess could be traced. Now, it's not uncommon for a criminal who is looking for lenient treatment to try to implicate more important people in his crime. This will sometimes cause the prosecution to land some pretty big fish. It can also ruin the reputation of innocent folks who are unjustly accused and never fully exonerated. I wasn't rightly sure which situation we had here, but McCord's testimony was pretty sensational in a couple of respects. When Danny Inouye tried to find out why such an upstanding citizen would be involved in burglaries and the like, McCord said that he was working with John Mitchell and John Dean to try to head off violent demonstrations during the presidential campaign. If that was true, the Attorney General of the United States (Mitchell) and the president's official lawyer (Dean) had knowledge of illegal campaign activities, if not of the Watergate break-in itself. Something else McCord said was potentially even more devastating. He told of clandestine meetings with a Treasury Department official by the name of Jack Caulfield. The purpose of these meetings was to offer McCord executive clemency in exchange for his silence. Only one person in the federal government would have had the power to grant clemency, and that was the President of the United States.

When Jack Caulfield came before the committee, he confirmed the fact that McCord had been offered clemency in exchange for silence. The offer, however, came from John Dean, who may only have been claiming to speak for the president. Now, we knew that if Caulfield was telling the truth, it was at the very least evidence of Dean's strong desire to save his own backside. It could be very damaging to him personally if McCord started squawking about some of Dean's activities. He was one of several opportunistic aides who were trying to get in good with their boss. It just so happened that their boss was a candidate for reelection to the office of president. What better way for Dean and his cohorts to ingratiate themselves with Nixon than by goosing that reelection effort along with some campaign high jinx? They probably knew that they could get fellows like McCord and the Cubans to go along by telling them it was all in the interest of national security. In this instance, "patriotism" may well have been the last refuge of scoundrels.

The middlemen between Nixon's lieutenants and the actual burglars were those two cloak-and-dagger types E. Howard Hunt and G. Gordon Liddy. Hunt had been in the CIA for so long that he was used to carrying out undercover operations to further our country's interests in the Cold War. The CIA, however, is meant to conduct its nefarious deeds overseas. It has such latitude in what it's allowed to do that it's specifically barred from operating in the United States. When Hunt went to work for Nixon, he carried the CIA mentality with him and did whatever he was told to do on the assumption that Nixon security and national security were one and the same. Hunt was a pretty fair spy novelist, but some of the things he did for the White House were more bizarre than fiction. It's easy to condemn a man like Hunt for thinking that the purity of his motives gave him a license to break the law, but you can't help feeling sorry for someone who suffered as much as he did. (His wife died in a plane crash at the height of the Watergate case, and his children were left as virtual orphans to see their daddy paraded from jail to courtroom and back in leg chains.) It was those cynical politicians in the White House and CREEP, who used Howard Hunt and then fed him to the wolves, that were the real villains here. We'd hear from just about every one of them before our hearings were through.

One fellow we never heard from, though, was Hunt's sidekick G. Gordon Liddy. If Hunt was a broken man, Liddy made it a point of honor not to break. And consequently, he didn't talk. He used to like to quote the German philosopher Frederich Neitzsche, who said, "Whatever doesn't destroy me makes me stronger."

I never met Gordon Liddy, but from what I hear I don't think he was wrapped too tight. He'd do things like hold his hand over a lighted candle until his flesh started to roast just to show how tough he was. He seemed to think that he was an old-time Prussian warrior who owed his loyalty and his very life to his commander-in-chief. We saw this kind of fierce devotion among the Japanese in the South Pacific during World War II. But from all accounts, I do believe that Liddy would have preferred serving a *fuhrer* to either an emperor or a president. They say that over at the Department of Justice he used to get a big kick out of showing Nazi propaganda films. If we had caught someone like that running around in Georgia, we would have had him locked up on the state farm in Milledgeville, where he couldn't do any harm to himself or others. He sure as hell wouldn't have had a sensitive position in any of *my* campaigns. Politics can be crazy enough when it's practiced by sane people. Those CREEP fellows should have known that keeping a bird like G. Gordon on the payroll was asking for trouble.

On June 14, the deputy director of Nixon's reelection committee took the stand. He was the highest ranking campaign official we had heard from up to that point and by far the most damaging. Jeb Stuart Magruder was a tall, smooth looking young man who resembled the actor Cliff Robertson. Everything about him made you think that he was the sort of fellow you'd want your daughter to marry. (The woman he did marry was an attractive brunette who sat quietly behind him throughout his testimony.) The boy was well educated and had an important position working for the President of the United States. He was a real comer in Washington. You have to wonder at the lack of judgment and common sense that would land a man like Jeb Stuart Magruder in the penitentiary. And with such an illustrious name to live up to at that.

What Magruder told us was enough to curl your hair, if not with moral indignation at least with shock at the stupidity of it all. According to Magruder, John Mitchell and various other individuals met with Gordon Liddy on three separate occasions to plan some pretty outrageous shenanigans. The first meeting took place on January 27, 1972, in Mitchell's office in the Justice Department. Liddy got him a bunch of charts on an easel and outlined a plan that involved wiretapping phones to gain information on political opponents, kidnapping left-wing radicals to keep them away from the Republican convention, and hiring call girls to "work with" prominent Democrats. Apparently, Mitchell just sat there puffing on his pipe and complaining about the $1 million price tag. At each of the subsequent meetings, both the plan and the price tag were scaled back until the only thing they finally agreed on was to bug the Democratic headquarters.

Nobody needed to tell me that Magruder was laying the responsibility for the Watergate break-in in the lap of the former Attorney General of the United States. But could Magruder be believed? He admitted that he had already committed perjury once. Maybe he figured he could earn himself a reduced sentence by frying some bigger fish. And there weren't many bigger fish than John N. Mitchell. Unless, of course, you count the president himself. That was the question on everybody's mind. As Howard Baker was to put it so many times to so many witnesses, "What did the president know and when did he know it?" I got the impression from the testimony given thus far that quite a bit of mischief could have been going on at both the White House and CREEP without Nixon's direct knowledge. God knows, even a senator can be at the mercy of his staff. Just to be sure, I phrased it this way to Magruder: "What you are saying, as I understand it, is that his staff was so completely remote, kept him so isolated, that this could have transpired without [the president's] knowledge, approval, and consent?" "Yes, sir," Magruder replied, "I can understand that very well."

Our next witness wouldn't have to express conjecture about the president's involvement in Watergate. John W. Dean III was counsel to the president and had kept him informed about developments in the case. Dean had resigned under pressure the previous spring at the same time that Nixon had had to dump his two top aides, Bob Haldeman and John Ehrlichman, and his attorney general, Richard Kleindienst. Nixon had told the nation how sorry he was to lose such fine men as Haldeman, Ehrlichman,

and Kleindienst, but all he said about Dean was that his resignation had been requested and accepted. Several of the witnesses
before our committee had implicated Dean in the cover-up. He
was already under federal indictment. Unless he had credible evidence incriminating persons higher up in the administration,
there was a good chance that the Watergate case would stop with
John Dean.

There had been so many leaks from our committee and Dean's
testimony was so sensitive that Sam Dash was meeting with him
in private to prepare for the public hearings. Sam told us that
Dean was the key to cracking this whole case, but we would have
to give him immunity before we could hear his testimony. In other
words, we were being asked to buy a pig in a poke. It's a tribute to
our great respect for Sam Ervin and to Ervin's confidence in Sam
Dash that we agreed to do so. The original vote on the committee
was 5-2 in favor of immunity, with the four Democrats and
Weicker voting "aye" and Baker and Gurney "nay." Seeing that he
was whipped, Howard moved to make the vote unanimous, and
Ed Gurney concurred. Had we not granted Dean immunity, he
might very well have declined to testify, citing his rights under the
fifth amendment. As it was, the path had been cleared for him to
take the stand, and the entire nation was waiting to hear what he
had to say.

The way things turned out, we had to wait a week longer than
anticipated for John Dean's testimony. On the very eve of Dean's
scheduled appearance before the committee, we received an
urgent request from majority leader Mike Mansfield and minority
leader Hugh Scott to delay the hearings for a week. Leonid Brezhnev, who was the top man in the Soviet Union, was coming to call
on President Nixon, and Mike and Hugh thought it might hamper
prospects for world peace if our commander-in-chief was under
fire during his negotiations with Brezhnev. This obviously put
Sam Dash in a bind, because he was doing his damnedest to keep
the details of Dean's testimony from leaking out to the press ahead
of time. But we'd just have to take that risk. I've always believed
that politics stops at the water's edge, and that's particularly true

when you're dealing with a mortal adversary like the Soviet Union.

Five other members of the committee saw things that way, too. Lowell Weicker was the lone holdout. He thought that if Brezhnev could hear Dean accuse our president of criminal acts, he would come away impressed with the strength of American democracy. I guess Lowell must have figured that the Politburo was sort of like a coffee klatch in Greenwich, Connecticut. He probably thought they would stand around saying, "You know, Nikolai, I'm right impressed with the openness of the American system of government. Why don't we abandon this Marxism-Leninism and get us a Bill of Rights?" Of course, anyone with a brain in his head knew that they'd be more likely to say, "Nixon's finished. Let's put the screws to him." Sometimes I think that Weicker was downright simple.

After the White House had appealed to our patriotism to postpone Dean's testimony for a week, it did everything it could during that week to try to discredit Dean. First they stressed his own involvement in the cover-up, which was beyond question. Then they started to leak stories about his personal life. The one that got the most circulation was that Dean had "borrowed" $4,850 from a cash fund at the campaign headquarters to pay for his wedding and honeymoon. At first glance, that might have seemed like a pretty lavish honeymoon, but once you got a look at Dean's wife, it began to make sense. She was a very stylish blonde lady, dressed fit to kill and wearing expensive jewels. I suspect that many men would have leaped at the chance to "borrow" $5,000 to keep that woman happy. In any event, John Dean's character was not at issue. If it turned out just to be his word against the president's, Watergate would be nothing more than a summer spectacular. Dean would need corroboration to be believed, but first we had to get his story. As expected, it was a real shocker.

John Dean appeared before our committee for a full week beginning on the morning of June 25. He wore well tailored Brooks Brothers suits and horn-rimmed glasses that gave him a kind of pointy-headed look, like a young and not very wise owl. He maintained remarkable poise throughout the ordeal. In fact, he was so calm he looked as if he could have performed heart surgery in the back of a pickup truck. He began by reading a six-hour opening statement in a dull monotone. He didn't have to add any drama to his voice, however, because the story itself was enough to keep us on the edge of our seats. Although there was nothing in Dean's testimony linking Nixon to the planning of the Watergate burglary, he told us of five separate meetings with the president—from September 15, 1972, to April 15, 1973—in which they discussed such things as executive clemency and hush money for the burglars. In the vernacular, that's a cover-up. In legal terms, it's obstruction of justice and compounding a felony. Any way you slice it, these were mighty serious charges.

The last three of Dean's meetings with the president occurred in the spring of 1973 as the cover-up was really starting to come apart. On March 13, Dean claims to have told the president that Howard Hunt was demanding money in exchange for his silence and that it might cost as much as a million dollars to keep Hunt and the others quiet. According to Dean, Nixon simply said that it would be no problem to raise that kind of money and then referred to the fact that Hunt had been promised clemency. On March 21, Dean really started getting antsy and told his boss that "there was a cancer growing on the Presidency and that if the cancer was not removed, that the President himself would be killed by it." Apparently, Nixon's solution to this dilemma was to blame John Mitchell. "If Mitchell takes the rap," the president is supposed to have said, "the public will have a high-level person and be satisfied, and the matter will end."

Dean's last meeting with Mr. Nixon occurred on April 15 (he got a "happy Easter" phone call on the 22nd and was sacked on the 30th). According to Dean, it was a right curious meeting from the outset, with the president asking him a whole passel of leading questions. This led Dean to suspect that the conversation was being recorded so that Nixon would have a record with which to protect himself. First off, the president brought up the million dollars in hush money and started to laugh like he was nervous. You, of course, realized I was only joking, he said. Then a bit later, he got up from his desk and walked over to a corner of his office and, "in a barely audible tone," said "he was probably foolish to have discussed Hunt's clemency with [Chuck] Colson." The way Dean described the president's behavior, he sounded every bit like a guilty man trying to cover his tracks. We couldn't know if this was true without hearing the president's side of things. However, our immediate task was to do what we could to test John Dean's credibility.

Dean's five days on the witness stand did nothing to enhance our opinion of his personal ethics. He was an ambitious young lawyer who had been caught concealing evidence of a crime to save his own skin and, now that the circumstances had changed, was revealing everything he knew (or claimed to know) for the same purpose. And he didn't make any bones about it either. At one point, I said, "It seems like to me after finding evidence of a conspiracy of this magnitude it was incumbent upon you as counsel to the President to make every possible effort to see that he got that information at that time." Without blinking an eye, Dean said, "Senator, I was *participating* in the cover-up at that time." We were not impressed with Dean because he was making lurid charges. No, it was his memory and his consistency that impressed us. He cited names and dates and places, and after four days of intensive grilling by the committee's lawyers and the seven senators, there was no substantial discrepency in his testimony. My God, I thought, either this boy's telling the truth or he's the most gifted liar since Ananias.

President Nixon declined to appear before our committee to answer the charges John Dean had made against him, but there were more than enough past and present officials of his administration available to do so. The first one was former attorney general John Mitchell. Upon taking the stand, Mitchell spent a good deal of time denying accusations made against him by Magruder and Dean and countering Dean's contention that the president was involved in the cover-up. Still, what he did admit to was enough to raise serious questions about Mitchell's own judgment. If, for example, he was outraged by the plans that Liddy was cooking up, why did he meet with that screwball three times and keep him on the payroll? In addition, there were several

outright contradictions between things Mitchell told us and statements he had made elsewhere. For example, in senate hearings to
confirm Richard Kleindienst, his successor as attorney general,
Mitchell had claimed that he had had *no political responsibilities*
connected with the Nixon reelection effort while he was still running the Department of Justice. He tried to weasle out of that by
saying that all he had denied was having *duties with the Republican
Party* during that time. I got out the official transcript of that hearing and said, "Let's read a little further, Mr. Mitchell." It was right
there in the record that sixteen months earlier Mitchell had denied
to another senate committee the campaign activity he had just
admitted to us.

John Mitchell had been Attorney General of the United States
until April of 1972, when he left to direct the Nixon reelection campaign. He had subsequently been forced to leave that position
because of marital problems. But during his time in the cabinet
and at the head of the reelection committee, Mitchell knew of
numerous criminal acts that had been performed on behalf of the
president. Not only had he done nothing about them himself, but
he had failed to inform the president of them. His rationale was
pretty cynical to say the least. If the president didn't know about
these deeds, he couldn't be held accountable for them. If he
were informed, he would feel obliged to expose them by "lower-
ing the boom" on his guilty subordinates. That might be politically
embarrassing and endanger his chances of reelection. I pressed
Mitchell on that point to be absolutely sure of what he meant.
Here's how it went:

> TALMADGE: Am I to understand from your response
> that you placed the expediency of the next election
> above your responsibilities as an intimate to advise the
> President of the peril that surrounded him? Here was
> the deputy campaign director involved, here were his
> two closest associates in his office involved, all around
> him were people involved in crime, perjury, accessory
> after the fact, and you deliberately refused to tell him
> that.
>
> Would you state that the expediency of the election

was more important than that?

MITCHELL: Senator, I think you have put it exactly correct. In my mind, the reelection of Richard Nixon, compared with what was available on the other side, was so much more important that I put it in just that context.

The next witness we heard was White House special counsel Richard A. Moore. He was a befuddled white-haired gentleman who looked older than his fifty-eight years. He was supposed to be a strong rebuttal witness to John Dean, but the man's obvious confusion and lack of memory made Dean seem all the more credible by contrast. You had to feel a little sorry for Moore, however; he got a pretty rough going over from Terry Lenzer. Still, at this point, Nixon needed something a little more substantial than pity to counteract John Dean. And he wasn't likely to get it from the next scheduled witness. Herbert W. Kalmbach was the man who had paid the hush money to the Watergate burglars. He was also the president's personal attorney. (I never knew a man to have so damn many lawyers working for him as Nixon did.) Anyway, when we got to the hearings on July 16, Kalmbach wasn't there. Sam Dash had replaced him with a surprise witness. It was a fellow by the name of Alexander P. Butterfield, who was head of the Federal Aviation Administration. It wasn't immediately apparent what the FAA had to do with Watergate, but I got wind of the fact that Butterfield had been some kind of custodian over at the White House. I wondered if this was another of Nixon's stalwart defenders or simply one of Sam Dash's insignificant "foundation-laying" witnesses.

Fred Thompson opened up the questioning by asking Butterfield if he was "aware of the installation of any listening devices in the oval office of the President." To which Butterfield replied, "I was aware of listening devices, yes sir." As it turned out, the committee staff had discovered in its interrogation of Butterfield that Nixon had been secretly recording all of his conversations in the White House since the spring of 1971. At the time, I thought that was an unusual practice, but I have since learned that Kennedy and Johnson had done pretty much the same thing. There was no question that such tapes could serve as a valuable resource when a president sat down to write his memoirs, and any president's memoirs command a good price in the literary marketplace. However, if I were a White House aide or a visitor to the Oval Office giving the president confidential advice, I'm not sure that I would want to be recorded without my knowledge or consent. There's a story that when Lyndon Johnson was president he called Bobby Kennedy into the Oval Office and got him to make all sorts of embarrassing and incriminating statements. Then when Lyndon went to play back the tapes, he found that they were inaudible. You see, Bobby had figured out what was up and had him a little jamming device in his pocket. Unfortunately, even in Washington, D.C., there have never been many individuals as sagacious as Bobby Kennedy.

Beyond the ethics of the situation, that taping system had a very practical bearing on our committee's work. If conversations in the White House had been recorded, then the evidence existed that would either confirm or refute John Dean's testimony. The issue of presidential involvement in Watergate could be settled one way or the other overnight. If Nixon was telling the truth, he could exonerate himself and put this whole sordid affair behind him by sending the relevant tapes over to the committee and insisting that we play them on national TV. Or if he was afraid that extraneous information contained in the tapes might leak out and damage the country or embarrass him personally, he could call Sam Ervin and Howard Baker over to the White House and play the tapes for them. Instead, he claimed that the tapes were protected by executive privilege and that neither the legislative nor the judicial branches of government had any right to them. He might as well have claimed the protection of the fifth amendment against self incrimination, because at that point lots of folks who had loyally backed him began to think that the man had something to hide. We were bound and determined to find out what that was. When the president refused to provide any access to the tapes, we subpoenaed them. As Howard Baker put it, the issue had been joined. We were primed for one of the biggest constitutional rows in the history of this nation.

☆ ☆ ☆

The next major witness to appear before our committee was John Ehrlichman. Up until a few months earlier, he and his buddy H. R. "Bob" Haldeman had been President Nixon's two closest aides. Senator Bill Saxbe of Ohio, who became attorney general after Elliot Richardson quit, used to call Haldeman and Ehrlichman "Hans and Fritz," after the Katzenjammer Kids. They were the keepers of the palace guard and were reputed to be the two most arrogant men in Washington, which was saying a lot, because our nation's capital isn't known for harboring shrinking violets. Ehrlichman more than lived up to his advance billing. He was sarcastic and argumentative and didn't give an inch on anything. However, if we were to believe Ehrlichman, we would have to disbelieve at least ten other witnesses. Danny Inouye expressed the sentiments of many of us when he inadvertently muttered into a live microphone, "What a liar!"

In questioning Ehrlichman, we got into some areas that were unrelated to the Watergate break-in itself, but shed a good deal of light on what those boys in the White House thought they could get away with in the name of national security. If you recall, back in 1971, a former defense department official by the name of Daniel Ellsberg had given the *The New York Times* some secret documents relating to the history of the Vietnam War. The actual contents of the documents weren't all that sensitive, but the very fact that they were being leaked made our government look like a sieve and caused other countries to think twice about sharing intelligence with us. Nixon was hopping mad, as well he should have been. Now, Ehrlichman's response to the situation was to try to discredit Ellsberg by getting derogatory information on the man from his psychiatrist's office. Specifically, he authorized "a covert operation ... to examine all the medical files still held by Ellsberg's psychoanalyst," just so long as it was "not traceable." With that go-ahead, Hunt and Liddy pulled off a burglary. Ehrlichman tried to tell us that he had only meant for them to do something "routine," like bribe a nurse, and that, in any event, the president (and presumably his subordinates) have the constitutional right to break the law if they think it's in the country's best interest to do so.

This discussion of burglaries and the like caused something that John Mitchell had said in his testimony to make a good deal more sense. Mitchell allowed as how the administration was less interested in covering up the Watergate burglary *per se* than in keeping the lid on other "White House horrors." You see, Nixon had gotten so fed up with leaks of confidential information from the government to the news media that he decided he would do whatever it took to stop them. He felt that the FBI had become a bit lax as J. Edgar Hoover was getting up in years, so he organized his own top secret band of sleuths in the White House. They were under the nominal control of a couple of youthful bureaucrats named Egil Krogh and David Young, but oftentimes their orders originated higher up in the administration, at least at the level of Haldeman, Ehrlichman, and Mitchell. (Fellows like Hunt and Liddy did the actual dirty work.) Since the original purpose of the group was to plug leaks, it was called the "plumbers." As time went on, its activities extended beyond the wiretapping of top government officials, which the president probably had the right to do to protect national security, to include burglary, kidnapping, and other crimes. As an act of petty political espionage, the Watergate break-in *was* essentially a third-rate burglary. But because it involved Hunt and Liddy, there was grave danger that some of these other unsavory escapades might be exposed. Hence, the massive cover-up.

When I heard Ehrlichman justify the president's right to authorize burglary and to invade the privacy of law-abiding citizens in order to smear his political opponents, I couldn't help being reminded of something William Pitt the Elder once said: "The poorest man in his cottage may bid defiance to all the forces of the crown. It may be frail, its roof may shake, the wind may blow through it, the storm may enter, but the King of England cannot enter. All his forces dare not cross the threshold of the ruined tenement." I began to wonder just how far this man Ehrlichman thought the powers of *our* sovereign extended. So I probed him on the matter.

TALMADGE: Now if the President could authorize a covert break-in, and you do not know exactly what that

290

power would be limited [to], you do not think it could include murder or other crimes beyond covert break-ins, do you?

EHRLICHMAN: I do not know where the line is, Senator.

TALMADGE: You are a lawyer, and I understand a good one.

EHRLICHMAN: Well, I am certainly not a constitutional lawyer, Senator. Far from it.

TALMADGE: Do you remember when we were in law school, we studied a famous principle of law that came from England and also is well known in this country, that no matter how humble a man's cottage is, that even the King of England cannot enter without his consent?

EHRLICHMAN: I am afraid that has been considerably eroded over the years, has it not?

TALMADGE: Down in my country we still think it is a pretty legitimate principle of law.

Much to my surprise, that little exchange was greeted with a spontaneous ovation from the audience in the hearing room.

Ehrlichman's defiant stance before the committee may have won him a few debating points, but it didn't win the administration much support among the American people. Ordinarily, folks don't take too well to a fellow who's always got a smirk on his face and his nose up in the air. From all reports, his sidekick Haldeman was even more arrogant. Tales of Haldeman's brusque and imperious ways were almost legendary. He had a crewcut that made him look like a porcupine and an advertising man's grasp of politics. That's not hard to understand, because his professional career had been divided between working as an advance man for Nixon and as an advertising executive for J. Walter Thompson. That outfit will be remembered for its Tidy Bowl commercials, which featured a colloquy between a housewife and a fellow navigating a tug boat through her toilet bowl. I'm not sure if Haldeman had anything to do with that commercial, but we were ready for just about anything from him as a witness. To the surprise of many, he acted less like a Nazi stormtrooper than a gee-whiz All American boy. I guess those ad men know how to size up an audience.

Haldeman gave his personal account of several of the meetings John Dean had told us about. Much to our surprise, Haldeman had been allowed to refresh his memory by listening to White House tapes of a couple of those meetings. Here was a man who was now a private citizen being allowed access to evidence that the president was denying to a duly authorized committee of the U.S. Senate. All this talk of executive privilege and separation of powers was just a constitutional smokescreen to cover up the fact that Nixon viewed Watergate not as a crime to be solved, but as a public relations problem to be handled. Nixon's faith in Haldeman, even after the man had resigned from the government under a cloud, spoke volumes about the extent to which politics in this country has been taken over by advertising. Not too long ago, I read a story about a political candidate named Mulligan. He was running for some county office out in California and turned himself over to one of these high-powered advertising agencies. They immediately sized him up as a complete idiot and sent him out of town for the duration of the campaign. Then they flooded the airwaves with a jingle—"Three cheers for Mulligan." Needless to say, Mulligan led the ticket. Nixon needed someone with good political horse sense, not some Tidy Bowl man, giving him advice. I think it was Howard Baker who said that Watergate might never have happened if some of those boys in the White House had ever run for sheriff.

After interrogating several more witnesses, we recessed our public hearings on August 7. The hearings resumed on September 24 and continued for several months thereafter. Watergate itself remained a national obsession for another year, until Richard Nixon resigned the presidency on August 9, 1974. However, the senate select committee faded from the national spotlight as the focus of the Watergate case shifted to the courts and, finally, to the house Judiciary Committee, which voted three articles of impeachment in late July, 1974. This progression in the case was proper and inevitable. The role of our committee was not to try, or even indict, anyone. It was simply to investigate the facts of the case. Several witnesses, particularly John Dean, made serious accusations of wrongdoing against the president and various members of his administration. Other witnesses, principally John Ehrlichman and Bob Haldeman, had vigorously denied those charges. We had given the public an opportunity to hear these witnesses and to weigh their testimony. We had also uncovered the means by which the truth of all their competing claims could finally be established. Going into the fall of 1973, both our committee and Special Prosecutor Archibald Cox were in court seeking access to the White House tapes. The special prosecutor's quest would cost him his job and lead to a fracas that made Nixon's departure from office a virtual inevitability.

When we reconvened our hearings on September 24, we concluded the Watergate phase of the investigation by questioning E. Howard Hunt and then moved on to a consideration of dirty tricks played during the presidential campaign. The first witness we heard from in that regard was White House speechwriter Patrick J. Buchanan. Now, Sam Dash wasn't alleging any improprieties on Buchanan's part; he was only trying to lay the general foundation for Nixon's campaign strategy and tactics. Unfortunately, in a battle of wits, the committee more than met its match in Patrick J. Buchanan. Having done nothing wrong, Pat was not contrite and apologetic as so many other witnesses had been. And unlike Ehrlichman, he didn't get real snooty and try to split hairs like a Philadelphia lawyer. He spoke with enough common sense and humor to deflate a lot of the moral demagoguery we had seen from some of the senators and the committee staff. He also put quite a few things in perspective when he identified "four gradations" of campaign activities: outrageous behavior, dirty tricks, political hardball, and pranks. It's not always clear where the line is to be drawn between permissible and impermissible behavior. Nevertheless, he conceded that "the line was probably breached in both campaigns in 1972, and perhaps previous ones." When asked what tactics he would be willing to use, Buchanan said, "Anything that is not immoral, unethical, illegal, or unprecedented in previous Democratic campaigns." As they had so many times before, the folks in the caucus room burst into laughter. However, this time they were not laughing with the committee

293

but at us. For our reputations and egos, that day's testimony was an unmitigated disaster.

It was typical of the way things were going for the administration that approximately two weeks after Buchanan's feisty testimony, Vice President Spiro T. Agnew—who had become a temporary American folk hero delivering speeches Buchanan had written for him—resigned from office to avoid impeachment for bribery and tax evasion. Agnew's crimes had occurred while he was Governor of Maryland and didn't have a damn thing to do with Watergate, but the whole affair further damaged the image of the administration at a time when that was the last thing it needed. Not since Aaron Burr had a sitting vice president been indicted for a felony, and never had one resigned from office. But no sooner had Agnew departed from the national scene than an even more historic crisis occurred. For a few hours on Saturday night, October 20, 1973, it looked as if the American government was coming apart at the seams.

Back in the spring of '73, it had become apparent to just about everyone that the Nixon Justice Department couldn't be trusted to investigate Watergate. So the new attorney general Elliot Richardson, who had just replaced Richard Kleindienst, appointed a special independent prosecutor to get to the bottom of the case. That seemed a pretty fair and hard-nosed thing to do, but, as an appointee of the Justice Department, the special prosecutor could only be as independent as the administration would let him be. That presented no problem until the existence of the White House tapes became known and the special prosecutor, Archibald Cox, went to court to try to get access to them. Finally, on Friday, October 19, Nixon offered to let Senator John Stennis listen to the tapes and authenticate White House summaries of their contents. These summaries would then be turned over to Archie Cox and to the senate committee. The president discussed this plan with Sam Ervin and Howard Baker that afternoon and then presented it to Cox as part of a direct order—accept the Stennis "compromise" *and* drop your suit at once. Sam Ervin appeared to accept the proposal for us under the mistaken impression that our committee would be getting verbatim transcripts prepared by Stennis. Archie Cox rejected the proposal outright, which put him in direct defiance of a command from his ultimate superior in the executive branch of government. In one bold move, Richard Nixon tried to put the tapes controversy and Watergate itself behind him by ordering his attorney general to fire Archibald Cox.

As everyone knows, this ploy backfired. Feeling that his honor was on the line, Elliot Richardson resigned rather than remove the special prosecutor whose independence he had guaranteed. The president then directed Assistant Attorney General Bill Ruckels-haus to fire Cox. When Ruckelshaus refused, the president fired him. Finally, Solicitor General Robert Bork, who was next in line at the Justice Department, agreed to do the bidding of his commander-in-chief. With the special prosecutor and the two top officials at the Justice Department removed from office, the president dispatched FBI agents to seal off the files of the special prosecutor. A lot of folks started wondering whether we were on the verge of martial law. Half a million telegrams arrived in congressional offices that weekend, the vast majority of them urging Nixon's removal from office. And the house Judiciary Committee began an impeachment investigation. Within a period of ten days, the vice president had been forced from office and the president himself had lost the confidence of the American people. Over in the Middle East, Israel and Egypt were engaged in a war that would threaten world peace and produce an energy crisis that permanently changed the way we live in this country. At a time of grave national and international peril, no one seemed in charge of the American government.

When Gerald Ford assumed the office of president on August 9, 1974, he told his countrymen, "Our long national nightmare is over." That nightmare had started over two years earlier with a third-rate burglary that nearly everyone, myself included, dismissed as low-level political chicanery. It began to seem more ominous with James McCord's letter to Judge Sirica in March of 1973 and the charges and countercharges made in our committee hearings that summer. It took a decided turn for the worse in the fall when the resignation of Agnew and the firing of Cox seriously eroded Nixon's political support, and the house Judiciary Committee undertook its impeachment investigation. However, the president's doom was not finally sealed until July 24, 1974, when the Supreme Court voted unanimously that he must relinquish all subpoenaed tapes. One of those tapes was of a June 23, 1972, conversation, in which Nixon and Bob Haldeman plotted to use the CIA to block the FBI's investigation of Watergate. This was clear, incontrovertible evidence—the so-called "smoking pistol"—that the President of the United States had been involved in a conspiracy to obstruct justice. When the contents of this tape became public knowledge, Charles Wiggins, who had been Nixon's staunchest defender on the Judiciary Committee, wept, and the ten committee members who had voted against all the articles of impeachment said there was now cause to remove the president from office. On the afternoon of August 7, the Republican leaders of the House and Senate, John Rhodes and Hugh Scott, along with Senator Barry Goldwater, went to the White House to tell the president that it was all over. Two days later he was gone.

Our select committee had submitted its final report to the Clerk of the Senate on June 27, some six weeks before the Nixon resignation. Having completed my official involvement with the case, I watched that transfer of power as most citizens did—from a distance and with a mixture of sorrow and relief, along with a measure of pride in the stability of our democratic system of government. Also like most citizens, I have since thought long and hard about the historical and political implications of that bizarre and tragic series of events called Watergate.

The first question a lot of people ask is: How serious was Watergate? Didn't previous administrations do things as bad, if not worse? If we confine ourselves to the Watergate break-in, the White House horrors, and the political dirty tricks, the Nixon administration probably didn't do anything unprecedented. The Nixon plumbers may have burglarized a psychiatrist's office, but the Kennedy administration had tried to get the Mafia to assassinate Fidel Castro. (When Lyndon Johnson came into office, he said he found that his predecessor had been running a "damn Murder Incorporated in the Caribbean.") From all reports, fellows like Haldeman, Ehrlichman, and Mitchell did their best to keep the president from knowing about some of the seamier things that were being done on his behalf. Where Nixon was culpable was in trying to cover up the truth when he finally did learn what was going on. And it was just plain dumb for him to preserve tape recorded evidence of his guilt.

I suppose that cover-up revealed Richard Nixon's own personal sense of insecurity. Suppose he had "lowered the boom" when he found out about some of the things being done at the White House and CREEP. He might have gone on television and said, "While I was concerned with weightier matters of state, some of my aides have engaged in unethical and even illegal activities. I will cooperate fully with the investigation to see that the guilty are punished and the innocent cleared. Also, I'll run a much tighter ship in the future and promise you that nothing like this will ever happen again." Had he done that, two things would have happened: (1) the New York-Washington media would have given him unshirted hell; and (2) the vast majority of the American people would have stood by him. (If Lyndon Johnson could win a landslide election after his press secretary was caught committing homosexual acts in the YMCA at the height of the political campaign, Nixon could have weathered Watergate—especially against the likes of George McGovern.) Surprisingly, Nixon put too much stock in what the media thought of him (if those boys were actually running things, the Checkers speech would have been his last public appearance) and too little confidence in the American people. It was only after he lied to the people and tried to put himself above the law that they finally turned on him.

Another question that always comes up when people talk about Watergate is whether Gerald Ford did right in pardoning Nixon. At the time, the majority of the American people thought not, but in recent years sentiment has begun to swing the other way. Every day criminals escape punishment through plea bargaining because prosecutors feel that there are sometimes higher social goals than extracting a pound of flesh from a particular wrongdoer. Ideally, criminal punishment should serve three ends: it should rehabilitate the criminal so he will not break the law again; it should deter others from breaking the law; and it should exact retribution on behalf of those who have been wronged. Nixon's resignation served the first and second of these ends. He seems personally to be a sadder and wiser man for the experience, and other politicians have been put on notice that misconduct in office is likely to ruin their careers. That leaves the question of whether Nixon has "suffered enough" for his crimes. Many would regard the disgrace of having to resign from office and accept a pardon to have been punishment enough. Whether it was or not, Jerry Ford obviously thought that putting Watergate behind us was a higher national priority than putting Richard Nixon in the penitentiary. That one act probably cost him the 1976 presidential election, thus making him the final political casualty of Watergate.

Mark Twain once observed that a cat who has sat on a hot stove will never do so again. Nor will he sit on a cold one either. The problem with learning from history is that we sometimes learn the wrong things. The public reaction to Watergate may have made the press too strong and the presidency too weak. It may have made congressmen and senators too eager to get their names in the paper and their pictures on TV. It may have put a higher premium on self righteousness and moral posturing than on genuine public virtue. But whatever else it may have done, Watergate did prove that our system of government works and that no man is above the law. For that reason, the entire Watergate affair, and particularly the senate hearings, constituted a remarkable lesson in civics.

There are questions about Watergate that remain unanswered, that may never be answered. What were those burglars looking for in Larry O'Brien's office? Why didn't Nixon burn all the tapes before they were subpoenaed? Who was Deep Throat? Indeed, was there a Deep Throat, or was he simply an imaginary or composite figure to lend credibility to the reporting of two relatively unknown journalists for the *Washington Post*? Finally, how did a politician as astute as Richard Nixon allow all of this to happen? Perhaps the most plausible answer to this last question involves a man who has followed Nixon's career from the very beginning, a political prankster named Dick Tuck.

For years Tuck plagued Nixon. Once when Nixon was making a speech on the back of a train, Tuck put on a railroadman's cap and signalled the train to pull out of the station. When Nixon was running for Governor of California in 1962, Tuck showed up at a rally in the Chinatown section of Los Angeles and gave a banner to some children to wave when the candidate showed up. "Let's get a picture," Nixon said. What he didn't realize was that the banner read, in Chinese, "WHAT ABOUT THE HUGHES TOOL LOAN?" (A $205,000 loan that Nixon's brother Donald had received from Howard Hughes was a major issue in the campaign.) When someone translated the banner for him, Nixon tore it up in front of TV cameras. As recently as the 1968 presidential campaign, Tuck had hired a bunch of pregnant black women to march around wearing buttons that said, "Nixon's The One!" Nineteen seventy-two would finally be Nixon's year to get even. His campaign plan called for developing his own bag of dirty tricks, what he called a "Dick Tuck capability." What it turned into was Watergate. *Time* magazine reported that one day during our hearings, Tuck and Bob Haldeman ran into each other in the halls of the Capitol. "You started all this," Haldeman said. "Yeah, Bob," Tuck replied, "but you guys ran it into the ground."

16

Politics in the New South

Back in early 1966 I got a call at my office in Washington from my old friend Ernie Vandiver. Ernie had been out of the governor's office for four years and was now constitutionally eligible to run for another term. Since I had brought him into politics twenty years earlier, I figured that Ernie was calling to seek my advice on campaign strategy. So I was a little taken aback when he said that he had to see me in Washington as soon as possible. I told him to take the next plane out of Atlanta and I would meet him at the airport. When Ernie arrived, he had some shocking news. His doctor had told him that he had a heart condition and that if he made another statewide political race, he was likely to be leaving a widow and orphans behind. My old enemy Ellis Arnall was preparing to run again, and in the wake of the Goldwater campaign, the Republicans had become a force to be reckoned with. If Ernie had to drop out of the race, there was no one left to carry the Talmadge banner. "Herman," he said, "you've got to come home and be governor again."

THE POLITICAL LANDSCAPE HAD CHANGED considerably since Ellis Arnall and I had faced each other across the threshold of the Georgia governor's office in January, 1947. At that time the only politicians in Georgia who did not call themselves Democrats were cranks like D. Talmadge Bowers. It wasn't just that

Republicans had exploited the South socially and economically during Reconstruction or that Franklin Roosevelt was seen as the Great White Father in the 1930's. It was more a case of political inertia. Southerners might cuss and moan about the national Democratic Party, and they might even strike out on their own as they had in 1948, but in the end they were always back pulling the Democratic lever—even if they had to hold their noses to do it. The national Republican candidates were Wall Street, Eastern Seaboard types like Wendell Willkie and Thomas Dewey, not conservatives like Robert Taft or John Bricker. As offensive as some of the liberal Democrats might be, it seemed better to try to reform the majority party from within than join the ranks of Jacob Javits, Nelson Rockefeller, and Clifford Case.

In 1964, however, both the South and the Republican Party changed for good. For the first time since 1936, the Eastern Seaboard Republicans failed to nominate one of their own for president. A grassroots coalition of Western and Midwestern conservatives carried the day for Senator Barry Goldwater of Arizona. Unfortunately, in the general election Barry lost to Lyndon Johnson in one of the biggest landslides in American history. But of the six states he carried, five were in the Deep South. In the five presidential elections since 1964, the South has gone Democratic only once (for Carter in 1976) and seems perfectly comfortable voting for a national party that used to be seen as a nest of carpetbaggers and scalawags. Now, there aren't nearly enough patronage positions to turn an entire region into post office Republicans. What happened was that Goldwater finally made the Republican Party stand for something. It cost them an election, but it also changed the face of American politics.

Some sourgrapes liberals will tell you that the Deep South went for Goldwater because of race. (What they're saying is that the South was so obsessed with race it didn't know that there were any other issues.) That's just plain wrong. Not only was Barry Goldwater not a racist, he wasn't even a segregationist. He had been instrumental in integrating the Arizona National Guard and the restaurant facilities at the airport in Phoenix. His personal record on matters of racial justice was a hell of a lot better than Lyndon Johnson's. The difference was that Lyndon was a politician and Barry a man of principle. When politicians of both parties were jumping on the bandwagon of civil rights, Barry queered his own political future by taking a stand for states rights and constitutional government. But he struck a responsive chord in the South because, like most Southerners, Barry was essentially a Jeffersonian Democrat. And with the leftward drift of the national Democratic Party, Jeffersonian Democrats began to feel more and more at home in the party of Goldwater.

If Southerners needed a signal that it was all right to become Republicans, they got it when my cousin Strom Thurmond switched his registration so he could campaign for Goldwater. In Strom's opinion, it was not so much a case of his leaving the Democratic Party as it was of the party leaving him. "The party of our fathers is dead," Strom said when he announced his defection. And those "who took its name are engaged in another reconstruction, this time not only in the South, but in the entire nation." He went on to say that, "If the American people permit the Democratic Party to return to power, freedom as we have known it in this country is doomed, and individuals will be destined to live lives of regulation, control, coercion, intimidation, and subservience to a power elite who shall rule from Washington." Those were mighty strong words, but with Lyndon's Great Society and new found devotion to "civil rights," they made sense to a lot of Southerners. And they carried that much more weight for having been spoken by Strom Thurmond.

Strom is a remarkable fellow. He isn't the greatest orator in the world, and he doesn't have the keenest intellect in the Senate, but his devotion to principle is absolute. He's a physical fitness fanatic and a man of great personal charm, who apparently has a good deal of sex appeal. I remember back in the late sixties my son Bobby came home from school one summer and asked me to help him meet some girls. I said, "Why don't you call up Miss Workman, who's a secretary in Cousin Strom's office, and have her introduce you to that real cute Miss South Carolina who works over there?" Well, Bobby did just that, but it seems he couldn't get anywhere with the young lady in question. A few weeks later I found out why. I picked up the paper and read that Miss Nancy Moore's parents were pleased to announce their daughter's engagement to Senator J. Strom Thurmond. It's enough to make you start cold showers and pushups in the morning.

As it turns out, I did not run for Governor of Georgia in 1966. When the word got around that I was thinking about it, I got a tremendous show of support from the state's political leaders. But the ordinary citizens of Georgia—what we call the butcher, the baker, and the candlestick maker—were of a different mind. They wrote me saying that I had now been in Washington long enough to acquire some seniority and a sense of how things were done in the Senate. That's where I was needed, and that's where I should stay. Dick Russell wasn't getting any younger, and it wouldn't do the state any good to have to break in two rookie senators. I took that advice to heart and remained in the Senate. With the tremendous increase in federal power in the twelve years since I had left the governor's mansion, the political action was all in Washington, anyway.

With Ernie Vandiver out of the race, there were three major Democratic candidates for governor—Ellis Arnall, state senator Jimmy Carter, and an Atlanta restaurant owner by the name of Lester Maddox. I considered all three to be personal friends, but Lester was the one who was closest to my political philosophy. He was a lifelong native of Atlanta who had had to drop out of school in the tenth grade to support his family when his father lost his job in a steel mill. He worked his way up from poverty to being the proprietor of a very popular fast food place over near Georgia Tech. It was called the Pickrick, and I used to eat there quite a bit when I was in Atlanta. Lester served good food at reasonable prices and made his customers feel at home. He was living testimony to the merits of the free enterprise system, which he extolled in newspaper ads for his restaurant. Lester included forty-five blacks among his sixty-five employees, many in supervisory capacities. But like so many self-made businessmen, he felt that private property rights entitled him to run his business any way he saw fit, even if it meant serving whites only. That notion had never been legally challenged in this country until the civil

rights movement began calling a lot of our constitutional principles into question. Not being a professional politician, Lester saw
no reason to abandon those principles just because the winds of
popular sentiment were blowing in the other direction.

As soon as the ink was dry on the 1964 Civil Rights Act, with its
provision about public accommodations, integrationists began
targeting Lester's restaurant. For several weeks, FBI agents
snooped around the place, taking down license numbers from
cars in the parking lot and even questioning customers after they
left the Pickrick. What they were trying to do was establish that
Lester was involved in interstate commerce and was thus subject
to the federal Civil Rights Act. When Lester was hauled into court
for refusing to serve some black agitators who tried to cause trouble at his place, those same FBI agents were called to testify on
behalf of the agitators. At that point, Lester either had to knuckle
under to the feds or close the business that he had spent his entire
life trying to build. Faced with that sort of decision, only one man
in a thousand would have stuck to his principles. But Lester was
that one man. At the time, a far-seeing friend predicted that his
stand would make Lester Governor of Georgia.

Up through early 1966, any man who seriously predicted a
political future for Lester Garfield Maddox would have been sent
to the state farm in Milledgeville for psychiatric examination.
Lester had run for Mayor of Atlanta against Bill Hartsfield in 1957
and Ivan Allen, Jr., in 1961 and had been defeated both times.
When he took his act statewide in 1962, running for lieutenant
governor against Peter Zack Geer, he lost that race as well. A three-
time loser who is considered something of a crackpot by the
newspapers and the established political powers is not exactly the
odds-on favorite to be elected governor—especially not against a
popular former governor like Ellis Arnall and a progressive state
legislator like Jimmy Carter. And if Lester should be lucky enough
to force a run-off with one of those two and actually secure the
Democratic nomination, he would then have to face Howard
"Bo" Callaway, a well educated and articulate textile heir who had
been elected as a Republican member of Congress during the
Goldwater campaign of 1964. With virtually no money and the
support of only a few loyal friends, Lester proceeded to take

his message to the people, much as Gene Talmadge had done when he ran for agriculture commissioner forty years before.

Ellis Arnall had been out of politics for twenty years in 1966. He had been mentioned as a possible vice presidential candidate in the Henry Wallace campaign of 1948 and was seen as the best hope of the anti-Talmadge faction in every gubernatorial election since he left office. But Ellis had himself a lucrative law practice and stayed on the political sidelines as a kind of elder statesman. (He had become so non-partisan that he even supported me when I ran for reelection to the Senate in 1962.) I'm not sure why he returned to politics in 1966, but he may have figured that the Democratic Party in Georgia was now liberal enough to welcome him back as its leader and that the people of the state were not ready to vote for a Republican governor regardless of what they might do in presidential elections. The incumbent governor, Carl Sanders, was a popular moderate who had worked with Ernie Vandiver to see that the integration of our schools was as peaceful and orderly as possible; however, Carl was ineligible to succeed himself. So with Ernie out of the race because of his heart and me not running, Ellis was the only big name willing and able to run. Besides, he had reached an age where if he was going to make a political comeback, he would have to do it soon.

To the surprise of no one, Ellis Arnall finished first in the Democratic primary. All he needed to do was whip Lester Maddox in the run-off, and the state would be treated to a classic confrontation between liberal and conservative in the general election. (Bo Callaway had won the Republican nomination in that party's state convention.) But a funny thing happened in that run-off: A lot of people who work for a living, go to church, obey the law, and believe in what this country is supposed to stand for started listening to Lester. He was not a big city lawyer, and he had no experience in public office, but they had entrusted their government to lawyers and politicians for years, and what had it got them? Nothing but unsafe streets, give-away welfare programs, and a federal bureaucracy that would destroy a man's business and rob him of his life savings to appease a bunch of special interest agitators. Lester might not have been brilliant, articulate, or well bred, but he had loads of honesty and common sense.

He was also a gutsy little fellow who wasn't afraid to stand up to the big boys. The pick handle (which Lester had used to protect his restaurant before the feds made him shut it down) had replaced red suspenders as the badge of the common man.

With the Democratic nomination in hand, Lester now had to face a better financed Republican candidate who had the solid backing of his own political party. At that, Lester was such an improbable candidate that some folks thought he never would have gotten the nomination had large numbers of Republicans not crossed over and voted for him in the Democratic run-off, figuring that he'd be easier to beat than Ellis. I have no way of knowing if that was true, but a lot of liberals and middle-of-the-roaders were convinced that either fate or deliberate chicanery had robbed them of a choice in the general election. It was like having to choose between George Wallace and Barry Goldwater, only worse. George had stepped aside after standing in the school-house door, whereas Lester had closed his restaurant rather than integrate it. And as for Howard Callaway, he might not have been more conservative than Goldwater, but liberals considered him more dangerous—if only because he had a better chance of winning.

I had known Bo Callaway all his life and his father, Cason, before him. Cason came from a very wealthy family in La Grange, Georgia, and had retired at about the age of forty from managing the mill that his daddy founded. Cason was very much interested in the economic plight of the Georgia farmer and figured that with some capital and business expertise he could do something about it. So he went around to most of the counties in the state and picked out a group of seven or eight business people who could spare a little capital and had them put a thousand or two dollars apiece in some farming operation, with Cason supplying the expertise. Unfortunately, most of those farms fell by the wayside within five to ten years. I remember once hearing Cason tell a farmer that the buttermilk on his farm was so good he'd pay a dollar a glass for it. "I'll bet you would," the farmer said. "It costs me two dollars a glass to produce it." Farming just wasn't as simple as Cason Callaway thought.

Cason had been appointed to the state Board of Regents by Ellis

Arnall and was still there when I became governor. He was a good regent and a nice fellow (we used to fish together at Blue Springs), and as far as I was concerned, he could stay on the board as long as he wanted to. Well, one day, he came into my office and said, "Herman, the doctor says I've got glaucoma. I'll have to leave the Regents. I've got a son that you know. He's a combat veteran of Korea, commander of a troop of South Koreans, graduate of West Point. I wish you'd appoint him in my place." I did just that, and Bo served with great distinction. Until the Goldwater campaign, Bo was a Talmadge Democrat. Had he remained one, I'm sure he could have had any office he wanted in the state.

So with Lester and Bo running against each other, the liberals in Georgia were fit to be tied. They decided that their only hope was to mount a massive write-in campaign for Ellis Arnall. Of course, there was no realistic chance that a write-in candidate would get a majority of the vote for governor. The only hope the liberals had was to deny either of the major party candidates a clear majority and thus throw the election into the state legislature. Even if that were to happen, the liberals would have to hope that enough conservative Democrats would desert Maddox for Callaway to enable Arnall to come in second in the voting. Then an overwhelmingly Democratic legislature would presumably vote for Ellis over Bo and return Arnall to the governor's mansion. Since Ellis refused to cooperate with the write-in effort, it fell far short of achieving its goal. But it did succeed in throwing the election into the legislature, which then proceeded to elect Lester Maddox Governor of Georgia. When asked to account for his victory, Lester summed it up right well: "It wasn't very difficult," he said. "All that was necessary was to defeat the Democrats, the Republicans—on the state and national levels—159 county courthouses, several hundred city halls, the major banks, the railroads, the utility companies, major industry, and all the daily newspapers and television stations in Georgia."

During the next four years, Lester surprised a lot of people by being a fair and moderate governor. He also had a way of irritating the big shots who were always used to having things their way. Once he got so tired of being preached to by the Atlanta papers on the issue of race that he went over to their building on Forsyth

Street and worked his way through the place, starting at the front door, to see how many black secretaries, office workers, and reporters were employed by the papers. What he found were a few black fellows pushing brooms. Another time, he met with a group of black legislators and ordinary citizens to discuss the agenda for his administration. When he told them that he intended to do as much for them as his predecessor had done, someone said, "Lord, Governor, *please* do more than that!" He promised that he would, and he did. The black people of Georgia made some of their greatest strides under the administration of Lester Maddox.

After nearly winning the governorship in 1966, the Republican Party in Georgia has fallen on hard times in its quest for state house offices. On the whole, the Democrats in Georgia have remained more conservative than the national party and have provided good government on a state, county, and local level. The people are willing to vote Republican for federal offices, while staying with the Democratic Party closer to home. Moreover, Georgia Republicans seem much more interested in internal squabbles than in winning elections. This was dramatically demonstrated in October 1968, when Jimmy Bentley, who was then comptroller-general, and four other state house officials switched to the Republican Party. Rather than welcoming them with open arms, the state's Republicans acted as if they were being attacked by alien beings. As Jimmy said, "I didn't give a damn who the state chairman of the Republican Party was… I wanted to see a hundred Republicans in the state legislature… I wanted to see a [Republican] governor and a lieutenant governor and some Republican state house offices… The Republicans just couldn't see that. They could never grasp that vision… I told them they'd either take over the state government in 1970 or they'd lose it for twenty years." As usual, Jimmy was right on the money.

When Jimmy Bentley was losing his race for the Republican gubernatorial nomination in 1970, one of the defeated Democrats from 1966 was ready to run again. He was a peanut warehouser and former state senator from Plains, Georgia, by the name of

309

Jimmy Carter. Although I didn't know Carter well at the time, his daddy, Earl Carter, had been a strong supporter of mine in the state legislature back when I was governor. By that time Jimmy was away making a career for himself as a young naval officer. He was a protégé of Admiral Hyman Rickover and seemed to have quite a future as a nuclear engineer. Had he stayed in the service, he might have risen to be Head of Naval Operations and retired as a young admiral with a good pension and excellent prospects for a second career in industry. Instead, when his father died of cancer, Jimmy resigned his commission and came home to Plains to run the family business. It was hard going at first, but he and his wife Rosalynn made a go of things and eventually got right prosperous. Jimmy was elected to the State Senate in 1962 and then left the legislature to run for governor in '66.

That 1966 race taught Jimmy a valuable lesson—Georgians like progressive government but conservative politics. He had tried to run by wooing blacks and white liberals and telling the folks about all the wonderful things he would do as governor. Well, Ellis Arnall had him outflanked on the left and Lester Maddox on the right. When he ran for governor again, Jimmy would have to make sure that history did not repeat itself. Since his major opponent this time was Carl Sanders, he had plenty of room on the right, which is where the majority of Georgians were, anyway. Jimmy had a smart young campaign manager in Hamilton Jordan and a shrewd advertising man in Gerald Rafshoon. Without making any overt appeals to race, those boys put Carter across as a kind of George Wallace clone and portrayed Sanders as a silk stocking liberal. The fact that Carl came from humbler origins than Jimmy and had done all he could for the little man when he was in office was beside the point. They had him branded as "Cuff Links Carl" and circulated a picture of him being doused with champagne by some black basketball players in the Atlanta Hawks dressing room. Jimmy nearly won a majority in the first primary, trounced Carl in the run-off, and swamped his Republican opponent in the general election.

No sooner had Jimmy Carter taken the oath as governor than he began reverting to the image he had projected in losing the 1966 race. His inaugural address and his subsequent administration surprised everyone who had followed the campaign. Liberals were delighted and began treating him as the voice of the New South (he even got his picture on the cover of *Time* magazine), and the conservatives who had supported him figured they'd been had. Probably no segment of the population was more pleased with Carter's performance as governor than the blacks. With the desegregation of our schools under Vandiver and the passage of three sweeping civil rights bills on the federal level, segregation had become a thing of the past. That enabled Carter to appear quite liberal on the race issue without having to make any hard substantive decisions. But he was great on symbolism. When he hung Dr. Martin Luther King, Jr.'s picture in the Georgia Capitol, that won Daddy King and Coretta, and with them came the majority of blacks in Georgia. By this time, however, Jimmy was looking beyond the Georgia electorate. He was constitutionally ineligible to run for a second term as governor. But as a native born American who was over thirty-five years of age, he was legally entitled to seek the highest office in the land.

There may have been nothing to prevent a Southerner from running for president, but none had been elected since James K. Polk in 1844. (Andrew Johnson had been the last Southerner to serve in the White House, and he had come within a single vote of being impeached.) There were just too many Yankees who wanted to feel morally superior to us on the race issue. The only way that would change would be if the rest of the country became more like the South or the South became more like the rest of the country. The most prominent Southern presidential candidate prior to Carter was banking on the first of these. George Corley Wallace figured that there were quite a few ordinary folks in the North who were tired of seeing their hard-earned tax dollars going to support loafers on welfare, who didn't want their children bused to unsafe and substandard schools, and who wanted to be able to walk down a city street without fear of being robbed, raped, or killed. No national Democrat was willing to run on these issues in 1964, '68, or '72, so George threw his hat in the ring. And millions of voters, North and South, responded.

I have known George Wallace since he was a judge in Alabama during the 1950's. Like Jimmy Carter, he lost his first race for governor because he was too liberal. And like Carter, he rectified that situation the second time around. As governor, he protested the integration of the University of Alabama but allowed it to take place without violent resistance. He took his crusade for state rights to some Democratic primaries in 1964 (including several in the North), even though he knew he had no chance of denying Lyndon Johnson the nomination. Then in 1968, George ran nationwide on a third-party ticket, sending a message to the political establishment that quite a few working Americans were mad as hell with the way things were going in this country. (Unlike Strom Thurmond's Dixiecrat campaign of twenty years earlier, this was a national race on national issues.) George returned to the Democratic fold in 1972 and seemed to be positioning himself for a spot on the national ticket when he was shot and paralyzed in a Maryland shopping center.

Although George did run again in 1976, the parade had passed him by. It wasn't just that he was confined to a wheel chair (that hadn't stopped Franklin Roosevelt), but that he was talking about issues that no longer stirred the old passions. Nixon and Ford may not have dismantled the welfare state, but they weren't building it up the way LBJ had. Folks were still bothered by crime and lawlessness, but the ghetto riots were over and, with the end of the Vietnam War, the campuses were quiet. George was reduced to the single issue of busing and, potent as that was, it just wasn't enough to sustain his candidacy. In going for Nixon in '72, the South had been on the winning side of a presidential election for the first time in twelve years. It was no longer that different from the rest of the nation, and it was no longer content simply to "send a message" to Washington. Not when it could send a president, instead.

Back in Georgia, Jimmy had done a pretty slick job of talking right and acting left. In the '76 campaign for president, however, he set himself the more difficult task of outflanking the opposition on both the left and the right simultaneously. He managed to shore up his strength on the left by winning endorsements from Andy Young and the King family. Moreover, as a non-Washington politician, he did not have a public record on Vietnam to live down. That same identity as a Washington outsider also enabled Jimmy to court the populist constituency that had always belonged to Wallace. (They figured why stick with George and raise hell when they could go with Jimmy and win.) You don't like the Washington bureaucracy? Jimmy would say. Well, back in Georgia I reorganized and streamlined state government—eliminating 278 of three hundred state agencies. (What he did not say was that after he moved the boxes around on the organizational chart, the state government was costing more to operate and employing more people than before.) Finally, Jimmy appealed to social conservatives, whom McGovern and other liberals had alienated, by stressing his evangelical religious views. This strengthened his standing among blacks and made in-roads among the white evangelicals who had yet to be organized for the Republicans by Jerry Falwell and Pat Robertson.

But in the last analysis, it wasn't issues than won Jimmy Carter the presidency in 1976. After Vietnam and Watergate, the people were looking for a politician they could trust. Anyone who had experience in Washington was automatically suspect. It was almost as if their positions on the issues didn't matter. (If you can't believe them, what difference does it make what they say?) In order for Carter to win, he needed to convince people that they could trust him when they couldn't trust anyone else. It was a brilliant strategy for getting elected but a disastrous one for governing. In a democracy people have to have confidence in more than one man. But in the post-Watergate era, too many folks believed Mark Twain was right when he said that America's only native criminal class is Congress.

17

Trial By Ordeal

It could be a room in any neighborhood in America. It could be located in a business or professional building, on a college campus, in a YMCA or other social club. But it is most likely to be in a church. A small group of men and women—eight or ten perhaps—have come together for a common purpose. Some of the people in the room are probably corporate executives. But you can also find entertainers, clergymen, judges, and skid row bums. There are no titles here and no social hierarchy. These people are on a first name basis because they have come to help each other with a problem none of them can deal with alone. It took me years of torment and denial before I was able to join them. In my life I have given thousands of speeches before crowds that sometimes numbered in the tens of thousands. But the most important and difficult words I ever uttered were before a handful of anonymous and caring people. When my turn came to speak, I stood up and said, "My name is Herman, and I'm an alcoholic."

PEOPLE DRINK FOR A LOT OF REASONS. Sometimes it just seems like a natural part of what they do for a living. I suspect, for example, that alcoholism is as much of an occupational disease among politicians as black lung is among coal miners—you can get it just by breathing the air. A person living and working in Washington, D.C., could attend receptions and parties night and day seven days a week. Many of these are social gatherings, but quite a few are also occasions where political business is transacted. (Congressional opposition to doing away with the tax deduction for the three-martini lunch was personal as well as philosophical.) A teetotaler could survive in this atmosphere by simply not drinking, but someone who genuinely liked to drink and socialize was in constant danger of getting hooked on the stuff. People outside of politics don't always realize what a stressful life elected officials lead. Along with being in combat during wartime, fighting forest fires, and killing rattlesnakes, running for public office is about the most demanding activity known to man. The temptation to ease the stress with a good stiff drink can be overwhelming. Before you know it, it has become a habit. Then a personal crisis comes along, and that habit turns into an uncontrollable addiction. Such a crisis occurred in my life on the evening of May 26, 1975.

It was Memorial Day weekend, and I was asleep at my home in Lovejoy. At about ten o'clock that night, I was awakened by our family maid Lucille Kelly. I knew that something terrible had happened because she was just standing out in the yard shouting, "Mr. Herman, Mr. Herman," as if she were too alarmed and distressed even to come into the house. I was by myself (Betty had stayed at our apartment in Washington), so I was totally unprepared for what Lucille had to tell me. My twenty-nine-year-old son Robert, who was on a holiday outing with his family at Lake Lanier, had drowned earlier that day. The authorities wanted me to come to Gainesville to identify the body. I called Lowell Conner, who was in charge of my Atlanta office, and asked him to meet me on the way. When I finished the two-hour drive to Gainesville, the people at the hospital took me into the room where my son's body lay. There was no mistaking that it was Bobby. I touched his cold forehead and knew that I had awakened to a nightmare.

Bobby had always been a bright boy, but for some reason he had had trouble learning how to read. I suppose that I was too busy being Governor of Georgia to realize this. All I knew was that his report card wasn't as good as it should have been. When I went to the Senate, we had him tested at a special school in Washington and discovered that he had a learning disability called dyslexia. Dyslexics are not stupid people; they just can't see letters on a page the way normal people do. To them it's all jumbled up. Albert Einstein, Nelson Rockefeller, and General Patton were all dyslexics who managed to make significant contributions to society. I don't know what Bobby would have done had he lived, but I was proud of him for what he had already accomplished. With the help of special tutors and recordings, he learned how to read well enough to graduate from the University of Georgia. At the time of his death he was running a real estate business in DeKalb County. He left a wife and two children behind.

From what I've been able to piece together, Bobby had been swimming for several hours in a cove near the Holiday Marina, where he and his family were visiting friends at their lakeside home. He must have become exhausted in the water and was too far out to make it back to shore. A fellow named Gene White, who was cooking steaks on the patio across the cove from where Bobby was visiting, said that he saw some "arms waving like in slow motion." And then they just disappeared into the water. White and his teenage son got into a boat and went out to where Bobby had gone down. They dived to the bottom several times, but to no avail. It finally took professional divers to retrieve the body. The funeral was held in a Methodist church in Atlanta large enough to accommodate the many friends who came from all over the state to share our grief. It was raining heavily on the day we buried my son in Lovejoy, a little ways behind the first home he ever knew.

After Bobby's death, I went into a period of depression where I was hitting the bottle. My drinking was beginning earlier in the day, and I was frequently drinking by myself. Also, I found that whenever I would have as many as two or three drinks, I would feel a compulsion to have more. Before, I had always persuaded myself that I didn't have a problem because I was able to do a first-rate job in my chosen profession. But even that was ceasing to be the case. I was spending too much time drunk or hungover to be the sort of senator I wanted to be. I could see it, my col-

317

leagues could see it, and I knew it was only a matter of time before my constituents would be able to see it too.

Now, it would make for a much better story if I could say that there was some dramatic incident that alerted me to my drinking problem and helped me turn my life around. But that's not the way it happened. The realization dawned on me gradually that I was a sick man. For a long while I told myself that I was using booze to get over some rough periods in my life, that when things got better I would sober up. But when things didn't get better, I had to admit that drinking wasn't helping me deal with my other problems. Instead, it was itself a problem—the *main problem* in my life. I could keep checking into hospitals to dry out, but that would do little good if I started boozing again as soon as I was released. So when I checked into the Bethesda Naval Hospital in January of 1979, I knew that a turning point was near.

One of the most difficult things for an alcoholic to do is to admit that he has a problem. The next thing he has to do, and this is sometimes even more difficult, is to admit that he can't solve that problem by himself. I have always been a resourceful and independent person. Sure, I've delegated responsibilities to others, but those were only things I didn't have time to be bothered with personally. I never asked an aide to do anything I didn't feel I was capable of doing myself (or that I hadn't already done for my father when I was working for him). So having to accept help in dealing with something as personal as alcoholism was in many ways a humiliating experience. But sometimes humiliation is necessary to produce true humility. And without humility, alcoholism is an untreatable disease. While I was in the hospital in Bethesda, people on my staff and political colleagues (some of whom had overcome drinking problems themselves) encouraged me to check into the alcohol treatment program at the naval hospital in Long Beach, California. Taking their advice probably saved my life.

Like so many youngsters, I had started drinking in college. Booze was a social lubricant that was an essential part of a good time. Although I could take a drink or leave it back then, I took more than I left. Sometimes I had more than my limit and got into minor mischief. But it never occurred to me then that I had a "drinking problem." After all, I kept my grades up and functioned well in loads of extracurricular activities. If I had given the matter any thought at all, I would have said that a true alcoholic couldn't do a tenth of what I did. Alcoholics are fellows who lie in the gutter choking on their own vomit. They are not big men on campus or successful young lawyers. And they certainly aren't hardworking and progressive governors. I may have relaxed a bit after a grueling day at the office or on the campaign trail, but I could always hold my liquor. Exaggerated stories about my drinking never really bothered me, because that was part of the image and legend of the Southern politician.

Our society has strange, hypocritical attitudes toward drink. We heap contempt on the wino and skid row bum, but our movies and television programs make booze seem glamorous and treat intoxication as a joke. Folks want their politicians to be sober on the job but interesting and colorful on the campaign trail. A candidate who isn't too uppity to drink with his constituents seems like a regular fellow. People got a laugh at Big Jim Folsom falling out of a jeep while reviewing R.O.T.C. troops and at Huey Long taking a leak on some heckler in the men's room and then went out and voted for more of the same. Jimmy Carter's brother Billy even had his own line of beer before he took the cure.

Some politicians practically make a career out of doing outrageous things when they're drunk. Take Earl Long, for instance. He beat a regular path back and forth between various mental hospitals and the Louisiana governor's mansion. (In his later years he took up with a New Orleans stripper named Blaze Star, and the two of them entertained the whole nation with their escapades.) Once when his wife Blanche had him committed to an asylum, Earl got out by exercising his power as governor and firing the administrator of the place. His more normal procedure, however, was to get the highway patrol to rescue him or his lawyer to file a writ of *habeas corpus*. At the end of his life, Earl was constitutionally barred from seeking reelection as governor, so he set his sights on the seat of a well-respected congressman by the name of Herbert B. McSween. When people accused Earl of being crazy, he met the issue head-on and said that when he got to Washington no one would be able to tell the difference. The voters bought that line and elected Earl by a landslide. Unfortunately, he died before he was able to take his seat.

Another politician who created a good deal of amusement with his drinking antics was Congressman Wilbur Mills of Arkansas. Up until the early morning of October 2, 1974, most Americans who knew Wilbur thought of him as pretty strait-laced, maybe even a little bit of a stick-in-the-mud. He had gone to Congress in 1938 and had been reelected seventeen times with little or no opposition. He wore conservative suits, had his hair slicked back, and stirred so little enthusiasm on the stump that when he tried to run for president in 1972 he drew less than one percent of the vote in some primaries. But as chairman of the Ways and Means Committee since 1958, Wilbur was the most powerful member of the House of Representatives. His committee was responsible for making all other committee assignments in the House and for writing the nation's tax laws. Of the countless public officials I have known at a local, state, and national level, none was more capable than Wilbur Mills.

Well, on that early October morning in 1974, the Washington, D.C., park police chased down a blue Lincoln Continental that was speeding with its headlights out over near the Jefferson Memorial. When they got the car pulled over, this spitfire blonde with a couple of black eyes jumped out, ran hysterically toward the Potomac River Tidal Basin, and fell in. There were two men and two other women in the car, all pretty juiced up. One was an old fellow with a nosebleed and scratches all over his face. The park police couldn't believe their eyes. It was Wilbur Mills.

This incident got folks to snickering inside the Washington, D.C., Beltway and created quite a bit of embarrassment for Wilbur back home in Arkansas—especially when it turned out that the blonde lady was an Argentine stripper by the name of Fanne Fox. However, things seemed to have blown over when Wilbur won reelection a month later with the campaign slogan "Never Drink Champagne with a Foreigner." But, as a few of us in Washington knew, Wilbur's problems went deeper than just a few too many toasts at a party one night. He had been operated on for a ruptured spinal disk in 1973 and started treating the pain with larger and larger quantities of vodka. Once during that period, when Russell Long was campaigning down in Louisiana and I was temporarily chairing the senate Finance Committee, we had some sort of conference with the house Ways and Means Committee. Wilbur confided to me later that at that time he was putting away a quart of vodka a day. Although he still seemed to me to be a walking encyclopedia, what I didn't know was that he was also suffering from periodic blackouts. One such blackout occurred about a month after his reelection to Congress in 1974. Having peeled her clothes in one of the sleaziest strip joints in Boston (she was now billed as the Tidal Basin Bombshell), Fanne Fox wrapped herself in a feathery pink negligee offstage and came back to take some bows. She peered down in the audience and said, "Mr. Mills, Mr. Mills, where are you?" Old Wilbur bounded up on stage and brought a distinguished political career to an end.

Folks laugh at Wilbur Mills and his "Argentine Firecracker," but what they often fail to see is the public and private tragedy of what happened to Wilbur. Publicly, the nation lost an extraordinarily knowledgeable and dedicated public servant. (Had it not been for his misfortune, Wilbur probably would have had a number of productive years ahead of him in Congress.) Personally, a genuinely good and decent man became something of a national laughingstock. But, thank God, this sordid incident was not the end of Wilbur Mills. As a politician Wilbur was finished, but as a human being he had just begun to live. Ever since he left politics, Wilbur has been working with Alcoholics Anonymous, trying to help people who suffer as he did from an inability to control their drinking. Wilbur no longer writes our tax laws. He is no longer in the public eye. And journalists no longer call him "the powerful Wilbur Mills." But over the past dozen years quite a few troubled men and women have felt the power of his counsel and drawn inspiration from his example. I know, because I'm one of them. As much as any individual Wilbur Mills helped me to face up to my affliction and take the necessary steps to turn my life around.

I checked into the Bethesda Naval Hospital in early January 1979, and by the end of the month I had decided to enter the alcohol treatment program that the Navy ran in Long Beach, California. It had been started because of a need within the Navy itself. The government spent hundreds of thousands of dollars to train a naval pilot to land on aircraft carriers and perform his other duties, and all that money was wasted when the pilot got so hooked on booze that he couldn't fly a plane straight. So even if you disregard humanitarian considerations, it made good economic sense for the Navy to try to salvage its investment by putting some money into alcohol treatment. By all reports, the program was a phenomenal success. That was, no doubt, due to the efforts of an amazing man by the name of Joe Pursch.

Joe was a naval officer who had been born and reared in Yugoslavia. His family was killed by Tito's people right after the Second World War, but Joe managed to escape and make his way to this country, where he ended up washing windows in Chicago, Illinois. By the time the Korean War rolled around, Joe had gotten himself into the naval medical corps and eventually earned his medical degree with a specialization in psychiatry. He started that alcohol treatment program out at Long Beach and was its driving force for a number of years. (When he retired from the Navy, Joe started a similar civilian program called Comprehensive Care.) It's the most successful and beneficial form of brainwashing I've ever run into.

I was out at Long Beach for about six weeks. For the most part they kept us too busy to have time to think about booze. At first it was hard not having a drink to relax with, but I came to learn that I had an addiction that could be controlled only if I stayed away from the addictive drug. They had us sleeping in a common room with about six other people. We each had responsibilities for keeping the area clean, and everyone had to keep his bed made. (If that was to teach us humility, it certainly did the trick.) We would have lectures and films during the day and Alcoholics Anonymous meetings at night. Although there was nothing sectarian about our treatment, we were taught to rely on a higher spiritual power. I have gone to church all my life and for a time as a boy even wanted to be a preacher. But I guess I never really took to heart Our Lord's admonition that you must become as a little child to enter the Kingdom of Heaven. At Long Beach I relearned a lesson I had forgotten along life's way—that we are all children of God. When I started having problems I couldn't handle myself, I had made the mistake of taking them to a bottle rather than to my Maker.

I suspect that military personnel being treated in the Long Beach program were assigned there by orders, but as a civilian, I was free to leave if I wanted to. I'm sure that the vast majority of patients would have stayed because of peer pressure, if nothing else. They used no medication out there at Long Beach, only group therapy, and it was the group dynamics that made the program so successful. When you are fighting in war, you don't consciously think of the Constitution or the flag or the American way of life. You think of that guy on your left and the one on your right. Your life depends on them and theirs on you. The French call it *esprit de corps*. But whatever label you put on it, it works. Of course, there were a few backsliders. (I heard of one Marine colonel who got drunk waiting on his plane to take him home.) But upwards of eighty percent of the patients who went through the program stayed off the sauce for good. Psychiatrists practicing individual therapy can't claim nearly that high a rate of success.

About the only advantage to being an alcoholic is that when you stop drinking you come to appreciate sobriety more than those who never suffered from this horrible addiction. Waking up in the morning without a hangover and being able to call your life your own are simple blessings that the non-alcoholic takes for granted. January 1987 marked my eighth year of sobriety. I don't feel the compulsion to drink, but I keep liquor at the house for those who do wish to partake. Part of the treatment for alcoholism is learning to live in a society where people who can handle booze continue to enjoy drinking it. A cripple has to live with people who can walk. A blind man has to live with people who can see. And an alcoholic has to live with people who can drink. It would be nice if I could drink moderately, but I can't. Instead, I savor the taste of food, I enjoy the natural beauty of the woods, and I remember a time when I was separated from those and other pleasures by a cloud of booze. I literally thank God that that time is gone forever.

There is a definite euphoria experienced by any alcoholic who goes on the wagon and stays there. But that euphoria can be deceptive and dangerous. Booze may no longer be a problem for the recovering alcoholic (there is no such thing as a *recovered* alcoholic, because alcoholism cannot be cured—only controlled). Still, he will continue to have his share of normal human problems, just as other folks do. Before, he tried to deal with those problems by drinking. Now he must find other ways of coping. Just about every recovering alcoholic has had a day when he says, "That used to drive me to drink." When that happens, he will experience many of the same physical and psychological symptoms that he did when he'd be on a binge. That's what's known as a "dry drunk." At such times, the support of family, friends, and other alcoholics can be invaluable. It is at such times that I remember the prayer of Saint Francis of Assisi that has become a sort of motto for Alcoholics Anonymous: "Lord, grant me the serenity to accept those things I cannot change, the courage to change those things I can, and the wisdom to know the difference."

As I've said, the period following Bobby's death was a dark time when my drinking really started getting out of hand. Also, Betty and I were drifting apart, and the dissolution of our marriage seemed imminent. I doubt that there are many professions that put as much strain on a marriage as politics does. It's a terribly unpredictable life. When I left home in the morning, I knew that I'd be eating lunch in the senate dining room, but I had no idea where I'd be having supper. If the Senate ran late, which was most of the time, I'd eat downtown. Only rarely would I be able to go home. Back in the early days, when I was running for Governor of Georgia, I would sometimes be on the road all week and come home only on weekends. The wife of a politician marries not just her husband but his career as well. There's an old saying that Caesar's wife must be beyond reproach. In a democracy, all politicians are potential caesars, and their wives are always in the public eye. That has ruined the marriages of many politicians.

For a public person, divorce is never a purely private matter. When my first marriage fell apart, I had the good fortune to be an obscure Atlanta lawyer whose life was still his own. But when Betty and I parted ways nearly forty years later, I was probably the best known man in all of Georgia. It's true that divorce had become commonplace and that most people were broad-minded enough to realize that politicians are human beings, not gods. Still, I knew that I would have to deal with that small minority of voters who were reluctant to entrust the affairs of state to a man with a troubled home life. What I didn't expect, and found infinitely more difficult to bear, was the obscene public scrutiny that comes with a divorce trial. I was soon to discover that in such a trial nothing about one's personal life is private any longer. Media vultures pick through a divorce petition until they find something they can exploit to sell newspapers or boost television ratings. These days cub reporters are no longer content to cover fires and ribbon cuttings. Too many see themselves as potential Woodward and Bernsteins, ready to send some corrupt public official to the penitentiary. And if the public official happens to be innocent, that's just too bad. The Supreme Court has virtually robbed him of the protection of the libel laws.

My divorce from Betty became final on October 19, 1977. Many longtime residents of Georgia viewed that tragedy as if it had occurred in their own family. If I was the best known man in Georgia at the time, Betty was certainly one of the best known women. She had been my first lady when I was governor and had received a good deal of favorable publicity as a charming hostess and shrewd businesswoman. Oldtimers around the state would find it hard to imagine either one of us without the other.

The personal aspects of my former marriage and eventual divorce will just have to remain personal. I know that my conscience is clear, and now that I am out of politics, it really doesn't matter what people think of me. For most of our marriage Betty was a good wife. In memory of those years and for the sake of our surviving son and grandchildren, I have not made and will not make public attacks on her. Besides, I was raised to believe that whatever else a gentleman might do, he does not insult a lady. And at age seventy-four, I'm not about to start now.

☆ ☆ ☆

For the growing thousands who were newly arrived in Georgia, press coverage of that divorce was their introduction to the character of Herman Talmadge. Mention my name to someone who first heard about me then, and he is likely to say, "Isn't that the fellow who kept his money in an old overcoat?" What they'd be referring to is the allegation, which surfaced during the divorce, that I paid my personal expenses out of a large horde of cash stuffed in the pocket of an old overcoat. That charge was embellished with some pretty good theatrics (which I'll be a-comin' to) and made for sensational copy in the anti-Talmadge press—particularly the Atlanta papers. But there was a hell of a lot less to it than most people were willing to believe. I've never denied that I found it more convenient to pay recurring personal expenses with cash rather than writing a lot of checks. It's an old-fashioned habit I probably acquired as a young man in the Depression. What I've always denied is that there were *huge amounts of cash* around the house, in an overcoat or anywhere else. With each retelling, that pile of cash kept getting bigger and bigger. "Where'd he get all that money?" people would ask. My answer was too simple and guileless to be believed by anyone who didn't know the traditions of Georgia politics.

As I've already mentioned in an earlier chapter, campaign financing back in the early days used to be pretty informal, to say the least. After a campaign speech, you'd pass the hat, or sometimes folks would just come up and shove money at you. They didn't ask for a receipt or demand to see your income tax returns. (That was before people had begun to believe that politicians were all crooks.) They knew that you would spend the money on campaign posters or bumper stickers or gas to get your car to the next rally. Those were the days before political action committees and negative TV advertising. It was also before Watergate and the new financial disclosure laws. Ellis Arnall, who has said some pretty rough things about the Talmadges over the years, testified to the senate Ethics Committee about the way things used to be. But in the political climate of the mid-seventies, those old ways of doing things looked mighty suspicious. In retrospect, I wish that I'd burned that damn overcoat and charged everything on American Express.

There's a pervasive notion among quite a few media folks that all politicians are on the take and getting rich at the public expense. That's a lot of hogwash. People who leave a successful career for a job in government service usually take a substantial cut in pay. Those who have been in politics all their lives invariably have made less money than they would have in some other line of work. The cash gifts I've received over the years (at birthday parties and the like) were unsolicited gestures of friendship that were individually so small they wouldn't tempt any but the neediest and stupidest politician to produce favors in return. Although I wasn't as rich as some, I was far from needy. And even my worst enemies have never accused me of being stupid.

Well, shortly after my divorce, some reporters from the *Washington Star* figured that if they snooped around long enough they would find hard evidence of my financial misconduct. What they found was pretty distressing. And no one was more surprised or upset than I was. My reputation for frugality with the taxpayer's money went back to my years as governor. While I was in office, the legislature had voted against my will to raise my salary by over $10,000. Feeling that was unwarranted, I refused to take the extra money, and as far as I know it is still in the Georgia treasury. Whenever I traveled on public business, I rode tourist class. And in my twenty-four years in the Senate, I went overseas exactly three times at taxpayers' expense. (Wyche Fowler, the fellow who holds my seat now, went overseas nearly forty times during his nine years in the House of Representatives.) If I was that scrupulous about taking money I was legally entitled to, I sure as hell wasn't about to lay claim to money that was not legally mine. But it appeared that for several years my senate office had been filing for reimbursement for expenses that were either unauthorized or non-existent. When I got wind of this, I hired one of the best public accounting firms in America to make a complete audit. As a result we discovered $37,125 in excess expense claims, which I promptly repaid to the federal treasury. The big unanswered questions, though, were, Who made the fraudulent claims and what was done with the money?

Throughout my career in public life, I had been blessed with extraordinarily competent and honest staff. From my first administrative assistant, Benton Odum, to my last, Will Ball, I had reliable subordinates to whom I could entrust matters great and small. No person in a position of leadership will do for himself what he can get others to do for him. That philosophy freed me to devote my attention to the issues the voters elected me to deal with. Only once did I make a serious mistake in selecting a key aide. Unfortunately, that one mistake led to the scandal that ended my political career.

I had known Daniel Minchew for several years as a lobbyist, and I found him to be an enormously bright and attractive fellow. He had a winning personality and quite a bit of drive and ambition. He was also a native Georgian. So when I had a vacancy in my senate office, I thought that Minchew would make an ideal administrative assistant. Ordinarily, I would have checked his background, but I felt I knew Daniel Minchew well enough to dispense with the formality. That bit of laxity was easily the biggest blunder of all my years in public life. Had I checked Minchew out, I would have discovered that he had been involved in some shady dealings when he tried to set up a travel bureau in Athens, Georgia, back when he was a student at the University. (I would later learn that affair almost landed him in the penitentiary.) During the time he worked for me, however, I had no occasion to suspect Minchew of any improper activity. In fact, I was so pleased with his work that I recommended him for a job with the International Trade Commission. It wasn't until we uncovered the overdrawn office expenses that I began to have second thoughts about Minchew. By this time (June, 1978), the senate Ethics Committee had launched its own investigation. The evidence it turned up revealed just how devious Mr. Minchew had been.

During the time he worked for me, Minchew was in charge of funds for both my senate office and my campaign committee. I naturally assumed that both were being handled properly. That was before the senate Ethics Committee discovered a Talmadge Campaign account at the Riggs Bank in Washington. Instead of using the office expense money for office expenses and depositing campaign contributions into my account with the Trust Company of Georgia, Minchew had been diverting money from both sources into this secret account that he had set up and then using it for his own speculation in real estate. Minchew was eventually convicted and sent to prison for doing this. But like so many small time crooks, he felt that he would make things easier on himself if he could drag a big name down with him. So he told the senate investigators that he had set up the account at my instructions and for my personal benefit. I remember that when Minchew's statement came out, my administrative assistant Rogers Wade came bursting into my office and said, "He's trying to cover his own ass!"

The senate Ethics Committee opened formal hearings on my case in May of 1979, a little less than four years after Bobby had drowned, over a year and a half after my divorce from Betty, and just a few months after my return from the alcohol treatment program at Long Beach, California. It was also six years after the opening of the senate Watergate hearings. I didn't relish being cast as the villain in this drama after having been a shining knight in the earlier one, but I knew that I was innocent of intentional wrongdoing and was certain that my colleagues would exonerate me. That is why I refused the committee's offer to plead guilty and submit to a senate censure without public hearings. My attorney, Jim Hamilton, had established a reputation for integrity during the Watergate hearings, and no one would suspect him of wanting to cover up the sort of crimes I had been charged with. Let the committee dig all it wanted to, the case finally came down to the question of whether Daniel Minchew or Herman Talmadge was telling the truth.

Unfortunately for me, the membership of the Senate Ethics Committee was pretty lackluster at the time. The chairman of the committee was Adlai Stevenson III. His great-grandfather had been vice president under Grover Cleveland, and his father was the fellow who twice ran for president against Eisenhower and later served as Kennedy's Ambassador to the United Nations. Like his father, young Adlai had about as much force of character as a jellyfish that had washed up on shore. But he lacked his daddy's wit and intellect and had real trouble thinking for himself. He formed too many of his judgments on the basis of what he read in the newspapers. And at this time the newspapers weren't exactly singing my praises.

The vice chairman of the committee was a New Mexico Republican by the name of Harrison "Jack" Schmitt. Since Adlai wasn't the most dynamic chairman in the world, Schmitt figured he could fill the leadership vacuum by making partisan attacks on me. Jack Schmitt was a former astronaut with a squeaky clean image and loads of ambition. He had lobbied for the hearings to be televised, presumably so he could demagogue in front of the entire nation. Fortunately, the majority of the committee would not go along, so Schmitt had to play to the audience in the hearing room and to the newspapers. From his conduct in those hearings, I got the impression that he thought any public official accused of wrongdoing was guilty until proven innocent. In fact, I'm not sure he even understood the charges that had been brought against me.

The other two Republicans on the committee were about as different as any two men in the Senate. Jesse Helms was a former radio and television commentator who had been elected to the Senate from North Carolina in the Nixon landslide of 1972. Jesse was so conservative he made me look like a leftwinger by comparison. He got a lot of folks riled up by taking the most extreme right-wing position on any issue. But I always found him to be a man of conviction and integrity. Unlike Schmitt, he wasn't out to lynch me. Still, Jesse was more interested in raising money for conservative causes and in his other senate chores than in the work of the Ethics Committee. So, in my case, he seemed willing to go along with whatever his colleagues thought proper.

Then there was Mark Hatfield. Today, Hatfield has more seniority in the Senate than any Republican other than Strom Thurmond, but he is far out of the mainstream for both his party and the nation as a whole. Hatfield was Governor of Oregon from 1959-67 and then came to the Senate as an outspoken critic of the Vietnam War. On foreign policy and military issues, Hatfield is probably the most liberal member of the Senate. (Next to him Ted Kennedy is a hawk.) He's one of those holier-than-thou fellows who thinks he has a direct pipeline to Heaven. Hatfield probably enjoyed being on the Ethics Committee because it gave him a license to be self-righteous. I'm sure that no Pharisee in the temple ever thought more highly of his own character.

Rounding out the committee were two more Democrats— Quentin Burdick of North Dakota and Robert Morgan of North Carolina. One was a political lightweight and the other a man of substance. Burdick was a former star football player from the University of Minnesota, who was clearly out of his depth in the U.S. Senate. During the hearings he was heard to say that the newspapers back in North Dakota were giving me hell, so he'd have to toe the line. Robert Morgan, however, was a man capable of thinking for himself. He had been attorney general in North Carolina before replacing Sam Ervin in the Senate when Sam retired in 1974. Morgan was the only member of that committee who spent more time studying the facts of the case than reading sensational newspaper stories. He knew what questions to ask and how to keep after a witness until he got the information he was looking for. He was the only committee member who had anything approaching a judicial temperament. The rest were willing to let the committee staff prepare a gallows and then turn out to see me hung.

There were about a hundred spectators in Room 1202 of the Dirksen Senate Office Building when the Ethics Committee opened its hearings on May 1, 1979. The case against me was made by the committee's chief counsel, a vindictive old man by the name of Carl Eardley. Mr. Eardley had left this country during the Vietnam War so he wouldn't have to prosecute draft dodgers (which was understandable, since two of his sons had fled to Canada to evade the draft). He had also traveled with the Freedom Riders down south in the early sixties. It was hard to believe that a man of his background could be fair and objective in judging a man of my background. But after I heard Eardley's opening statement, I breathed a sigh of relief. Not only was his case incredibly weak, but Eardley was befuddled and tongue-tied. By the time he had finished, I was chomping on the bit to show my senate colleagues and the American people just how baseless his accusations were.

After answering three petty charges against me, I reminded the committee that the excess office reimbursements had been discovered by an audit I had ordered and paid for and that I had willingly repaid the federal treasury all the money I was alleged to owe. I then turned my attention to the final, most serious, charge against me. Here are some excerpts from my statement to the committee:

> Daniel Minchew admits diverting nearly $13,000 of senate funds and about $26,000 of campaign contributions into [a secret bank] account. The accusation brought against me rests on the word of Daniel Minchew. But no one—after hearing all the facts—could possibly believe his story.
>
> Undisputed evidence will show that Minchew opened the secret Riggs account by forging my signature.
>
> That he obtained $13,000 in senate funds by forging my signature to two senate vouchers.
>
> That he alone made all the deposits into the account.
>
> And that he alone made all withdrawals by forging my signature to checks made out to cash.

I went on to show how my various actions in this matter were inconsistent with Minchew's allegations that I knew about the secret account and was profiting from it. Why, for example, would I have ordered an independent audit (which Minchew tried to talk me out of) if I knew that it would reveal a secret bank account that would incriminate me? Why, when I learned that two senate checks had been processed at the Riggs Bank, did I promptly turn them over to the Ethics Committee and the Department of Justice? If I had intended to steal money, I would not have taken on an accomplice who could later implicate me. I would not have opened a bank account that left a paper trail so easily discovered. (Hell, if I had wanted to divert campaign funds for personal use, I could have simply endorsed the checks to cash and pocketed the money.) And I certainly would not have insisted, as Minchew claims I did, that money from a milk cooperative be put in that account at a time when the Watergate Committee, on which I served, was scrutinizing the political contributions of that same cooperative. To believe Daniel Minchew, one would have to believe that in addition to being a crook, I was also a fool.

Simply on the basis of my reputation for honesty against Minchew's, the charges should have been dropped then and there. It was a matter of record that Minchew had lied to financial institutions from which he had borrowed money, to the Department of Justice, and repeatedly to the Internal Revenue Service. He had failed three FBI lie detector tests, and even his own hired polygraphers agreed that his answers to the FBI were deceptive. His travel agency license had been revoked because of his misuse of funds due the airlines; he was hounded by creditors; he had tried to defraud his real estate partner of tens of thousands of dollars; and he had bounced checks all over town. Moreover, in 1974, when most of the money was taken from the secret Riggs account, Minchew's obligations and expenditures exceeded his legitimate income by more than $40,000. And yet, he expected the authorities to believe that he was stealing money for my benefit.

What possible motivation did I have to misuse public funds? My income exceeded $70,000 in 1973 and $80,000 in 1974. In both years my wife's separate income exceeded $80,000, and my son Bobby's $50,000. (Bobby, Betty, and I were the three people Minchew alleged were benefiting from the Riggs account.) Furthermore, my net worth in those years was over $1.5 million, and I had ample funds in the bank. Had I needed more money during those years, I could have accepted numerous speaking engagements offering generous honoraria. These facts were matters of public record unchallenged by even my bitterest enemies.

I concluded my opening statement by framing the issue as I saw it:

> Mr. Chairman and members of the committee, to find me guilty of complicity in the Riggs account, you would have to accept the word of a proven liar, cheat, and embezzler. You would have to accept his word against

that of a senator who has held the trust of his colleagues and his constituents for 23 years—a senator who would not have jeopardized his career, betrayed his colleagues, and abused the trust of his beloved state of Georgia for any reason, let alone a few dollars.

After my opening statement, the hearings dragged on as Eardley vainly tried to make a case against me. Everyone was waiting for Minchew to take the stand and do his best to pull me in the quagmire with him. But the committee didn't even get to him until after the Memorial Day recess. (The investigation had already cost over $100,000 of the taxpayer's money with no end in sight.) When they finally called him to testify, Minchew did his case no good. After listening to him for eight days (six under cross examination), no person in his right mind would have believed Minchew when he said "good morning" without calling the Weather Bureau to make sure.

At first, Minchew told the authorities he had taken for his personal use $7200 of the nearly $40,000 he claims to have stolen for me. After accountants for both myself and the committee began tracing the paths of the money in and out of the secret account, Minchew was forced to admit that he had taken $16-18,000. (I wouldn't be surprised if the actual figure was twice that high.) Even Carl Eardley seemed put off by his star witness. After Minchew finished testifying, Eardley said to him, "The record in this case has indicated to me at least that you have been deceptive in some of your business relationships. As a consequence, your credibility as a witness has been eroded."

At that point I figured my troubles were over. What I hadn't counted on was the impact of the testimony my former wife would give the following week. Under Georgia law, a wife cannot be compelled to testify about confidential marital communications. Betty had tried to invoke the spirit of that law to be excused from appearing before the senate Ethics Committee. But Eardley wouldn't hear of it. Because my difficulties had begun with allegations made during the divorce trial, it was assumed that Betty knew some deep dark secret that would resolve the issue of my guilt or innocence. As it turned out, her testimony was spectacular but almost totally irrelevant.

When Betty entered the hearing room on the morning of June 12, I got out of my seat and walked over to greet her. It was an awkward moment, with about a dozen camera lights glaring at us. (Reporters who had been dozing through weeks of testimony more interminable than a Wayne Morse filibuster snapped to attention to see what would happen next.) I stuck out my hand and said, "Good morning." She took it and said, "Hello, Herman." After she was sworn in, Betty proceeded to give her version of events that everyone else remembered differently. One example was a little altercation in my senate office on January 21, 1974.

As Betty recalled that incident, she had come to my office to get a look at some financial records of a business she was involved in. When she didn't get the cooperation she sought from Daniel Minchew, she started to fuss at him and eventually "slapped" him in frustration. As I recall that confrontation, however, Betty came storming into the office telling everyone that she had put me where I was and that from then on everyone—"including Herman"—worked for her. The next thing she did was to "fire" Minchew and begin to clear out his desk. When he took exception to her behavior, she picked up a wood carving and started to throw it at him. I tried to restrain her and hurt my shoulder in the process. (If I had known then what I know now, I would have left her alone or actually helped her go after the s.o.b.) Betty commandeered Minchew's desk and sat there on and off for three days as everyone in the office tried to work around her.

Although my secretary Allyne Tisdale, who was also an eyewitness, testified to the details of that little fracas, the committee didn't seem to have any reservations at all about swallowing whatever cock-and-bull story Betty was of a mind to tell them. They were also impressed as hell by a little visual aid she brought along with her—a stack of seventy-seven $100 bills that she claimed to have taken from my overcoat in early 1974. The bills were in an envelope with the name of "Harry Anestos" written on the outside. Harry was a supporter of mine who had a good deal of influence in the Greek-American community in Savannah. So the implication was that I was taking secret payoffs from Harry and doing favors for him in return.

Well, I was sure that I had never gotten a contribution from Harry as large as $7,700, and certainly not in cash. When we looked into the matter further, it was established that the handwriting on the outside of the envelope belonged to Rogers Wade, who hadn't come to work for me until 1975— *a year and a half after Betty claims to have found the money.* What the envelope actually had contained was not cash at all, but a note requesting that I speak at a Greek Orthodox Church in Savannah. Betty may have been convinced that she was telling the truth, but any objective observer could see that she was simply deluding herself. (She once told my press secretary Gordon Roberts that she would make me sorry if I ever divorced her.) However, the majority of the committee was so bug-eyed from looking at those $100-bills they probably would have believed Betty had she sworn I'd printed them up in the senate basement.

Betty's testimony concluded Eardley's case against me. In a regular trial, where a man is judged innocent until proven guilty, the defense would have rested at that point and asked for a dismissal of all charges. But constitutional rights and the tradition of English common law carried very little weight in what amounted to a public inquisition. It was up to me to prove that I was not only innocent of the specific charges brought against me, but that I was a paragon of civic virtue. (To ask a man to *prove* his virtue is sort of like asking a woman to prove her beauty.) I had an impressive array of character witnesses to help me do just that, but the investigation had gone on for too long and had cost too much for the committee and the press to admit that it was hounding an innocent man. (If I had had Jesus Christ and the twelve apostles testifying on my behalf, the Atlanta papers probably would have run a headline saying, "Religious Leader and Cohorts Implicated in Talmadge Scam.") Jack Schmitt wanted to hang me out to dry and pushed for an outright censure, but he couldn't get a majority of the committee to go along. What they decided to do was split the difference between a censure and a reprimand and vote to "denounce" me for reprehensible conduct. That recommendation went before the full Senate, which voted on the matter on October 10, 1979.

Looking back on it, I wish that I had carried my fight to the senate floor. It's ironic, but a couple of years before I came to the Senate, Joe McCarthy was censured for making wild charges against government officials, and the people he had accused were held up as innocent victims, if not national heroes. What a difference twenty-five years makes. It was now the innocent victim who was subjected to a public flogging and the reckless accusers who were seen as the conscience of the nation. I think many of my senate colleagues, who had no great love for that Ethics Committee, anyway, might have understood what a travesty was being perpetrated, if I had only made the effort to reason with them. But the preceding four years had taken a lot of the fight out of me. When friends came up and said, "Herman, how do you want me to vote on this?" I replied, "Any way you see fit." The vote was eighty-one to fifteen in favor of the resolution, with four senators voting "present."

Although I had not been officially vindicated, neither had I been convicted of any intentional wrongdoing. Daniel Minchew went to the penitentiary, while not so much as an indictment was brought against me. Some would say that merely staying out of jail is not a high enough standard of conduct to expect of public officials. But what the folks who say that really want to do is substitute their own partisan political judgment for the objectivity that is supposed to prevail in the criminal justice system. (If they can't put you behind bars, the gossips simply will defame your character, knowing that it's nearly impossible for a public person to win a libel suit.) Beyond the press and the Ethics Committee, however, there was a court of last resort that had always found in my favor. Always when the going was roughest, the Talmadges had drawn their strength from the ordinary people of Georgia. What I didn't realize was that those ordinary people were slowly being outnumbered by folks who had recently come to the state because they heard that it was a good place to live. For the most part, they had no idea how it got that way, and the *Atlanta Constitution* wasn't about to tell them.

18

My Last Campaign

It was August 19, 1978. Seven hundred folks had gathered at the Atlanta Hilton to wish me a happy birthday. I had turned sixty-five ten days earlier, and I'd been in the Senate for twenty-two years. Papa would have been proud. He only made it to sixty-two himself, and he lost both his races for the Senate. He'd been dead for over thirty years, but there were still people who loved or hated me because of him. I hadn't had any happy birthdays of late. Bobby had died three years earlier. Then, there was the divorce, and this ethics thing was coming up in the Senate. But life couldn't be all bad if so many people would pay twenty-five dollars a head to be seen in public with me. Right after the war, my birthday was celebrated with just a few fellows out at the farm in Lovejoy. Then, as now, they'd sing: "For he's a jolly good fellow. For he's a jolly good fellow. For he's a jolly good fellow. That nobody can deny..." But some were denying it. The Atlanta papers just wouldn't let up or give me the benefit of the doubt. Neither their owner Mrs. Anne Cox Chambers nor her hired guns. I got up to speak and took off my coat. That's right—red galluses. They came for a stemwinder, that's what they'll get. "When Papa used to get mad," I said, "he'd take off his coat, snap his suspenders, and shell down the corn."

I DECLARED MY CANDIDACY FOR REELECTION at that birthday dinner in 1978. People who didn't know me had started to spread the rumor that I might not run again, that I might even resign before my term was up. The political maneuvering had already begun. No one was willing to challenge me yet, but quite a few were ready to jump in if I pulled out. Maynard Jackson would have loved to run again, but he knew that I could still take him with one arm behind my back. Wyche Fowler, a white liberal who had replaced Andy Young in Congress, was a possibility, but I'd have to be a hell of a lot more wounded for Wyche to give up a safe congressional seat to run statewide in conservative Georgia. If anything, the opposition might try to outflank me on the right. Larry McDonald (a Democratic congressman and leader of the John Birch Society) was giving me unshirted hell for voting to "give away" the Panama Canal. And J.B. Stoner was doing his best to stir up race hatred. I was too liberal for the bigots when I was equalizing facilities and services for blacks back when I was governor. And now that I was supporting extension of the Voting Rights Act, they figured I was a wild-eyed revolutionary.

My previous campaigns for the Senate had been pretty prefunctory. In 1956 and '62, I had no Republican opposition in the general election and very little competition in the Democratic Primary. After Senator George dropped out of the race in '56, what was left of the anti-Talmadge forces had no one to turn to but M.E. Thompson, and M.E. hadn't won anything since his 1946 campaign for lieutenant governor. (I carried every county in the state and ended his career.) In '62 I had token opposition from an old college friend by the name of Hank Henderson. I have no idea why Hank ran against me, unless he just wanted to be a footnote in the history books. He lived most of the time in his automobile and didn't carry a single precinct in the state.

Nineteen sixty-eight was only slightly different. Although the Voting Rights Act was passed in 1965, it was largely superfluous in Georgia. We had had a large black registration ever since the White Primary was outlawed in the late forties, and I had courted the black vote from then on. Still, some blacks felt they had to make a kind of crusade of opposing me. Take Maynard Jackson. He ran against me in the 1968 senatorial primary. Then as Mayor of Atlanta, he began to equate being pro-black with being anti-white. Maynard thought that any black who supported me had sold out to the enemy. (He realized that his career wasn't going anywhere after he left the mayor's office, so maybe he thought that finding someone to beat me in 1980 was the only political vindication he would ever get.) It's the sort of philosophy that says, "Unless you're my enemy's enemy, you can't be my friend."

After beating Maynard in 1968, I ran for a fourth term in the Senate in 1974 and again won in a landslide. That was the year after the televised Watergate hearings, and I was at the height of my popularity. All I really remember about that campaign was that I had to face two crank candidates—one in the primary and one in the general election. In the primary my opponent was Dr. Carlton Myers, who was a veterinarian with the U. S. Department of Agriculture. He had been fired from his job as a poultry inspector and was mad at me because I had either been unable or unwilling to help him get his job back. So he ran against me and spent the whole campaign talking about poultry inspection. I figured that was a good issue for him to talk about and left him alone.

In the general election that year the Republicans ran a fellow by the name of Jerry Johnson. Now, Jerry didn't talk about poultry inspection, but he was real big on financial disclosure. He had revealed his income tax returns to the press and was insisting that I do the same. I'd already told him that I didn't believe in that kind of Peeping Tom politics and that he'd just have to play by himself. (He reminded me of a little kid saying, "I've shown you mine, you show me yours.") Well, that didn't go down too well with Jerry, so he alerted the press and the TV stations that he was going to confront me when I went to speak before a group at one of the hotels in Atlanta. And sure enough, he was there blocking my entrance, shouting, "When are you going to disclose your taxes?" I told him I wasn't and that it was none of his business. About that time Lowell Conner, who was one of my aides, sort of pushed Jerry aside so that we could get to the meeting. Next thing I knew, Jerry had gone down and sworn out a warrant against Conner for assault and battery. Fortunately, Lowell was acquitted of the charge, and I won the election handily. But this salacious interest in my personal finances would plague me for the rest of my political career.

☆ ☆ ☆

After the ethics investigation and the Senate's denouncement of me in October 1979, the sharks smelled blood in the water. Any politician who wanted my seat knew that he could get front-page coverage in the Atlanta papers simply by attacking me. By the same token, anyone who supported me was subjected to vicious abuse. This was particularly true of the blacks who were for me. The August 9, 1980, "Weekend" edition of the Atlanta papers ran a cartoon showing state representative Billy McKinney shuffling into a smoke-filled room to serve drinks to me and my cohorts as we sat around a table counting huge bags of money. That was shortly after Maynard Jackson had said that voting for Herman Talmadge was like spitting on Martin Luther King's grave. In spite of that organized hate campaign, Dr. King's niece, Alveda King Beal, endorsed me. And Daddy King never wavered in his friendship.

Of the Democrats seeking to replace me, the one who was closest to my political philosophy was Dawson Mathis, a congressman from Albany, Georgia. Dawson was a former TV anchorman who came across quite well on the air. He was bright, articulate, and a good campaigner. But he made a serious misjudgment when he gave up a safe congressional seat to enter the senate race. Even if I was hurting among liberals and city folk, the conservative rural constituency had not abandoned me. Dawson would have been a formidable candidate in the general election, but the arithmetic just wasn't with him in the primary. Also, he wasn't able to raise the money needed to compete in a statewide race.

I knew that I'd probably face stiffer competition from a New South moderate by the name of Norman Underwood. Norman had served as Governor George Busbee's top aide for several years before Busbee appointed him to the state Court of Appeals. Underwood was a dull campaigner, so he tried to appeal to the white collar crowd as a competent, no-frills executive, just like his mentor. That strategy was designed to make Norman an attractive prospect for governor in 1982, but when I began to look vulnerable, he immediately set his sights on the Senate. (Unlike the governorship, the senate terms were six years with unlimited prospects for reelection.) Norman's game plan was to stay in the middle of the road, make me an issue, and hope for a runoff where he could unite folks of various political philosophies who believed that I was every evil thing the Atlanta papers accused me of being. One particularly scurrilous television ad showed a bunch of hands stuffing money into an overcoat. That was my introduction to the sort of high tech mudslinging that passes for campaign tactics these days.

On their editorial pages, the Atlanta papers let it be known that while they would be delighted to see me lose to either Mathis or Underwood, their fairhaired boy was Lieutenant Governor Zell Miller. Zell was still a relatively young man in 1980, but he had been around Georgia politics for the better part of twenty years. During that time he had managed to take just about every position on every issue. I don't have to agree with a man to respect his views, but when he has no principle other than expediency, that's where I draw the line. Norman Underwood called Miller "Zig Zag Zell," and that just about summed up the man's character.

Zell was a history professor who came to the State Senate in the early sixties after having served as Mayor of Young Harris, up in the Georgia mountains. He ran for Congress twice against Phil Landrum. Once he tried to outflank Phil on the left, another time on the right. He was on the state pardon and parole board for awhile and later worked as Lester Maddox's top aide when Lester was lieutenant governor. Zell won the lieutenant governorship himself in 1974, and then he immediately went to badmouthing Lester, who had given him a job when he needed it. Like Norman Underwood, Zell was planning to run for governor (just as soon as Busbee finished his second term), but changed his mind when it looked as if I could be beaten in the senate race. So "Zig Zag Zell" traded in his credentials as a redneck segregationist and climbed in bed politically with Maynard Jackson and Julian Bond.

Everybody figured that I'd come in first in the primary election, but my opposition hoped that I could be held under fifty percent. Under Georgia law that would force a runoff, and runoffs had been historically unkind to well-known incumbents. Since I was the central issue in this campaign, a lot of folks assumed that the candidates eliminated in the first primary would rally around my opponent in the runoff to present a united anti-Talmadge front. So when I got forty-two percent of the vote in the first primary, the pundits started writing my political obituary. To them that primary meant only one thing—that well over half the Democrats in Georgia wanted Herman Talmadge out of the Senate.

Before the first Democratic Primary in 1980, I had never gotten less than fifty percent of the vote in any election for public office. (In fact, I was used to piling up totals in the seventy percent range and higher.) So I was disappointed to have to face a runoff, but not dismayed. I thought that it would be easier for me to hold my people than for my opponents to close ranks against me. My nearest competition in the primary (and opponent in the runoff) was Zell Miller, who had twenty-five percent of the vote. Zell had done that well by mobilizing a hard core of blacks, labor union bosses, and liberal activists. They had voted for him once and would probably do so again. But where would he make up his seventeen-point deficit? He wouldn't get it from the Mathis camp (Dawson was backing me in the runoff), and there simply weren't enough Underwood people to make the difference. The Talmadge-Mathis vote constituted a solid (55 percent) majority for conservative government. Where would Maynard Jackson, Julian Bond, and Zell Miller go to beat that?

Perhaps without realizing it, Zell had painted himself into a corner. He was so deathly afraid I would win the first primary outright that he had pulled out all stops to force a runoff. That meant mobilizing the big-name Atlanta blacks and calling me every vile name in the book. But once he *had* forced the runoff, he had to convince folks that he was really a moderate who possessed qualifications other than his dislike of me. Whatever anti-Talmadge feeling there was in the Democratic Party had peaked during the first primary. For three years the Atlanta papers and assorted politicians had been telling the electorate what a scoundrel Herman Talmadge was. If they didn't believe it by now, nothing Zell said was likely to change their minds. In fact, now that it was one-on-one instead of three-against-one, Zell would have to defend his own record rather than just attack mine. If he stuck with his ultra-liberal positions, he risked alienating the moderate voters he had to attract. But if he moved too far away from his platform of the first primary, he would appear opportunistic. Zig or zag, Zell was a sitting duck.

Because the Talmadges had been dominating state politics for over fifty years, some folks thought that I was a throwback to another age. What they didn't realize was that Zell was, too. Just as surely as I was Gene Talmadge's son, Zell was the political offspring of Eurith Dickinson Rivers. Zell's father had worked for the Rivers administration, and Zell idolized Ed when he was growing up. Although Ed *was* a likable fellow, most historians agree that he was a disaster as governor. The one notable exception to that consensus was Professor Zell Miller. Zell's master's thesis is a defense of the Rivers administration. Zell regards Ed as a far-seeing liberal statesman who had the misfortune of being ahead of his time. (Considering Ed's fondness for give-away welfare programs and deficit financing, Zell may have something of a point.) Since Papa cleaned up the mess that Ed made in state government and then ruined Ed's political comeback in 1946, the triumph of the Talmadges was also the end of Ed Rivers. What better way to avenge Ed than for his most ardent admirer to bring down the last of the Talmadges? Zell was too much of an historian not to appreciate the irony of the situation.

There was a series of four televised debates in the three-week runoff campaign. The conventional political wisdom held that a well-known incumbent who was ahead in the polls didn't give his opponent free exposure by agreeing to debate. But I thought that the more exposure Zell got, the less people would find to admire in him. Besides, with the *Atlanta Constitution* running daily attacks on me, I needed the chance to show people who didn't know me well that I wasn't the clown they saw in the editorial cartoons of their daily newspaper. One point I insisted on was that the debates be face-to-face confrontations of the Lincoln-Douglas variety, not glorified press conferences. Zell didn't like the idea of having to go against me without his press buddies around to support him, but after all his squawking about debates, he had no choice but to accept my terms.

Like his mentor Ed Rivers, Zell was incapable of saying "no" to any special interest group. A candidate running for public office will get mailings from different constituencies, each with its own legislative program. Since the candidate wants to make friends and win votes, he is sorely tempted to endorse every proposal that comes along. With the size of our national budget, a few billion dollars more or less doesn't seem like all that much. But as Everett Dirksen used to say, "A billion here and a billion there, and pretty soon you're talking about real money!" If the people could be made to see that, "Zig Zag Zell" would not only *teach* history, he would *be* history. We counted up the price tag for the programs Zell was endorsing and got a figure of $156.8 billion, which was more than seven hundred dollars for every man, woman, and child in the United States. When I pointed that out in our second televised debate, the small lead I had enjoyed started to grow. It was gradually dawning on the people of Georgia that behind the cowboy boots and the mountain twang, Zell Miller was such a reckless spender that he made a sailor on shore leave look like a tightwad by comparison.

When Georgia Democrats went to the polls on August 26, 1980, 58.5 percent of them voted to return me to the Senate. I carried 140 of 159 counties and left Zell sucking air. I had been used to large victories, but under the circumstances, this one had to be one of the sweetest of my career. Although winning the Democratic Primary was no longer tantamount to election in Georgia, I couldn't see where my Republican opponent, Mack Mattingly, could put together a coalition capable of beating me. He wouldn't dare run to my left, and there wasn't much room on my right. Some die-hard Miller supporters might vote for Mattingly out of spite, but I assumed I could count on a good majority of rural Democrats and blacks. Conservatives who knew the value of seniority would surely stick with a four-term veteran over a rookie. The only strategy open to my opponent was to repeat all the stale personal attacks on me. If it hadn't worked for more quick-witted candidates, it seemed like desperate tactics for someone as inarticulate as Mack Mattingly. What I underestimated was the power of a hostile press.

☆ ☆ ☆

The treatment I received from the Atlanta papers during the last three or four years of my political career made me miss Ralph McGill and the civility he brought to journalism. Ralph gave the Talmadges a lot of grief over the years, but Papa and I both considered him a decent human being and a worthy adversary. His death in February, 1969, marked the end of an era in Southern journalism. Sure, I know that the first amendment guarantees freedom of the press and that our political traditions assure a lively debate on public issues. But one thing Ralph McGill knew that the current crop of reporters has never learned is that you can disagree with a man's views without being personally vindictive. Once when Lester Maddox's son was accused of stealing a TV set and Lester was thinking about disowning him, Ralph wrote Lester a letter urging him to stand by the boy in his difficulties. According to Ralph's biographer Harold Martin, Lester showed up at Ralph's office the next morning and thanked him with tears in his eyes. Lester then went on the air to ask the people of Georgia to pray for his son.

I don't know why journalism has turned as nasty as it has in recent years. Maybe the papers feel they have to be "hard-hitting" to compete with radio and television. Maybe Vietnam and Watergate have made reporters more cynical about politicians. In my case, however, I think that personal factors were involved. Editorially, the *Atlanta Journal* and *Constitution* are separate newspapers (the *Journal* tends to be conservative and the *Constitution* liberal), but both are owned by the Atlanta Newspaper Corporation, which is in turn controlled by the Cox family. When two papers with vastly different philosophies start going after the same public official, you have to wonder if the motivation isn't coming from the board room rather than the editorial offices. It may be only coincidence, but the vendetta waged against me by the Atlanta papers began at the time of my divorce. It didn't help my cause any that the principal owner of the two papers, Mrs. Anne Cox Chambers, was a close friend of my former wife's.

The *Constitution* comes out on weekday mornings and the *Journal* in the afternoons. Then on Saturday and Sunday, the papers put out combined editions. That meant that each week there were a dozen opportunities to tell the people of metropolitan Atlanta that their senior senator was a disgrace to the state of Georgia. I'm sure that if I had moved to Oregon and read this sort of garbage day in and day out about one of their politicians, I would be ready to vote the rascal out myself. When the folks over at the *Constitution* ran out of accusations to make about my current conduct in office, they took to running a little editorial feature called "Lest We Forget." The purpose was to rattle every skeleton in my closet—real or imagined. They even went back to the mid-fifties to remind their readers that I used to be a segregationist. They neglected to mention any of the positive things I had done for blacks or to acknowledge that my position on race was no different from that of the vast majority of white Southerners, including their beloved Zell Miller. But then, why let the facts stand in the way of a good story?

I suppose the gravest omission of all was in the way the press covered the outcome of the ethics hearing. I knew that the hearing itself and the subsequent vote by the Senate would get front page coverage in the Atlanta papers. Those events were news, and it's the business of newspapers to cover the news. However, the point of the hearing was not to bash Herman Talmadge but to see who was guilty of stealing approximately $40,000 from the United States Government. The committee turned all the evidence it had gathered over to the Justice Department for prosecution. As a result, Dan Minchew was tried, convicted, and sent to prison, while I was exonerated of wrongdoing. But that story got very little play in the Atlanta press. Instead, the papers went right on portraying me as a crooked politician who had gotten caught with his hand in the cookie jar. The truth is that I personally reimbursed the government for all the money Minchew stole and endured the humiliation of a Senate denunciation for what amounted to the crime of careless bookkeeping.

Sometime in late 1977 or early '78, the *Constitution* decided that my transgressions were so numerous that their present staff was inadequate to cover the story, so they went out and hired a professional gunslinger from Detroit, Michigan, by the name of Seth Kantor. He was on the *Constitution's* payroll for several years, and during that time I saw only one story under his byline that didn't relate to me. It's one thing for staff people who are already working on a paper to devote themselves to a single story, but when the paper has to reach into another part of the country to hire a character assassin, you begin to suspect that there is something more involved than a disinterested concern with the public's right to know.

For a while I thought that the regular working reporters might be more honorable and fairminded than the editorial writers and investigative muckrakers. In particular, I was impressed with a young man named Frederick Allen. Rick Allen is a bright fellow and a very capable writer. I got to know him fairly well when he was covering my senate campaign in 1980. Now, like everyone else, a politician will make casual comments in private that are not meant for public consumption. Most reporters respect that distinction and do not violate a man's confidence just because he happens to be a controversial politician. To my regret, I had assumed that to be true of Rick Allen. The incident that taught me better occurred one afternoon on my campaign plane.

A candidate for public office gets more speaking invitations than he can honor on his own, so he often has to send representatives to appear on his behalf. Well, I had just received a request to speak before a group of gays in the Atlanta area. They told me they had 250,000 members in metropolitan Atlanta and wanted to hear my views on issues affecting their welfare. One of my campaign aides at the time was Herman Coffer, former Commissioner of Public Safety for Georgia. Like many policemen, Herman took to gays about the way the Devil takes to holy water. So I called him over and said, "I need for you to go and address this important group of constituents for me." I told him that he would have to get him a new hair style, a bracelet, and a different style suit. Poor Herman thought I was dead serious and was absolutely terrified. Along about this time, Rick Allen picked up on what was happening and came over to join in the levity. He offered to help write Herman's speech and continued joking with us for the remainder of the trip. Then as soon as the plane touched down, Rick was on the phone to the head of the gays telling him everything I had said. As a result, I was publicly rebuked for being insensitive to another minority.

If I had to pick the one "journalist" who seemed most intent on slandering me, it would be Bill Shipp, then an editorial page columnist for the *Atlanta Constitution*. During the senate ethics investigation, he made up his mind that I was guilty of fraud, perjury, and contempt for the people of Georgia. Because the facts wouldn't bear him out, he simply distorted them to fit his thesis. He did what he could to make Zell Miller palatable to the people of Georgia, and when that proved too tall an order, he switched his allegiance to Mack Mattingly. Shipp's swing from the far left to the far right was motivated by nothing more than hatred of Herman Talmadge. If Miller couldn't rid the state of me by uniting the liberal forces, then the task would have to be entrusted to carpetbagger Mattingly and the Reagan Republicans.

Running for public office in 1980 was a vastly different affair from what it had been when I first ran for governor in 1948. Back then, you tried to meet as many people as you could and let them size you up. Folks would turn out by the thousands to hear a candidate speak in the town square on a hot summer afternoon. They would cheer him, talk back to him, and eat his barbecue. And hundreds of them would get in their cars and form a motorcade to follow him to his next stop. People read the newspapers and listened to radio back then, but they also had the evidence of their own senses. Because the candidate wasn't separated from them by a television screen, he was a flesh-and-blood human being. Today he's just a talking head dolled up by a bunch of ad men who probably couldn't get elected dogcatcher in their own right.

Television enables you to reach more people with a given message, but every minute of prime time is so expensive that you end up paying more to say less than ever before. You can't discuss issues in any depth in thirty seconds, so you're reduced to catchy slogans and oversimplifications or—as in the case of my opponents—personal mudslinging. Talk about tax or agricultural policy, and you put the TV audience to sleep. Show them a bunch of disembodied hands stuffing money into an overcoat, and you have them on the edge of their seats. When the national

Republicans took a poll and determined I was vulnerable, they poured hundreds of thousands of dollars into Georgia. Much of it went into TV ads featuring caricatures of me saying things I never said. In order to reach every household in Georgia with a TV set, it was necessary to run those ads on stations in Atlanta, Savannah, Columbus, Macon, Augusta, and Albany, Georgia; Greenville, South Carolina; Chattanooga, Tennessee; Tallahassee and Jacksonville, Florida; and Dothan, Alabama.

After my victory over Zell Miller in the Democratic runoff, I needed to pause and catch my breath before plunging into the general election campaign. I also needed to go back to Washington and tend to my job in the Senate. During my twenty-four years in Washington, I had had an eighty-five percent attendance record, but I knew that I had fallen considerably below that level in the preceding year. The rough primary campaign had forced me to come home and appear all over the state just to defend myself. Had I not done so, my opponents and the newspapers would have accused me of hiding from the people. But having come home to face the people, I was leaving myself open to charges of absenteeism from the Senate. What a neophyte like Mack Mattingly didn't realize was that the real business of the Senate was done in committees where important legislation was written. Floor votes on whether or not to have National Wildflower Week did not affect the crucial interests of Georgians or the American people as a whole.

While I was back in Washington allowing the wounds from the primary to heal, my Republican opponent was trying to gain some name recognition across the state. Mattingly was a pleasant looking fellow with a big dimple in his chin. He had come to Georgia from Indiana in the 1950's and worked for IBM for a number of years. His previous political experience consisted of a losing race for Congress and a stint as state chairman of the Republican Party. Although he faced token opposition in the Republican Primary, the senate nomination was pretty much his for the asking. What Mattingly was obviously banking on was the popularity of Ronald Reagan, who was heading the Republican ticket that year, and the negative feelings that some voters had about me. In fact, the animosity toward Washington was running so high that he even made his inexperience into something of a virtue.

Probably the biggest mistake I made in that campaign was to assume that folks would see through Mattingly's inexperience. The best way for me to have assured that would have been to debate him. However, my feeling at the time was that a televised debate would only give Mattingly free exposure and credibility. Because he had not had to spend his money in the primary, he was already in a position to outspend me by two-to-one in the closing weeks of the campaign. I wasn't about to hand him free air time on top of that. But in retrospect, I see that I was wrong. I had won the Democratic runoff in large part because of the debates with Zell Miller, and compared to Mattingly, Miller was a mental giant. Had I debated Mattingly, his ignorance of the issues would have been apparent. As it was, he stuck his foot in his mouth every time he had to go beyond a few platitudes about tax cuts and the economy. An audience of blacks at Morehouse College was appalled when he didn't know the difference between South Africa and Rhodesia. (The fact that he called the newly independent state of Zimbabwe by the colonial name of Rhodesia didn't help matters.) In fact, the only foreign policy issue on which he scored any points at all was attacking me for giving away the Panama Canal.

Going into the general election, I wasn't particularly afraid of the Atlanta newspapers or Mack Mattingly. (In the primaries I had taken all the abuse the Cox syndicate could dish out and still won going away; and as for Mr. Mattingly, he was about as prepossessing as a department store mannequin.) No, my principal fear was that my own troops would get so complacent that we'd throw the election away ourselves. When I'd go out on the campaign trail, Talmadge loyalists would be talking about the election as if it were a football game we had already won and the only thing left to be determined was the point spread. "Think you'll get sixty-five percent?" they'd say. "I might lose," I told them, "unless you get out to vote." They'd just laugh and say they didn't like Carter and weren't about to vote for a Republican, so they might just sit this one out. As things transpired, I spent so much time persuading my natural supporters to take the election seriously that I didn't campaign nearly enough in the Atlanta area. It looked like a contest between the two Georgias with the size of the turnout determining the results.

On Tuesday, November 4, I cast my vote in Henry County, then headed north to Atlanta to wait for the returns to come in. Going up the Jonesboro road, I could see how the fast food places and the shopping plazas were creeping into an area that was once totally rural. White collar folks who worked in the city were moving farther and farther into the surrounding area. Where once I would see only pickup trucks or a second-hand jalopy on cinder blocks, there were now more and more Volvos and BMW's. Designer jeans had replaced bib overalls, and it wasn't just poor farm kids who went several months without a haircut. Just a few miles onto I-75 North, there's the Hartsfield International Airport—the second busiest in the nation—complete with moving sidewalks and robot voices that tell passengers to steer clear of the subway doors. (How many of the millions of people who pass through there each year even know who Bill Hartsfield was?) Then, not too long after 75 merges with I-85, you have the Fulton County Stadium—home of the Braves. Like the nation itself, that team moved from the Northeast (Boston) to the Midwest (Milwaukee) to what used to be called the South. It's called the Sunbelt now, and Atlanta is its capital. I turned off the interstate and headed to the Atlanta Hilton. We had a suite of rooms on the seventeenth floor.

Before the network news was over and before the polls had closed in most of the nation, the experts were predicting a Reagan landslide. Until almost the very end it had been a close campaign, and then the hostage issue turned against Carter in a big way. Jimmy and I were never particularly close, but it was sad to see our first Southern president in over a hundred years humiliated at the polls. (And it was his native South as much as any region that was doing him in.) What was even more surprising, however, were the Republican gains in the Senate—in states like Alabama, North Carolina, and Florida. All across the country big-name Democrats were biting the dust: Bayh in Indiana, Nelson in Wisconsin, Church in Idaho, and McGovern in South Dakota. Even Warren Magnuson lost in Washington. He had been in the Senate a dozen years when I arrived in 1957 and was now President Pro Tem.

(Lyndon Johnson had been best man at his wedding.) The President Pro Tem of the Senate is supposed to retire or die in office, not be voted out.

A new broom was sweeping clean. By the time the evening was out, the Republicans had gained control of the Senate and deprived me of my committee chairmanship. The only thing that seemed safe was my seat itself. Two of the TV networks and both wire services had declared me the winner. My supporters were celebrating in the ballroom fifteen floors below, and the early morning edition of the *Atlanta Constitution* declared "Talmadge Walks Away With Fifth Term." I went to bed about the time I usually get up, 100,000 votes ahead and confident that I had won the most difficult race of my career.

After sleeping for a few hours at my home in Henry County, I got up Wednesday morning and took a walk with a couple of my aides. There had been computer breakdowns in Cobb and DeKalb Counties, two large and populous areas to the north and east of Atlanta, and the returns from there were just starting to come in. The vote for Mattingly was so overwhelming (a margin of about 150,000 in the metro Atlanta area) that my comfortable lead of the night before had evaporated. At 11:20 A.M. Mattingly appeared on television to claim victory. The margin was close but decisive. Georgia had its first Republican senator since Reconstruction, and a political dynasty that had lasted for fifty-four years was finally over.

If I had that race to run over, there are things I would do differently. I spent too much time in the regions where I was strongest and not enough in the ones where I was weakest. A hundred receptions in the Atlanta area might have made the difference. (Certainly, I should have debated Mattingly.) But there were also factors beyond my control. The heavy turnout brought a lot of voters to the polls who knew me only from what they read in the newspapers. Of these, too many Republicans and too few Democrats pulled the straight party lever. But I remember thinking: *What the hell? That's all behind me. No use playing it back over in my mind or brooding about what might have been. I entered politics dramatically and I guess I'm leaving the same way. Sure, it's been my life, but unlike Papa, I can live without it. At 67, I've still got*

354

a lot of living to do. I'm also Mama's son, after all. And she'll be a hundred years old on Friday.

Epilogue

Gone Fishing

A LOT HAS CHANGED IN THIS COUNTRY since I broke into politics managing my daddy's campaign against Walter George in 1938. We've landed a man on the moon, conquered once fatal diseases, and created a standard of living that is the envy of the world. In my native South every child, regardless of his race or the circumstances of his birth, now has the chance to get a good education and become a productive citizen. Infant mortality is down, family incomes are up, and mass communication has made us all better informed. But we also see alcoholism and drug abuse on the rise. In some of our major cities violent crime has reached epidemic proportions. Illegitimacy and abortion have become more socially accepted, and half our marriages end in divorce. Many of our churches stand half empty while psychiatrists' couches are filling up. Has America gained the whole world at the expense of its own soul? Is there any way for our country to get back on track?

I guess the first thing we need to do is admit that there's a problem. Then we have to realize that there are no novel and exotic solutions. Gary Hart ran for president in 1984 as the candidate of new ideas, and a lot of people bought that line, thinking that ideas are like clothing or automobiles—the newer they are, the better they are. In my book, that's not the way it is. We don't need to find new ideas; we need to recover old values. Now, I could give you a whole list of the values we seem to have lost during my years in public life, but for the moment let's just focus on three: hard work, thrift, and respect for the law. America became the economic leader of the world because her people worked harder and saved more than the folks in other countries. And our society remained peaceful and cohesive because people respected the rights and property of others. Unfortunately, it's not that way anymore.

Take the value of work. The Bible says that you shall earn your bread by the sweat of your brow. When I was a boy on the farm, we took that as a given. Families and local communities took care of their own when they got too aged, sick, or infirm to work. To accept charity was an admission that you couldn't make it on your own, and most able-bodied men would rather have starved than made that admission. The notion that someone had the *right* to be supported by the government in Washington was unheard of. We didn't have the benefit of advanced economic theories back where I grew up, but we did know that if you had more people sitting in the wagon than pulling it, it wasn't going to go anywhere. Today, half the people in this country are receiving some sort of government benefit. Since the government creates no wealth on its own, it has to pay for those benefits by taxing the productive segment of society and borrowing from future generations.

The trend of cradle-to-grave welfare began with the administration of Franklin D. Roosevelt. The people were demanding government action to deal with the economic crisis of the Great Depression. But when that crisis went away (primarily because of World War II), the government programs were still in place and growing. Up to that point, the federal government had been concerned primarily with maintaining an army, coining money, and running the post office. However, when the Supreme Court decided in the Baker Case that Congress could legislate in any area affecting public welfare, politicians began buying votes by promising something for nothing. Balanced budgets became a thing of the past, and far too many folks started seeing themselves not as citizens but as wards of the state. My first year in the United States Senate, I received forty thousand letters from constituents who felt they had business with the federal government.

By the time I left office, that number had risen to 240,000. The trend continues year in and year out—under Democrats and Republicans, liberals and conservatives alike.

You can't legislate a respect for hard work, but you can create a climate in which people who do work live better than those who won't. Historically, state and local governments have done the best job of running and monitoring welfare programs. They are closer to the people, and they can't paper over their debts by printing money. Also, states and localities are not shy about demanding that healthy welfare recipients be available for work or for job training. Back in the sixties and seventies, some "experts" were urging that welfare be federalized. The so-called Family Assistance Plan would even have resulted in a guaranteed annual income paid for by Uncle Sam. Twice when I was in the Senate, that hare-brained scheme was proposed by a supposedly conservative president, Richard Nixon. I'm glad to say that both times the Senate was able to keep it from becoming law. What we ought to do is dismantle many of the existing federal welfare programs and return their functions to state and local authorities.

As essential as it is to encourage people to work, they must also be allowed to benefit from the fruits of their labor. An inflated currency and high interest rates deprive them of that right. From the late sixties, when Lyndon Johnson pursued a policy of reckless federal spending for guns and butter, up through the early years of the Reagan administration, inflation and interest rates remained high in good times and bad. Those rates were brought down by a severe recession in 1982, but few economists are betting that they will stay down permanently. With a ballooning national debt, much of which is owed to foreigners, we're sitting on a time bomb in this country. And the political pressures for government spending are so great that that time bomb is liable to go off before our elected representatives take steps to correct the situation. The only way to avert disaster is to bind them down with the chains of the Constitution. For years I have advocated a constitutional amendment to mandate a balanced budget at the federal level. I'm glad to say that there is now broad grassroots support for that idea around the country. Only when we have a government that spends no more than it takes in and takes in no more than it needs to fulfill its constitutional functions will we have enough private capital left over to create prosperity for all.

Private debt is also a problem in this country. When I was a boy, we used an old blue-back speller that not only taught you spelling but also had some very profound words of wisdom in the back. One quotation I remember was from Benjamin Franklin's *Poor Richard's Almanac*. It said, "A penny saved is a penny earned." We don't use that blue-back speller anymore, and we have a generation of Americans who neither spell nor save very well. Too many young people today think that a penny saved is a waste of time. The government can't change the character of our people, but it *can* change the structure of incentives that make thrift less profitable than debt. It's a basic rule of economics that whatever you tax you get less of, and whatever you subsidize you get more of. For too long our federal tax system has punished earning and saving and rewarded borrowing. If we don't like the results of that policy, then maybe we ought to think about altering the causes.

I doubt that any other highly industrialized nation derives as much of its tax revenue as we do from the productivity of its people. Not only does the federal government take too much of the gross national product in taxes, but far too much of that is in taxes on income (principally, the personal and corporate income tax and the social security payroll tax). Almost all of our trading partners derive a substantial portion of their revenues from taxes on consumption. (In Western Europe it's called a Value Added Tax.) Although there are a number of ways that that could be done in this country, it is not my intention here to endorse any specific plan. I just think that it's an issue that our political leaders need to pay some attention to if we don't want to have to teach our children how to count in yens.

As serious as our economic problems are and as important as it is to try to solve them, the primary responsibility of government is to preserve domestic tranquility. When I was a boy in Telfair County, we hardly ever locked our doors, and crimes of violence were freak occurrences that folks didn't worry about any more than they worried about being hit by a meteor. By the time I went to the Senate I knew that things had changed, but that fact was really brought home to me one night in Atlanta. I was staying in town to give a speech, and I followed my usual habit of getting up well before dawn. I went to a diner to get breakfast and a newspaper and then prepared to walk back to my hotel. On the way I noticed that a patrol car was following me. I wondered whether the officer thought I was a mugger or some other criminal suspect. Then I realized what was happening. He had recognized me and was following me back to my hotel to see that no harm came to me. It's a sad state of affairs when a United States Senator can't walk the streets in the capital city of his home state without a police escort.

The crime wave in this country has been caused by a multitude of factors and isn't likely to be ended overnight, but there are things that can and must be done. First of all, we need to restore public confidence in the ability of the government to preserve law and order. That may require more prisons, more police, less probation, stiffer sentences, and a renewed vigilance on the part of the citizenry. Without public confidence in law enforcement, this nation will be reduced to armed camps with quite a few innocent bystanders caught in the crossfire. Over the long haul, however, we need to deal with the more deeply rooted causes of crime. Since most crimes are committed by young people, we must pay more attention to how character is formed at an early age.

It used to be that children learned their concept of right and wrong in their parents' home, but today too many children have no parental guidance. They either live in a single-parent home or in a household where both the mother and father work. They're called latchkey children, and they're left to raise themselves. In some communities, illegitimacy is so high that children have no idea who their fathers are, have never seen their mothers, and are shuffled back and forth between relatives and foster homes. These kids create a discipline problem in schools and are usually into drugs and other crimes by the time they reach adolescence. They're cradle criminals, and they account for a disproportionate amount of the lawlessness in this country. If we can get them and other young people started in the right direction, we can go a long way toward making the streets of our cities safe again. That means getting serious about the notion of individual responsibility.

For one thing, we need to eliminate government programs that promote illegitimacy and the breakup of the family. Under Aid to Families with Dependent Children, a man and a woman can produce as many babies as they like at government expense as long as the man doesn't live in the home. We need to start holding parents accountable for the care of their children and let the tax-payer off the hook. The government can't create a proper home environment, but it can at least stop subsidizing socially irrespon-sible behavior in the breeding and rearing of children.

We must also restore learning and discipline in the schools. Quite a few of our public schools have become little more than a glorified babysitting service where the worst students terrorize teachers and fellow students, and some high school graduates are so illiterate they can't even read their own diplomas. We need to expel the principal troublemakers, keep the other students in line with the carrot and the stick (including the hickory stick when necessary), and put an end to "social promotion." Over the past twenty-five years or so the children of America have been given every material advantage. What is needed are educational and moral standards for them to live up to. Far too many "educators" and social workers think that our primary responsibility to our young people is to teach them how to read the label on a package of condoms or a bottle of birth control pills. That's simply not good enough. Elections are won and lost on economic issues, but nations are won and lost on moral issues. That's something the politicians need to be talking about, and it's something the Ameri-can people need to hear. But from now on, I'll be offering my views on these and other public matters from the sidelines. My own political career is over.

At first it was strange having to adjust to private life. From the time I went into the Navy in 1941 until my senate defeat in 1980, I was on the go from eighty to a hundred hours a week year round. Practically every hour of the day was planned, and sometimes speeches were scheduled as much as two years in advance. To wake up and wonder what I was going to do that day was about as novel as waking up on Mars. But I got used to it awful quick. I now have time to read and think and walk in the woods. I've also managed to improve my financial situation. The life of leisure is so good that I now understand why welfare is so popular.

Some adjustments, however, have been more difficult than others. Without a full-time secretary, I started having to answer my mail by myself. I got to the point where my long letters were two sentences and my short letters were one. When I started getting bills, I figured I had to pay them to keep my credit from going bad. So I went down the road to the Jonesboro branch of the Trust Company of Georgia, walked up to the teller, and asked for some checks. Well, that teller looked at me as if I had just stuck a gun in her face and asked her to hand over a sack of money. "What kind of checks do you want?" she said.

"Counter checks, to pay some bills with," I replied.

"Do you bank with us?" she asked.

"I've been banking with your main office in Atlanta for forty years," I said.

"Well, what's your number?"

"My number? I didn't know I had a number."

So the teller got on the phone to Atlanta to see if she could get my number. She apparently got someone on the phone who was about as inexperienced as she was. By this time I was getting a little impatient. I knew that I could write a check on a paper bag or a fertilizer sack, and if I had the money to cover it, the bank was supposed to pay it. After about five minutes went by, I said, "Look here, you get Mr. Strickland, the chairman of the board, on the phone, and he and I can settle this matter right quick." Well, that wasn't necessary, because she finally got my number through regular channels and stamped it on to about ten or fifteen checks. A few weeks later I discovered the importance of that number when the bank paid a check I hadn't even signed.

A much more pleasant change occurred in March of 1984, when I was asked to speak before the Atlanta Farmer's Club. As it turned out, most of the audience were not farmers but folks connected in one way or another with agribusiness or food service. I couldn't help noticing a very pretty lady at a table up near the front. After the speech, I asked a friend of mine to introduce her to me. I found out that her name was Lynda Cowart Pierce, that she was a University of Georgia home economist with the Gwinnett

County Extension Service, and that she was unmarried. When I asked for her phone number, she probably didn't realize that when she got to work the next morning there would be a message waiting for her. She answered that message and several others over the course of the next few months. We were married in September of 1984 and are having a very happy life together.

In looking back over my life, I suppose I have the normal share of regrets. But if I had it all to do over again, I wouldn't hesitate to enter politics. The rewards far outweigh the price one has to pay. When I speak to a civic club or just walk down the street, I invariably run into someone who has benefited in some way from my three and a half decades in public life. Yes, it was a good life. But a political career, like all things, must finally come to an end. It's been nearly sixty years since my teacher, Mrs. Enda Ballard Duggan, took me away from my hunting and fishing. I've got a lot of catching up to do.

Index

INDEX

Jefferson, Thomas, 222-23
Jeffersonian, The, 37
Jekyll Island, 98
Johnson, Jerry, 341
Johnson, Lyndon B., 33, 147, 149, 171, 173,
    178, 297, 302, 312, 354, 359; as majority
    leader, 170, 185, 192, 228, 246; civil
    rights, 192, 226, 302-03; Vietnam, 167,
    226, 246-47, 252
Jones, J. Frank, 90
Jordan, Barbara, 261
Jordan, Hamilton, 310
Jupp, Commodore Stanley, 47, 50, 53-4

Kalmbach, Herbert, 287
Kantor, Seth, 348
Keating, Ken, 163
Kefauver, Estes, 151-52, 153, 178, 191, 254,
    257, 263
Kelly, Lucille, 316
Kennedy, Bobby, 33, 170-72, 192, 253, 288
Kennedy, John F., 147, 149, 162, 170, 173,
    191-92, 247, 251, 254, 287, 296; Bay of
    Pigs, 241-42, 245; civil rights, 191, 193,
    253; Cuban Missile Crisis, 241; death,
    172, 193, 283-89; presidential race (1960),
    192-93, 226, 238; Vietnam, 247, 253
Kennedy, Ted, 162, 170, 198, 239, 260, 330;
    as senator, 162, 170-72; Chappa-
    quiddick, 171, 254
Kerr, Bob, 168
Khomeini, Ayatollah, 240
Kimbrough, Bill, 133-34
King, A.D., 207
King, Coretta, 207, 311
King, Martin Luther, Jr., 192, 205-06, 207,
    208, 209, 212, 216, 217, 311, 342
King, Martin Luther, Sr., 206-07, 218, 311, 342
King, Primus, 69
Kirbo, Charles, 252
Kirby, John Henry, 33
Kissinger, Henry, 237, 247
Kleindienst, Richard, 281-82, 286, 294
Kopechne, Mary Jo, 254
Korean War, 237, 245
Krogh, Egil, 290
Krushchev, 173, 241
Ku Klux Klan, 18, 58
Kuchel, Tom, 195

LaFollette, Bob, 38, 166
Lance, Bert, 209
Landon, Alf, 148
Landrum, Phil, 161, 343
LaRouche, Lyndon, 145
Lawson, Frank, 37
Lenzer, Terry, 257, 258, 287
Levant, Oscar, 88
Lewis, J. Ham, 28

Lewis, John, 219, 215-17
Liddy, G. Gordon, 250, 256, 279-81, 280,
    285, 290
Little Rock, AR, 187
Long, Earl, 187, 319-20
Long, Huey, 18, 32-33, 34, 67, 185, 195, 262,
    319; *My First Days in the White House*,
    33
Long, Russell, 167, 321
Lott, Trent, 261
Loudermilk, Charlie, 219
Lucas, Scott, 168

MacArthur, Douglas, 50, 52, 147, 246
McCarthy, Eugene, 213, 252
McCarthy, Joe, 181, 196, 257, 337
McCord, James, 256, 278-79, 295
McDonald, Larry, 340
McFarland, Ernest, 168-69
McGill, Ralph, 73, 75-76, 86, 99, 132, 190,
    347
McGovern, George, 208, 297, 313; agricul-
    ture, 227, 251; foreign policy, 251;
    presidential race (1972), 148, 173, 250,
    251-52, 253, 254-55
McIntyre, Ed, 101
McKinney, Billy, 342
McLennan, Alex, 42
McNamara, Bob, 247
McRae, GA, 9, 12, 15, 16, 20, 27, 35, 66, 73,
    80, 81, 110, 113, 224
McSween, Herbert B., 319
Maddox, Lester Garfield, 95, 213, 215,
    304-07, 308-09, 310, 343, 347
Magnuson, Warren, 353
Magruder, Jeb Stuart, 280-81, 285
Maloy, Dr. J.C., 80
Mann, W.S., 80
Mansfield, Mike, 173, 227, 249, 255, 258,
    265, 282
Martin, Harold, 79, 81, 347
Mathis, Dawson, 342, 343, 344
Matthias, Charles "Mac," 261
Mattingly, Mack, 139, 346, 350, 351-52, 354
Mayaquez, 238
Maynard, Judge E.W., 29
Miller, W.L., 59
Miller, Zell, 343, 344-46, 348, 350, 351, 352
Millican, Everett, 85
Mills, Wilbur, 252, 320-21
Minchew, Daniel, 336, 332-34, 335, 348
Minimum Foundation Program, 135, 136
Mitchell, John, 278, 280, 284-87, 298, 296
Mitchell, Margaret, 199-200
Monaghan, John, 76
Mondale, Walter, 148, 208
Monroe Doctrine, 241
Monroe, James, 240
Montoya, Joe, 258-59